Simulation Engineering

Jim Ledin

CRC Press
Taylor & Francis Group
Boca Raton London New York

CRC Press is an imprint of the
Taylor & Francis Group, an **informa** business

CRC Press
Taylor & Francis Group
6000 Broken Sound Parkway NW, Suite 300
Boca Raton, FL 33487-2742

First issued in hardback 2018

ISBN-13: 978-1-57820-080-1 (pbk)
ISBN-13: 978-1-138-43641-1 (hbk)

Visit the Taylor & Francis Web site at
http://www.taylorandfrancis.com

and the CRC Press Web site at
http://www.crcpress.com

*Dedicated to the memory of my father,
John Ronald Ledin.*

Table of Contents

Preface

The title of this book, *Simulation Engineering*, is intended to convey two meanings. The first is the idea of applying engineering principles and techniques to the development of valid, useful simulations of complex dynamic systems operating under realistic conditions. In other words, this definition of simulation engineering is the application of engineering approaches to the development of good simulations. The second meaning of the phrase applies when simulations developed by the use of engineering methods are used as part of a product development and testing process. In this definition, simulation engineering occurs when simulations become part of an engineering process and are applied as tools to develop better products with greater efficiency.

The intent of this book is twofold. First, it provides an introduction and background to dynamic system simulation that covers both of the meanings discussed above. Second, it contains practical techniques and approaches that have been used successfully in the development and test processes for different types of complex embedded systems over many years. This book is intended for use by engineers, managers, and others involved in the development and test processes for embedded systems, as well as by students and anyone else with an interest in dynamic system simulation.

I would like to gratefully acknowledge the assistance provided by Dr. Jack Crenshaw in his incisive technical review of this material. I would also like to thank the staff at CMP Books for their support in this effort. Finally, I want to thank my lovely wife, Lynda, for the patience, encouragement, and help she has provided during the writing of this book.

Chapter 1

Simulation Engineering

1.1 Introduction

This book deals with the subject of simulation as it applies to the process of designing, developing, and testing complex dynamic embedded systems. A *dynamic system*[1] has behavior that is described by *differential equations* (for continuous-time systems) or by *difference equations* (for discrete-time systems). Dynamic embedded systems are dynamic systems that use computing resources to control their dynamic behavior. The number of applications for dynamic embedded systems is steadily increasing, and includes safety-critical systems and those that have the potential to cause large financial loss in the event of system failure. Because of these risks, system developers must provide a high level of assurance that the system hardware and software designs and implementations are free from serious errors. It is more important than ever to use development tools and processes that reduce the potential for serious design problems which may remain undetected until late in the development cycle or after the product is in customer hands.

Simulation is an approach that can significantly accelerate the product development cycle and provide higher quality in the final system. A simulation contains a set of mathematical models of one or more dynamic systems and the interactions between those systems and their environment. During execution, the simulation advances through time and solves the equations for all the models at each point in time. The equations that describe the behavior of

---

1. Italicized terms in the text are also found in the Glossary, beginning on page 285.

complex systems are complex themselves — so the approach used in simulation is often the only way to solve them with an acceptable degree of accuracy.

Simulation can play several roles during the development of a dynamic embedded system. It is useful for

- exploring design options,
- optimizing design parameters,
- as a tool for thoroughly testing the system under realistic conditions, and
- other applications such as failure analysis.

This book will discuss several ways simulation is used — including the use of real-time simulation for testing system hardware and software.

It is critically important that a simulation accurately reflect the behavior of the system and environment being simulated. It is crucial that each model in the simulation — as well as the complete simulation application itself — undergo a thorough procedure to demonstrate its accuracy. Chapter 7 is devoted to a discussion of simulation verification, validation, and accreditation, which are the processes used to demonstrate the degree to which each mathematical model (and the full simulation) are sufficiently correct and accurate for their intended uses.

Because simulation development and execution is commonly performed using an off-the-shelf simulation software package, Chapter 9 describes several current simulation tools and demonstrates the implementation of a simple yet nontrivial system simulation in each one. Demonstration versions of each of these packages, as well as others that are not discussed in this book, are generally available from vendors at no cost for a limited period. Developers considering which tool to buy should try out several and select the one that best meets their needs.

Before diving into the issues of modeling and simulating dynamic systems, it's important to discuss reasons why it is needed and identify some of the benefits that accrue from the use of simulation.

1.2 Embedded Systems

Embedded systems are products that contain computing resources. These systems are becoming more complex as the power of computing hardware and software increases. Moore's Law[2] states that the computing power of microprocessors doubles approximately every 18 months. As performance increases, the cost of computing power is decreasing. Therefore, it is becoming more feasible to implement high-performance, low-cost embedded computing technology into products. This abundance of computing capability can provide sophisticated new product features with low per-unit incremental cost. As always, the products that succeed in the marketplace will provide features that buyers want and are willing to pay for. The companies that succeed will make the best use of embedded computing power to develop products that become market leaders.

However, low-cost computing hardware is only one part of an embedded system. Before this hardware can do anything at all, someone must develop software to run on it. Embedded software must undergo a design, development, and testing process similar in many ways to

---

2. Gordon E. Moore, co-founder of Intel, made the observation in 1965 that the number of transistors per square inch on integrated circuits had doubled approximately every year since the integrated circuit was invented. In subsequent years, the pace slowed somewhat so that the current rate of transistor doubling is about every 18 months.

the hardware development process. As the complexity of the tasks performed by the software in an embedded system increases, so does the time and expense required for the development process. In many cases, the software development costs for an embedded project exceed the costs for hardware development, sometimes by a substantial amount [1]. Because of the large and growing percentage of product development resources expended on software, techniques for improving the software development process are becoming increasingly important.

In addition to the hardware and software development costs of a complex embedded product, hardware/software integration can also be a source of significant expense and risk. Often the hardware and software development efforts occur in parallel. This means that the software developers cannot run their code on the actual embedded hardware until a proto-type becomes available, which may not occur until *after* completion of the bulk of the software development. As anyone who has worked on a sizable software project knows, debugging a large, untested chunk of software is vastly more difficult than developing and debugging it a little bit at a time. Projects can become bogged down in problems during the hardware/software integration phase, frequently leading to lengthy delays, exploding costs, and outright project failure. There is a critical need for techniques that can reduce the risks associated with parallel hardware and software development. Simulation is one way to reduce these risks.

Users will continue to demand more product capabilities causing developers of competing products to strive to provide solutions that meet those needs. To flourish in this environment, companies must adapt themselves and their processes to the realities dictated by complex dynamic embedded systems. These large software projects will require the use of the best available development and test methodologies to *a*) minimize the number of software problems that occur in fielded systems, and *b*) to minimize the negative effects of those problems should they appear. Simulation is a useful tool for meeting these goals.

Software problems can arise from many sources, for example

- incorrect algorithm implementation,
- accessing hardware devices improperly,
- and failing to handle exceptional conditions (e.g., division by zero) properly.

Other software-related problems can arise in the larger project context. One area where problems frequently occur is in the specification of software requirements. During the early project phases when software requirements are defined, it can be very difficult to envision all the circumstances under which an embedded system will operate. If the requirements are set "in stone" at this early phase, it may be difficult to identify and implement requirement changes that could lead to a better product.

An example of a software requirements-related system problem occurred in the Patriot missile system used in the Gulf War. On February 25, 1991, a Patriot missile battery in Saudi Arabia was unable to engage an incoming Scud missile due to an excessive amount of clock drift in its target tracking system. The Scud subsequently struck a warehouse in Dhahran and killed 28 U.S. soldiers. An investigation determined that the real-time clock in the Patriot targeting system steadily drifted away from the correct time due to rounding error [2]. When the system had been running continuously for a long time (over 100 hours, in the case of the failure), sufficient clock error would accumulate so that the system could not acquire a target.

After this failure, the system developers produced a software patch that fixed the clock drift problem. This led to the popular belief that the root cause of the problem was a software error. However, the problem may not have just been a slowly drifting real-time clock. The original requirements for the Patriot system apparently did not envision that the missile batteries would remain in a continuously operational state for more than a few hours at a time. During the Gulf War, Patriot missile batteries often remained in the operational state for several days at a time. This allowed the clock error to grow to the point that the targeting system would not function. The conclusion in this affair appears to be that the system met its original requirements (even with the clock drift present), but in the operational situation, it was used in a manner that was not compatible with those requirements. This resulted in the complete failure of the system to perform its intended task.

The root problem in this case may have been a combination of a limitation in the original system requirements and improper operation by the end users (possibly due to inadequate user training or poor system documentation). It does not appear to have been a problem of software design or implementation, because all real systems are specified in terms of error tolerances. The developer must meet those tolerances, but it is not appropriate to expend resources in an attempt to further minimize errors once the tolerances are satisfied. If the system meets the specifications but still does not function correctly, the specified tolerances may not be tight enough.

Software development practices and tools are steadily evolving to increase the efficiency and quality of the development process, but there are no breakthroughs on the horizon that would dramatically improve the situation. Incremental enhancements will occur as software tools become available that improve some aspects of the software development and test processes. Better developer and management practices will improve their ability to meet project goals. Even with the use of refined tools and practices, however, the development and testing of software is likely to remain a slow, labor-intensive process for years to come.

Software development and test complexity, hardware/software integration, and requirements analysis can be major problems in the development of complex dynamic embedded systems. Cost-effective approaches must be developed and implemented to deal with these issues in ways that reduce the risk of encountering expensive and difficult-to-fix system errors during development and particularly after development is completed. The earlier in the cycle that meaningful system-level testing can be performed, the easier and less risky final system integration will be. Any approach that allows earlier testing of embedded software can improve the chances for a successful, on-time, on-budget development effort. As you will see, simulation is a technique that meets this need.

1.3 Simulation

Simulation is a vital tool for dealing with the problems discussed in the previous section. A *simulation* is defined as the reproduction of a situation with the use of models. A *model* is a physical, mathematical, or other logical representation of a system, process, or phenomenon. In this book, I will consider the development and use of models and simulations as computer programs. Many different kinds of simulation are used in product development today. Examples of simulation types include:

- Circuit simulation (Will the circuit meet timing requirements?)
- Thermal simulation (Will any of the chips on the board get too hot?)
- Network simulation (Will congestion be a problem?)

The focus of this book will be on the use of simulation at the system level. A system-level simulation models the behavior of an overall system as it operates in a realistic, simulated environment. The modeling of subsystems and components may be simplified significantly for a system-level simulation — as long as the essential behaviors of all components of the system and its operational environment are accurately modeled. Some types of simulation used in the product design process (such as thermal simulation) may not need to be included at all in a typical system-level simulation.

Dynamic system simulation focuses on the entire system as it operates in its intended environment. This type of simulation permits testing of the system in its designated operational modes as well as under dangerous emergency conditions without risking loss of life or valuable assets. Environmental conditions that may be difficult or impossible to reproduce for system tests (such as icy roads in the middle of summer, or the conditions of outer space) can be simulated using computers and appropriate software algorithms. Using simulation, we can perform intricate test sequences quickly and repeatably at relatively low cost.

We can test hardware and software at the subsystem level using *hardware-in-the-loop* (HIL) *simulations* long before a testable system prototype becomes available. HIL simulations run at real-time speeds and perform input/output operations with the system or subsystem so that the test item "thinks" it is operating as part of a real system in its operational environment. These systems or subsystems can then be tested under nominal conditions as well as beyond their intended operational boundaries. HIL simulation provides the ability to thoroughly test subsystems early in the development process. This can greatly reduce the debugging time and project risk compared to the alternative approach of waiting until a prototype is completed before performing integration and testing.

Many important ancillary issues must be addressed to gain the full set of potential benefits from a simulation effort. Two examples of these areas are simulation verification and validation. *Verification* is the process used to demonstrate that a simulation has been implemented according to its specifications. The *validation* process demonstrates that the simulation is a sufficiently good representation of the actual system it attempts to simulate. The primary goal of the verification and validation processes is to provide sufficient, convincing evidence of the correctness of the simulation so that even the most skeptical observers will agree that it is credible and accurate for its intended purposes.

Another issue involves the methods used to effectively analyze and process the large amounts of output data generated by a simulation. There must be adequate tools and techniques available for extracting useful information from all of the output data. Some of the data will need to be archived for later use for such purposes as regression testing (which verifies that the simulation continues to work correctly after undergoing significant modifications).

1.4 Complex Products

Dynamic embedded systems are constantly becoming more complex in terms of computing hardware and software. Many of these products become part of safety-critical systems such as aircraft, traffic signals, or medical instruments. Even for products that are not safety-critical, it is important that serious defects be identified and fixed before production begins. If a major problem is not detected until after the product is fielded, the effects can be financially devastating for the company that produced it.

Many new products are being developed that would not be economically feasible without the availability of low-cost embedded computing power. One example is the handheld GPS

(Global Positioning System) receiver. Other embedded computing products have evolved from designs that did not include any form of digital electronics in earlier designs, such as electronic controllers for automotive engines.

An example of a complex embedded product that evolved from a simpler system design is the John Deere combine harvester. The current model contains 10 microprocessors connected by a CAN[3] network. The harvester includes a GPS receiver, sensors that measure the quantity of grain as it is harvested, and a sensor that measures the humidity of the grain bin. Using this information, the system computes an estimate of the dry weight of the harvested grain in real-time. After completing the harvest, the system can produce a map that shows the yield at each location in the field. This example demonstrates how low-cost, high-performance embedded computing can add important new features to a mature product.

Embedded computing is also becoming a critical part of many safety-critical systems. Safety-critical software must undergo a rigorous development and testing process to ensure that software errors do not create risks to users, innocent bystanders, or to valuable equipment [3]. These systems must be tolerant of failures in the embedded system hardware and software. For example, a redundant communication channel between the processor and a sensor can automatically switch into use if the primary channel fails.

Testing for correct system performance under potential failure conditions can require elaborate test sequences — beginning with system initialization followed by a period of operation with defined inputs that drive the system to a known state. The test sequence completes with the injection of a system failure and the monitoring of the system response. This type of test typically requires a significant development effort and may involve additional investments in hardware and software. Simpler tests should be used whenever possible because they are generally faster and cheaper to perform.

One relatively simple type of system testing is the stimulus–response test. In this type of test, a known set of inputs is applied to a system and the response to those inputs is measured. The measured response is compared with expectations (often by checking to see if the response lies within a tolerance band) to determine if the system is operating correctly. This is relatively easy to perform and can be automated efficiently.

Stimulus–response testing may be difficult to use if the system is a dynamic system. In this situation, the state of the system cannot be specified completely by the inputs at a given time. Additional state information internal to the system exists that determines its response to a set of inputs. This state information complicates the process significantly, and makes the use of stimulus–response testing less attractive.

An example that demonstrates the difficulties with stimulus–response testing is the automobile. A very simple model of automobile motion assumes that a car is moving along a straight road (i.e., no steering is involved) and only the accelerator and brake affect the speed (wind resistance, slope, and rolling resistance are ignored). In this model, the internal state information is the car's speed and its position along the road. The system inputs are the accelerator and brake. The position and speed of the car at any moment will depend on the entire time history of accelerator and brake inputs since it first began moving. A stimulus–response

---

3.   The CAN (Controller Area Network) protocol is an ISO standard (ISO 11898) for serial communication. It has gained widespread use in industrial automation as well as in automobiles and mobile machines.

test of this system would not make much sense, because the car does not respond instantaneously to accelerator and brake inputs. Rather, it responds over time. Therefore, any useful test must observe system response over a period of time.

The necessity to perform a test over a period of time while providing inputs to the embedded system that mimic those in the real-world leads naturally to the use of simulation as a test methodology. Simulation testing approaches will be discussed in later chapters, particularly in Chapter 4, which focuses on hardware-in-the-loop simulation.

1.5 Short Development Cycle

Another trend in embedded systems development is that the time available to develop new products is decreasing in many application areas due to intense competition. Any group using tools that speed the development process and that allow quick identification and resolution of problems will be ahead in the game. Simulation can provide these benefits.

It is standard engineering procedure that a project team develops mathematical models of system components and their interactions with the environment at an early stage in the design process. The team then analyzes these models using techniques that depend on the particular branches of engineering (electrical, mechanical, etc.) to which the models relate. After the system designers have scrutinized the models and deemed them to be of adequate fidelity, the simulation developers combine the models into a complete simulation of the overall system. A *non-real-time simulation* is a computer program that simulates a dynamic system beginning from a specified initial state and operating over a period of simulated time. A non-real-time simulation may execute at a faster or slower rate than real-time. After the simulation has been developed, it must undergo a verification and validation process to build confidence in the correctness of its results before using those results in making critical project decisions.

With the completion of simulation development, verification, and validation, the project team will have a tool for performing comprehensive system testing. As changes are made to the system design, parallel changes must be incorporated into the simulation, which permits an early evaluation of the effects of changes on system performance.

The system simulation provides a robust and flexible tool for examining design tradeoffs early in product development. When used effectively, simulation can speed the design evaluation process and avoid the need for expensive changes that might otherwise have been necessary at a later development stage.

A non-real-time simulation is useful as the basis for a real-time HIL simulation. The steps in developing an HIL simulation typically include porting the simulation to a suitable real-time computer system and the addition of input/output devices to communicate with the embedded system. It is often necessary to adapt the mathematical models to the requirements of real-time operation, for example, by eliminating disk accesses during model execution. Some simplification of the models may be necessary if they cannot execute fast enough for real-time operation. These issues and others related to HIL simulation will be discussed in Chapter 4.

As subsystem hardware prototypes become available, the developers integrate them into the HIL simulation, which enables system-level simulation using *actual* embedded hardware and software. The ability to perform system-level testing in a simulation environment early in the development cycle can provide tremendous benefits to the project. System problems detected early can often be fixed at a relatively low cost.

Integrating the subsystems into the known environment of the HIL simulation can significantly reduce risks as compared to the approach of integrating subsystems into a full system prototype. The HIL simulation methodology leads to reduced project risks and increased speed of system integration compared with alternative approaches and, therefore, a shorter product development cycle which may pay for the investment in simulation many times over.

1.6 Improved Quality

Quality can be defined in several ways as it applies to the complex embedded systems discussed in this book. A straightforward definition states that a product has high quality if it performs its intended functions adequately without any significant negative attributes or behaviors from the user's point of view. This is a goal pursued by the developers of essentially any embedded system.

One way to ensure that a product has high quality is to perform thorough testing during initial development and following each change in the system design. A set of *regression tests* is performed following a product change with the intention of verifying that previously existing functionality has not been disturbed. Ideally, regression testing is carried out in a way that can be completed as quickly as possible and in as automated a manner as possible. If regression testing is fast and somewhat automated, developers will do it more often — which will lead to the early discovery of some types of problems.

With the use of simulation, it is possible to perform a great deal of thorough, repeatable testing in an automated fashion. Following a product change, a suite of regression tests can be run using the simulation to verify that previous functionality has been maintained. This is a powerful method for maintaining quality in the face of ongoing product upgrades and problem fixes.

A fundamental method for performing system tests is to take the thing out and fly it, or drive it, or do whatever it does under a specified set of real world test conditions. This type of testing is referred to as *operational testing*. While operational testing is unquestionably a highly realistic way to test the system, the method does present some problems.

For one thing, operational testing can take a long time and cost a lot of money. Commercial airliners receive airworthiness certification after passing a rigorous series of flight tests. These tests may take over a year to complete. Great patience and deep pockets are required to conduct an operational test series of this magnitude. It makes sense to replace or augment operational tests with faster and lower-cost forms of testing whenever appropriate.

Another problem with operational testing is that it may be difficult to perform the tests repeatably. In a flight test, for example, the wind conditions and air temperature are factors that cannot be duplicated from one day to another. When performing a regression test in an operational environment, it may be difficult to determine if deviations from previously achieved behavior are due to system problems or to differences in test conditions.

Simulation can help with both of these problems. Once a simulation has been developed and validated, test runs can be performed quickly and at low cost. This can eliminate the need for some operational tests, though not all of them. A number of real world tests will always be required to validate the simulation.

The problem of test repeatability for regression testing purposes is greatly reduced when simulation is used. If well-documented hardware and software configurations for the simulation are maintained, it should be possible to return to any previous test configuration and re-run the test under virtually identical conditions. Sometimes this will be impossible due to changes that have been made to the embedded system hardware or in the simulation computing environment. In these cases, repeatability of regression test results can be demonstrated by showing that the new configuration produces results that match the old configuration within an acceptable margin.

Using simulation, complex test series can be set up and executed in an automated manner. This can make the process of regression testing relatively fast and inexpensive. As new capabilities are added to the embedded system, new tests can be added to the regression test suite. The ability to perform regression testing in a somewhat automated manner can result in a higher quality system because existing functions are thoroughly retested each time the system goes through an update cycle.

1.7 Lower Total Cost

The expense and effort that go into developing a simulation can be viewed as an investment. In order for this investment to pay off, there must be benefits at the end of the product development process that exceed the costs. Many companies are using simulation as a tool in the development process because they have evaluated its costs and benefits. They realize that effective simulation usage is critical if they are to achieve their goals of high product quality and reasonable development cost.

The most significant expenses in developing a simulation fall into two categories.

1. The time and other resources required for system experts and simulation engineers to develop models and assemble them into a simulation.
2. The effort to perform verification and validation of those models in the full simulation.

In some cases, computing hardware costs for a digital simulation may be insignificant, such as when it runs on an ordinary PC. An HIL simulation can cost anywhere from less than $10,000 to millions of dollars. The costs for the HIL simulation hardware will depend on the level of real-time performance required and the complexity of the simulator hardware and software used to generate the signals for use with the embedded system under test.

The expense required for developing models suitable for simulation is often a relatively small addition to the comparable project cost without a simulation effort. Even when simulation is not extensively used during product development, engineering models of system components are frequently developed in the analysis and design phases of complex products. The initial versions of these models may be simple linear representations used for tasks such as stability analysis, time constant estimation, etc. It may not take a great deal of effort to combine a set of these simple models into a simulation — thus providing an initial tool for examining the workings of the entire system as it operates in a simulated environment. While this early simulation may be necessarily incomplete and simplified, it provides a framework and a baseline for the development of higher-fidelity versions.

As the design of the embedded system proceeds, the initial simple models can be enhanced to include more complex behavior such as friction, limits, latencies, and quantization, for example. Alternatively, simple models can be removed and replaced with more elaborate versions that are higher-fidelity representations of the system elements. For example, a parameter that was modeled as a constant in an early model version may be represented as a curve-fit equation or an interpolated lookup table in a more realistic model.

A certain amount of simulation verification work must be part of the ongoing simulation development process. Each change to a model must be tested to show that it is correct in its effects both internal to the model and in interactions with other models. The compatibility of the various models in the simulation must be demonstrated each time a change is made to an interface. Testing must also be done to ensure that one model does not depend on effects from another model that have not been implemented as expected. The interfaces between models should be specified carefully so that there is no need for assumptions about the inner workings of other models.

If the simulation development effort is well integrated into the overall product design process, the additional cost can be minimized. The verification and validation process must proceed during simulation development. These tasks will require a commitment of time from the embedded system design experts who must examine the simulation design and output data to develop confidence in its correctness and usefulness.

The benefits of using simulation will start appearing right away if the initial, relatively simple engineering models are implemented into an early digital simulation and made available to the system designers for analyzing system behavior. If the designers come to see the simulation as a useful tool that they understand from the beginning, they tend to be supportive of its future development and more willing to put their efforts into improving it.

As more realistic models of subsystems and environmental effects are developed and added to the simulation, it can be used to refine the system design parameters and to identify the areas where performance is weak. Identification of areas of performance uncertainty can be a guide for the testing of subsystems and the planning for operational tests to be performed once system prototypes become available.

As the simulation matures into a robust, high-fidelity representation of system performance, an HIL simulation can be developed using the non-real-time simulation as a basis. The HIL simulation may require the simplification of some models in order to meet the requirements of real-time operation. Any simplifications should be thoroughly tested by comparison with the complete non-real-time simulation to ensure they are reasonable for the intended application. After the HIL simulation becomes operational, subsystem hardware can be integrated into the simulation as prototypes become available. Examples of subsystems suitable for testing in an HIL environment for an aircraft include

- the inertial navigation system (though not the inertial sensors, which are typically simulated),
- the autopilot, and
- the control surface actuators.

After a full system prototype is available, the non-real-time and HIL simulations can be used in the planning for operational tests. The simulations can predict system performance under planned test scenarios as well as under variations that are likely to occur while the test is in progress. After an operational test is complete, the collected data is used for simulation validation. A standard validation comparison is performed by running each simulation under the conditions that occurred in the actual test and comparing simulated system performance to actual performance.

Careful use of system simulations in the planning for operational tests can reduce the number of expensive operational tests required, leading to significant savings. Depending on the type of system under development, this alone may pay for the cost of simulation development. This approach also provides significant savings by preventing costly test failures or disastrous problems in fielded systems. The use of simulation can greatly reduce the risk of these types of problems occurring in the development of a complex dynamic embedded system.

1.8 Resistance Against Simulation

Given that simulation results are "just" output data from a computer program, there are likely to be people who are skeptical of the usefulness of this information. Sometimes a simulation developer may work with people who are dead set against the use of simulation under any circumstances. In my experience, people have developed this attitude after an experience where the validity of some simulation data was oversold and the conclusions derived from that data turned out to be incorrect. This situation may have had a variety of negative consequences, ranging from embarrassment to a costly test failure.

The best way to overcome an "anti-simulation" attitude is by using a methodical simulation development process and performing careful simulation verification and validation. Later, when operating the simulation, care must be taken to keep the system behavior within the validated region, or adequate justification must be provided when operating outside the validated region. Properly applied, simulation can provide reliable predictions of system behavior. Credibility will follow from a careful simulation development process combined with a thorough verification and validation procedure.

Project managers must instill a sense that simulation is an integral part of the product development process and not just something added as an afterthought. This may be a difficult task if the team members have been burned by bad simulation experiences in the past. Under these conditions, the simulation developers must proceed with extra care and make sure that the skeptics remain aware of and involved in simulation development plans, model development and validation techniques, and the results of ongoing simulation work. It may be necessary to deliver frequent progress updates so that all those concerned with the simulation work are aware of its status.

Successful integration of simulation into a development project will be unlikely if simulation work proceeds independently and without frequent review and feedback from the embedded system developers. If the results of simulation runs are presented to the embedded system developers without a clear explanation of how the simulation was developed and how the results were generated, the developers will likely dismiss those results if they deviate in any way from expectations. When this happens, the expense and effort that went into developing the simulation is essentially wasted. The system developers proceed as if no simulation work had taken place, and none of the benefits of simulation will be achieved. Project managers may see the failure to integrate the simulation effort into the development process as an indication that simulation is unnecessary and avoid its use in the future. This unfortunate conclusion can be avoided if effective communication takes place between the simulation developers and the product developers.

A related problem can occur if the embedded system developers accept simulation results too readily and apply insufficient scrutiny to the simulation development process and results. When this difficulty arises, there may be undetected errors or deficiencies in the simulation modeling or data analysis process that could have been discovered with a more rigorous examination. These shortcomings may lead to problems in the embedded system that remain undetected until they cause costly test failures or problems in fielded systems.

The ideal situation is to reach a balance between having system experts and managers who are neither overly skeptical of simulation results nor too willing to accept results that they do not fully understand. A significant amount of additional effort and perseverance may be required on the part of the simulation managers and developers to reach this state. If the primary benefits of simulation use are achieved (shortened development cycle, increased product quality, lower total development cost), the added work will have been justified.

1.9   Simulation Planning

Before simulation development begins, the developers must create a plan identifying

- what is to be simulated,
- the degree of simulation fidelity required, and
- the ways in which the resulting output data will be used.

In addition to describing the products of the simulation development effort, the plan must also describe the simulation software development process, including such issues such as configuration management, version release criteria, and problem reporting and resolution processes. The plan must also define a manageable process for operating the simulation that includes procedures for defining input data sets, performing simulation runs, analyzing simulation results, and using those results as input for project decision making.

To achieve maximum value from the simulation effort, the simulation plan must be thoroughly integrated into the larger project plan. The structure of the project development plan must also be defined in a way that maximizes the benefits of the simulation effort. There are a number of different approaches, but I will examine two of the most popular ones: the waterfall approach and the iterative approach.

1.9.1 The Waterfall Development Model

The waterfall development approach [1] is shown in diagram form in Figure 1.1. This approach has been used in the past for many large development projects. It presents the major tasks in the design and development process as a set of logical, orderly steps. In practice, projects that used this approach have frequently encountered problems that resulted in significant delays and cost overruns, as well as occasional failures that resulted in project cancellation.

The problems with the waterfall approach stem from the rigidity of the sequence of steps it uses. It assumes that all requirements are fully specified during the requirements analysis phase. Once the development project moves to the design step, no major changes to requirements are anticipated. In reality, changes to requirements occur frequently after they have been "frozen" in the requirements analysis phase. One reason these changes occur is because the people who identified the requirements could only imagine how the final system would behave. They did not have any way other than using their imaginations to test the assumptions that went into their decisions, or to verify that the final requirements were consistent or adequate for the system's tasks. Requirement changes can come about for many other reasons, such as advances in technology or new information that changes the goals for the system under development.

Figure 1.1 Waterfall development model.

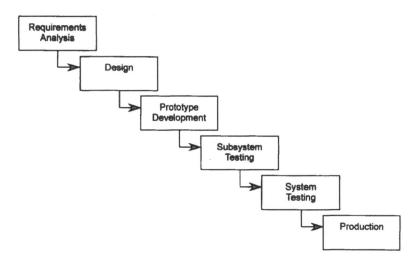

In the waterfall development approach, changes to requirements can result in major disruptions because once each phase is completed, the structure used in that phase may be disassembled and scattered. For example, if a requirement is changed considerably after the product design has been completed, it may be difficult to reassemble the design group to implement the change. The designers may have moved on to other projects or may be unavailable for other reasons. Bringing the designers back to implement unexpected requirements changes may in turn produce unacceptable delays for the other projects they are working on.

An additional problem with the waterfall approach is that project risk reduction does not occur until late in the development cycle. This is because comprehensive system testing does not begin until the requirements and design are largely completed and prototype hardware becomes available. If a significant design flaw is not detected until this late stage, the time and cost required to alter the design, implement it, and test it can be unacceptably high.

In summary, the waterfall development model assumes that the results of each step in the process are correct and complete as that step is finished. In a relatively small development project, this may not be an unreasonable assumption. If there are problems at some point in smaller project, it may be easy to go back to an earlier stage and fix things before continuing. In the development of a large, complex system, however, this approach may be unrealistic due to the difficulty involved in revisiting an earlier project phase.

1.9.2 The Iterative Development Model

An alternative to the waterfall model is the iterative development model [4], shown in Figure 1.2. The iterative model applies primarily to the software portion of a development project and is of limited use with hardware development issues. The model contains of a sequence of steps that the software developers repeat several times during a development project — shown in the circular part of Figure 1.2. The essential idea is that at the end of each pass through the cycle, a working prototype of the software has been produced and tested. The lack of prototype hardware may present problems with testing during these phases, but as you will see, the use of simulation can mitigate this difficulty significantly.

Figure 1.2   Iterative development model.

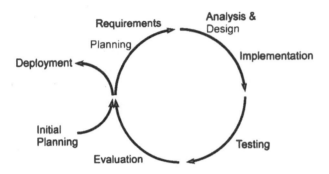

The results of each iteration are used as input to planning the next cycle, which includes possible requirement modifications and leads to the design and implementation of a new subset of system functionality. In the early cycles through the iterative loop, the software will have limited capability. If complex, high-risk capabilities are developed and tested during early passes through the cycle and tested again during later iterations, project risk is reduced. The addition of less complex, lower risk functions occurs later, after the more difficult aspects have been shown to work properly.

In the iterative development model, the integration of new requirements happens as part of the normal development cycle. The new requirements will have incremental costs associated with them, but they will not (usually) force drastic, disruptive changes to the development process. After a sufficient number of cycles through the iterative loop have occurred and all the software requirements have been implemented, the system will be ready for deployment. With the iterative model, the most complex and riskiest parts of the software will have been thoroughly tested several times as ancillary capabilities are added at each iteration.

Simulation is a natural complement to the iterative development model. Simulations can be developed during initial project planning to assist in requirement definitions. In this approach, the people specifying system requirements can observe the performance of the simulated system and use that information to assist in determining new requirements and revising existing ones.

During the early iterations of the software development cycle, prototype hardware may not be available for testing software builds. It may be possible to use a simulation as a testbed for evaluating these early builds. In this scenario, part or all of the system software can be implemented as modules in a complete system simulation. This "embedded" software receives inputs from the simulation, performs its processing, and produces outputs that drive the simulated system. This technique allows thorough testing of early versions of the embedded software in a simulated operational environment. Because this is a non-real-time simulation, full use can be made of debugging and execution analysis tools with no degradation of test capability.

Later in the development process, as prototype hardware becomes available, this hardware can be integrated into a real-time HIL simulation for testing the system software running on target hardware in a realistic simulated environment. The HIL simulation is a valuable tool for speeding the software/hardware integration process while making it relatively easy to identify and fix problems as they occur.

Simulation reduces uncertainty and risk at each development phase. The initial set of requirements is less likely to undergo major revisions if the developers have made effective use of a system simulation as part of the requirements definition phase. During system development, as prototype software and hardware become available, they can be placed in a simulated environment and tested under realistic conditions. By the time a full system prototype is ready for testing, it is possible to achieve a high level of confidence that no serious problems remain. The early reduction of risk is one of the best payoffs from the effective use of simulation from the beginning of the project.

1.10 Source Code and Examples

This book contains several models of system components and complete simulations as well. As you'll learn in Chapter 9, there are many tools and programming approaches used to develop simulations of dynamic systems. The software tools available for simulation development generally use text-based programming, graphical programming, or a combination of the two. I have chosen to use the C++ language for text-based examples and Simulink® for block diagram-based examples.

These tools will be used to present examples of the algorithms, models, and simulations in this book. The C++ language is used to demonstrate the detailed implementation of numerical algorithms related to simulation and it provides a way for those who do not have access to Simulink to gain experience.

Simulink provides a high-level, graphical modeling environment for simulation development that hides many of the numerical details from the user and allows quick model construction, execution, and simulation results analysis. Using other software tools available from The MathWorks, Inc.[4], it is possible to automatically translate Simulink models into C or Ada language source code and compile this code for execution on an HIL simulation computer or on an embedded processor.

1.10.1 Dynamic System Simulation Library

The Dynamic System Simulation Library (DSSL) is a library of C++ classes I have devloped that implement numerical algorithms useful for dynamic system simulation. The C++ examples presented in this book use the DSSL and are suitable for building both non-real-time and real-time simulations of dynamic systems. The source code for DSSL is provided on the CD-ROM included with this book.

The DSSL makes use of C++ features such as templates, class inheritance, and virtual functions to provide a tradeoff between execution performance and ease of program development. The use of templates avoids dynamic memory allocation that would otherwise be required and allows some error checking to occur at compile time rather than at run time. The use of potentially expensive features such as virtual functions is minimized, and occurs

---

4. http://www.mathworks.com

only where a genuine benefit is realized. Dynamic memory allocation is rarely used, and occurs during initialization rather than during the (possibly real-time) execution of the simulation models.

All components of the DSSL become accessible with the C++ statement #include <dssl.h>. The DSSL is contained in a set of header files and one C++ source file, which must be compiled and linked into the application. All fragmentary program listings in this book will assume that the #include <dssl.h> statement appears at the top of the source file.

The major elements of the Dynamic System Simulation Library are:

Matrix and vector data types and manipulation routines   The dimension(s) and element data types of vectors and matrices are specified as template arguments for the Vector and Matrix classes. The element data type specification is optional and defaults to double. The vector/matrix manipulation routines include addition, subtraction, and multiplication as well as matrix inversion and the solution of linear equations. Some example matrix and vector declarations are:

```
#include <dssl.h>     // Make the DSSL library available
#include <complex>     // Used by the complex vector below

Vector<2> v1;          // A 2-element vector of double elements
Vector<3, int> v2;     // A 3-element vector of int elements
Vector<3, std::complex<double> > v3; // A 3-element complex vector

Matrix<3,3> m1;        // A 3x3 matrix of double elements
Matrix<4,2, int> m2;   // A 4 row 2 column matrix of int elements
```

State variable integration   The template argument for the State class is the data type, which defaults to double. Each State variable is associated with a StateList, which is used in performing integration. By using multiple StateList variables, it is possible to develop a simulation containing multiple integration time step sizes.

A complete program that integrates the sin function from 0 to 10 with an integration step size of 0.01 using the default integration method (Adams-Bashforth 2nd order) appears below:

```
#include <dssl.h>     // Make the DSSL library available
#include <cmath>       // sin function

int main()
{
    // Declare a list of state variables and place one state variable in it
    StateList state_list;
    State s(&state_list);
```

```
// Define some constants
const double step_time = 0.01, end_time = 10.0;

// Specify the state initial value
s.ic = 0;

// Set the initial value of the variables in the state list
state_list.Initialize(step_time);

for(;;)
{
    // Compute the state derivative, which is sin(current time)
    s.der = sin(state_list.Time());

    // Check for end-of-run condition
    if (state_list.Time() >= end_time)
        break;

    // Integrate to the next time step
    state_list.Integrate();
}

return 0;
}
```

Linear function interpolation with equally- and unequally-spaced breakpoints. The number of function dimensions and the length of each dimension are limited only by available memory. Breakpoint and function data are loaded from text files during program initialization. A two-dimensional function example with four unequally-spaced breakpoints along each dimensions follows. Function interpolation will be discussed in Chapter 2.

```
// Declare two breakpoint lists and load the associated data files
UneqSpacedBkpt<4> x_bkpt("x_bkpt.dat"), y_bkpt("y_bkpt.dat");

LinearInterp<2> interp1; // Two-dimensional function

// Specify the breakpoint list for each function dimension
interp1.SetDimension(0, &x_bkpt);
interp1.SetDimension(1, &y_bkpt);
```

```
interp1.SetupData("interp2.dat"); // Load function data

double x = 3.4; // Define the function inputs
double y = 1.6;

x_bkpt.Eval(x); // Perform a breakpoint search for each dimension
y_bkpt.Eval(y);

double z = interp1.Eval(); // Compute the interpolated function result
```

Random number generation.   Both uniform and normal (Gaussian) pseudorandom number generators are provided. The core random number generator uses Knuth's subtractive method [5], which provides portability and avoids the serious limitations of some compiler-provided random number generators. Some examples of these routines follow.

```
Random r; // An instance of the random number generator class

double x = r.Uniform(); // Uniformly distributed value from the range (0,1)
double y = r.Normal();  // Normally distributed value with mean=0, std dev=1
```

Although the algorithms provided by the DSSL are by no means exhaustive, it does implement many of the numerical details required in performing a simulation of a complex dynamic system.

1.10.2 Simulink Examples

Simulink is a popular tool for developing simulations of complex dynamic systems. It is integrated with the MATLAB® numerical programming environment and uses many of the features of MATLAB. Simulink is a block diagram-oriented tool with an intuitive, mouse-driven user interface. The user constructs models by dragging and dropping blocks from a predefined library onto a diagram. These blocks are connected by drawing lines between outputs and inputs. Once all the inputs and outputs are joined, the user defines values for any parameters associated with each block and the simulation is ready to run.

Output data from simulation runs can be viewed during simulation execution on graphical "scopes" or it can be saved to the MATLAB environment for analysis and plotting using the comprehensive numerical capabilities of MATLAB.

Figure 1.3 is a Simulink model that performs the same sine wave integration that appeared in the state variable example beginning on page 16. The user selects parameters such as the simulation end time from dialog boxes prior to starting the simulation run and then clicks a button to start the simulation. In this example, the time history of the integrator output will be stored in a variable named result in the MATLAB workspace.

Figure 1.3   Example Simulink model.

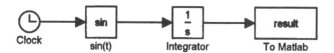

Note: This book will assume that Simulink users have a basic familiarity with the MAT-LAB and Simulink tools and can perform such tasks as creating Simulink diagrams, running simulations, and displaying time plots of signals on scope displays. For more information about these activities, see the documentation provided with Simulink.

1.11 Chapter Overview

Simulation Engineering focuses on dynamic system simulation as it is applied to the product development and testing process, beginning with the early stages of conceptual design through prototype hardware and on to a mature, fielded product. This book discusses the modeling and simulation techniques used to develop and execute non-real-time simulations as well as real-time HIL simulations of complex systems.

Chapters 2 through 9 each end with a number of exercises that allow you to apply the material presented in the chapter. A glossary of simulation-related terms is included at the back of the book (beginning on page 285).

The chapters are organized as follows:

Chapter 1, Simulation Engineering   A discussion of the importance of simulation in the design and development process for complex embedded systems.

Chapter 2, Modeling Dynamic Systems   Describes mathematical models of dynamic systems and the basic techniques used in their development.

Chapter 3, Non-Real-Time Simulation   Outlines the numerical techniques used to turn a set of mathematical models into a simulation capable of producing useful results.

Chapter 4, HIL Simulation   This chapter describes how — beginning with a non-real-time simulation of a system — a simulation developer can create a real-time HIL simulation and use it effectively.

Chapter 5, Distributed Simulation   Describes distributed simulation, (which consists of separate components that run independently and communicate with each other over a network).

Chapter 6, Data Visualization and Analysis   Simulations can easily produce enormous quantities of output data. This chapter identifies strategies and techniques for extracting useful information from simulation output data.

Chapter 7, Verification, Validation, and Accreditation   A simulation only has value if it is an accurate representation of the simulated system. Verification, validation, and accreditation (VV&A) provide the techniques to determine and document the fidelity of a simulation.

Chapter 8, Simulation Throughout the Development Cycle   Simulation can provide valuable benefits from the concept definition phase of a project on to supporting a mature fielded product. This chapter discusses the uses for simulation at each phase in the development cycle.

Chapter 9, Simulation Tools   This chapter contains an overview of several currently available commercial software and hardware tools for dynamic system model development and simulation.

References

[1]   Boehm, Barry W., *Software Engineering Economics*. Upper Saddle River, NJ: Prentice-Hall, 1981.

[2]   U.S. General Accounting Office, *Patriot Missile Defense: Software Problem Led to System Failure at Dhahran, Saudi Arabia* (GAO/IMTEC-92-96). Washington, DC: U.S. General Accounting Office, 1992.

[3]   Leveson, Nancy G., *Safeware: System Safety and Computers*. Reading, MA: Addison Wesley, 1995.

[4]   Royce, Walker, *Software Project Management: A Unified Framework*. Reading, MA: Addison Wesley, 1998.

[5]   Knuth, D. E., *Seminumerical Algorithms*, 2nd ed., vol. 2 of *The Art of Computer Programming*, §3.2-3.3. Reading, MA: Addison Wesley, 1981.

Chapter 2

Modeling Dynamic Systems

2.1 Introduction

To develop a simulation of an interesting and complex dynamic system, one must begin by developing mathematical models of the system components and the interactions between the system and its operational environment. A *mathematical model* is an algorithm or a set of equations and a set of related data values that together represent the significant behavior of a system, process, or phenomenon.

Depending on the system to be modeled, the development of a representative set of mathematical models may be an easy task or it may require a great deal of work. In cases where the system's dynamics are not well understood, it will be necessary for the developer to design and execute a series of experiments to collect data that can be used for model development.

This chapter introduces concepts involved in the mathematical modeling of dynamic systems and presents some of the basic techniques used in their development. The relevant properties of dynamic systems will be examined and I will provide examples of engineering techniques for deriving mathematical representations of their behavior. The positive and negative attributes of commonly used modeling approaches will also be discussed.

2.2 Dynamic Systems

A *dynamic system* has behavior that evolves over time. This behavior is commonly represented by *differential equations* if the system is of the continuous-time type or by *difference equations* if the system is of the discrete-time type. I will use the phrase *dynamic equations* to indicate the set of differential or difference equations that describe a system's behavior.

A system is *continuous-time* if its dynamic equations are valid at all points in time. A *discrete-time* system has dynamic equations that are updated or used only at discrete points in time. A dynamic system that is modeled using both difference equations and differential equations is called a combined discrete-continuous system, or simply a *combined system*.

2.2.1 Continuous-Time Systems

Some examples of continuous-time dynamic behaviors include:

- the translational and rotational motion of an aircraft,
- the orbital motion of a satellite,
- the response of a robotic arm to the motion of its actuators, and
- the response of an op-amp bandpass filter to its input signal.

The behavior of these systems can be represented mathematically by *differential equations*. A differential equation contains an unknown function and one or more of the function's derivatives. The goal is to find the unknown function, which will determine the system behavior over time.

Systems containing distributed parameters are described using *partial differential equations*, which contain partial derivatives. An example of a distributed parameter system is an electrical transmission line, which has resistance and inductance distributed continuously along its length. It is possible to approximate a distributed parameter system with a lumped parameter model, which contains a finite number of discrete locations where energy can be stored and dissipated. Lumped parameter models can be represented by *ordinary differential equations*, which contain ordinary derivatives rather than partial derivatives.

Note: This book will consider the modeling of dynamic systems using ordinary differential equations rather than partial differential equations. Therefore, distributed parameter systems will always be represented by lumped parameter models. When the phrase "differential equation" appears, it will refer to an ordinary (rather than partial) differential equation.

It is often necessary to begin the simulation implementation process with a mathematical model that is in a format *other* than differential equations and transform it so that it becomes a set of differential equations. In engineering analysis and design processes, continuous-time dynamic systems are usually studied using one of three formats [1]. These are the *s*-plane, the frequency response, and state–space representations. These formats are usually used to represent systems as *linear time-invariant models*. Linear time-invariant models and the three model formats are discussed in the following sections.

Linear Time-Invariant Models

Mathematically, a model is *linear* if it satisfies the following condition. Start with two model input signals $x_1(t)$ and $x_2(t)$, and their corresponding output signals $y_1(t)$ and $y_2(t)$. Create a new input signal that is the sum $x_1(t) + x_2(t)$ and apply it as an input to the model. If the model output equals $y_1(t) + y_2(t)$ for any arbitrarily selected $x_1(t)$ and $x_2(t)$, the model is linear. A model is *time-invariant* if the dynamic equations that define its behavior do not change as a function of time. A linear time-invariant model combines both of these properties.

The s-plane Format

The *s*-plane format is based on the Laplace transformation [2]. This technique is widely applied in the areas of classical control system analysis and design, though it is used less often in the simulation of nonlinear systems. *s*-plane models are typically used to represent linear time-invariant models. These models possess desirable properties for system analysis and control system design.

Models in the *s*-plane format are often represented as *transfer functions* consisting of a ratio of polynomials in the complex variable *s*. A transfer function represents the ratio of output to input in the *s*-domain. An example linear differential equation is shown in Equation 2.1 and its equivalent transfer function is given in Equation 2.2. Lowercase *x* and *y* indicate the signals in the time domain and uppercase *X* and *Y* indicate the *s*-domain representation. A single prime over a variable indicates a first derivative with respect to time. Two primes indicate a second time derivative, and so on.

2.1 $\quad y'' + 1.8y' + 100y = 100x$

2.2 $\quad H(s) = \dfrac{Y}{X} = \dfrac{100}{s^2 + 1.8s + 100}$

In many simulation environments, it is possible to model systems using differential equations but not transfer functions. For these environments, it is necessary to convert transfer functions to differential equations. It is a straightforward procedure to convert from an *s*-plane transfer function to an equivalent differential equation, assuming zero initial conditions. The steps are:

1. Given a transfer function in the format of Equation 2.2, multiply through by both denominators.
2. Wherever the variable *s* multiplies a variable, replace that term with the derivative of the same order as the power of *s* that is multiplying it.
3. Change the uppercase *X* and *Y* variables to lowercase.

Equation 2.3 shows the intermediate step in converting Equation 2.2 to Equation 2.1 where the multiplication through by the denominators in Equation 2.2 has taken place. The next step is to replace the terms s^2Y and $1.8sY$ by $\ddot{y}$ and $1.8\dot{y}$. Finally, the remaining uppercase *X* and *Y* variables are changed to lowercase variables and the result differential equation is as shown in Equation 2.1.

2.3 $\quad s^2Y + 1.8sY + 100Y = 100X$

The Frequency Response Format

The frequency response format describes a system's behavior as its response in magnitude and phase to a sinusoidal input signal at various frequencies. The frequency response of a system can be determined empirically, which makes it useful for systems that are not understood well enough to model using the equations of physics.

Figure 2.1 shows a frequency response representation of the transfer function in Equation 2.2. The magnitude and phase of the transfer function are displayed in the form of *Bode plots*. Bode plots show the ratio of the magnitude of the output signal to the magnitude of the input signal in *decibels* and the phase lag of the output signal relative to the input signal in degrees. The horizontal axis in both plots is the frequency of the input signal in radians per second displayed on a logarithmic scale.

Figure 2.1 Bode plots of the response of Equation 2.2.

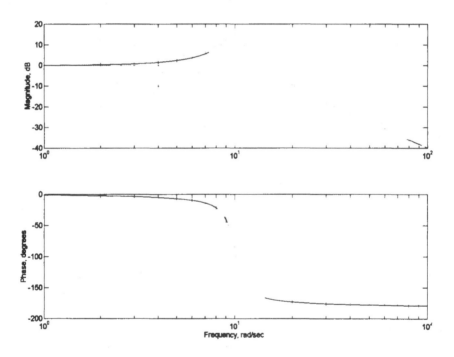

The decibel (or dB for short) is a way of expressing a ratio of two quantities. dBs are used instead of simple ratios because very large and very small ratios can be described with numbers of reasonable size. Another reason is that two ratios can be multiplied or divided by adding or subtracting their values in dB, which simplifies calculations. The mathematical definition of gain in dB appears in Equation 2.4, where z is the ratio of y to x in dB.

2.4 $z = 20\log_{10}\left|\dfrac{y}{x}\right|$ dB

The vertical bars around the quantity y/x in Equation 2.4 represent the absolute value of the ratio. z will be negative if the magnitude of y is smaller than that of x. Using this formula, if y is 1/1000 of x, z will equal –60 dB. Some other examples:

- If z is –1 dB, the ratio y/x is 0.89.
- If z is –6 dB, the ratio y/x is 0.50.
- If z is +6 dB, the ratio y/x is 2.0.

A frequency response cannot be used directly in a simulation. First, it must be transformed into a format suitable for implementing a simulation model. Assuming the system represented in the frequency response data is approximately linear, it is possible to develop an s-domain model that has a frequency response approximating the measured data. One (tedious) way to develop this model is by manually adjusting the coefficients of an s-domain model until its frequency response matches the system's frequency response to some degree.

Alternatively, the techniques of *system identification* [3] can be applied to develop a model from experimental data. System identification uses a computer program to process the sampled input signal and output signal from a test of the dynamic system. The system identification algorithms adjust the model parameters until the output of the model matches the output of the system as closely as possible. The model that results from system identification of a continuous system will typically be linear and time-invariant, and will usually be in the s-domain format. This approach will be discussed further in the section "System Identification" on page 52.

The State–Space Format

The state–space representation models a system as a set of first-order linear differential equations using matrix methods. As an example, Newton's law for a mass M moving in one dimension x under the influence of a force F is shown in Equation 2.5. A state–space representation of this second-order linear differential equation is shown in Equation 2.6. In this representation, the variable x_1 is the position of the mass and x_2 is its velocity.

2.5 $Mx'' = F$

2.6 $\begin{bmatrix} x'_1 \\ x'_2 \end{bmatrix} = \begin{bmatrix} 0 & 1 \\ 0 & 0 \end{bmatrix} \begin{bmatrix} x_1 \\ x_2 \end{bmatrix} + \begin{bmatrix} 0 \\ 1 \end{bmatrix} \dfrac{F}{M}$

When working with linear time-invariant systems it is possible to transform state–space models to equivalent transfer functions and vice versa. It is also possible to convert a state–space model containing N first-order equations into a single Nth-order differential equation. However, the state–space representation is ideal for simulation because the numerical algorithms that we use for solving differential equations apply only to first-order equations.

The three system representation formats described rely on the assumption that the system being modeled is linear and (often) time-invariant. These assumptions are only reasonable under specific conditions. For example, an aircraft can be represented as a linear time-invariant system when it is in a steady-state cruise condition, where the velocity, altitude, and pitch orientation are approximately constant over some period of time. Under these circumstances, it is reasonable (and accurate) for many purposes to assume that the response of the aircraft to the small control inputs used to maintain altitude, heading, and airspeed is linear.

It is not reasonable to expect a linear time-invariant model to be useful for simulating the flight of the aircraft from the start of the takeoff run until it reaches cruising altitude because the flight conditions change drastically in the transition from a low speed, low altitude take-off environment to a high speed, high altitude cruise condition. A high fidelity simulation model of this aircraft is necessarily nonlinear and time-varying to account for the changes in dynamic behavior as different flight regimes are encountered. Nonlinear and time-varying dynamic behavior can be modeled in a straightforward manner using differential equations, as the next section will show.

The Differential Equation Format

Differential equations are the general format for representing dynamic systems. They contain an unknown function and one or more of its derivatives. The *order* of a differential equation is the order of the highest derivative appearing in it. The solution of a differential equation is a function that satisfies the equation at all points and that also satisfies any associated boundary conditions.

High fidelity dynamic equations representing real-world systems tend to be nonlinear and time-varying. The formats for modeling dynamic systems discussed previously (s-plane, frequency response, and state–space) are usually limited to linear time-invariant models. This is because many engineering analysis and design techniques are available only for linear time-invariant models and are not applicable to nonlinear models.

A standard technique for developing a linear system model is to perform a *Taylor series expansion* of the nonlinear, time-varying dynamic equations about a stable operating point. An example of a stable operating point is the aircraft in a steady-state cruise condition as discussed in the previous section. A variety of analysis techniques can be used with the linearized system model.

Simulation uses a different approach for examining system behavior. A simulation can model the behavior of a nonlinear, time-varying system just as easily as it can model a linear, time-invariant system. The basic method used in simulation is to numerically compute estimates of the solutions of the system's dynamic equations. Although techniques exist for finding exact analytic solutions of some categories of dynamic equations, this is usually not possible unless the equations are linear and have mathematically simple input signals such as a step function or a sine wave. Dynamic systems often have input signals that are not simple in a mathematical sense. An example of a mathematically complex input function is the rotational position of an automobile steering wheel as the driver travels along a road. For these reasons, the approach most commonly used in dynamic system simulation is to perform approximate numerical integration of the dynamic equations. The details of several algorithms for numerical integration will be examined in Chapter 3.

Numerical integration algorithms operate on first-order differential equations only. This means that if a dynamic equation contains second (or higher) derivatives, it must be transformed into an equivalent set of first-order differential equations. This is a simple procedure.

1. Solve for the highest order derivative. This places the equation into the form $x^{(n)} = f(t, x, x',..., x^{(n-1)})$ where $x^{(n)}$ is the nth-order time derivative.
2. Make the following substitutions for the function and its derivatives: $x_1 = x$, $x_2 = x'$, $x_3 = x''$, and so on. This changes the equation into the form $x'_n = f(t, x_1, x_2,..., x_n)$, a first-order differential equation.
3. Write first-order differential equations for each of the variables x_1 through x_{n-1} as follows: $x'_1 = x_2, x'_2 = x_3..., x'_{n-1} = x_n$.

Here's an example. Equation 2.7 is a second-order nonlinear differential equation. The result of solving Equation 2.7 for the highest derivative appears in Equation 2.8. Equation 2.9 is a set of two first-order differential equations that are equivalent to Equation 2.7. In Equation 2.9, x_1 is equal to the solution function x of Equation 2.7 and x_2 is equal to the derivative x' in Equation 2.7. The variables x_1 and x_2 are referred to as *state variables*.

2.7 $\quad x'' + 3x'^2 + 5x = 1$

2.8 $\quad x'' = -3x'^2 - 5x + 1$

2.9 $\quad x'_2 = -3x'^2_2 - 5x_1 + 1$
$$x'_1 = x_2$$

In general, many different solution functions can satisfy a differential equation such as Equation 2.7. Additional information in the form of boundary conditions must be provided to identify the solution of interest. In dynamic system simulation, boundary conditions are specified as *initial conditions* on the state variables. The initial conditions are the values of the state variables at the start of simulation execution.

Equation 2.10 shows an example set of initial conditions at time zero that, combined with Equation 2.9, uniquely specify the solution to the dynamic equation represented by Equation 2.7.

2.10 $\quad x_2(0) = 0$
$$x'_1(0) = 0$$

2.2.2 Discrete-Time Systems

If the output of a system is updated or used only at discrete points in time, the system can be represented as a *discrete-time system*. A discrete-time system is described by a set of difference equations. One reason that this kind of modeling is of interest in the development of dynamic embedded systems is that the behavior of an embedded computer control system is well represented by a discrete-time model. This concept is applicable to embedded control systems that sample their inputs at discrete points in time, perform processing, and then update their outputs, with this cycle repeating at fixed time intervals.

In a general discrete-time system, the output at any time is some function of the current system input, previous input values, and previous output values. As with continuous systems described by differential equations in the previous section, difference equations can be linear or nonlinear and time-invariant or time-varying.

In engineering analysis and design, linear time-invariant models of discrete-time system are used in ways similar to the linear time-invariant models of continuous-time systems. For simulation purposes, it does not matter if the difference equation is linear and time-invariant or if it is nonlinear and time-varying. An example nonlinear difference equation is shown in Equation 2.11. The subscripts in Equation 2.11 represent the sample number in the discrete system's input and output sequences. y_{n+1} is the system output value at the next time step, x_n is the current input value, x_{n-1} is the input value of the previous step, y_n is the current output value, and y_{n-1} is the output value of the previous step.

$$2.11 \quad y_{n+1} = \frac{1}{2}x_n + \frac{1}{4}x_{n-1} + \frac{1}{8}y_n^2 + \frac{1}{16}y_{n-1}^2$$

The order of a difference equation is determined by the oldest previous output value that appears in the equation. Equation 2.11 is a second-order difference equation because y_{n-1} appears on the righthand side, which is two steps older than the equation output y_{n+1}. If no previous output values appear in the equation, the order of the difference equation is determined by the oldest previous input value instead.

Unlike the case of high order differential equations, there is no need to represent a high order difference equation as a set of first-order equations for simulation purposes. However, difference equations are similar to differential equations in that it is necessary to provide initial conditions to uniquely specify a solution. In Equation 2.11 — assuming that the system begins operating at $n = 0$ — the initial conditions would be y_0, y_{-1}, and x_{-1}.

2.3 Mathematical Modeling

A mathematical model is an algorithm or a set of equations that represents the interesting behavior of a system. Experts with thorough knowledge of the system and its interaction with the environment typically perform model creation tasks in development projects for complex dynamic systems. The development of a model for a complex dynamic system is an iterative process that involves significant effort to verify the correctness and accuracy of the resulting implementation.

The process of model development begins with a specification of the requirements the model must meet. The following are issues that must be addressed in developing a model of a complex system.

What effects should be included in the model? A system may exhibit many different kinds of behavior (for example, the motion of motors, vibration, wear of moving parts, etc.), but not all of these behaviors need to be modeled to produce an effective simulation. Limiting the effects modeled to only those that are truly necessary will make the model less complex and easier to build, test, and maintain — as well as requiring less computational resources to execute.

How detailed must the model be? In many cases, a simple model is all that is needed, but if precise determination of system behavior is required, the model may need to be very elaborate.

What interactions between the system and the outside environment must be modeled?   For example, a communication satellite motion model must operate in conjunction with a model of the earth's gravitational field, as well as with models of other relevant phenomena such as solar pressure.

What techniques will be used to develop the model?   A fundamental choice is whether to use physics-based equations or measured data as the basis for the model. The answer to this question is often obvious to those with expert knowledge of the system.

What data must be gathered to perform the modeling?   For example, an aerodynamic model of an aircraft may require extensive wind tunnel testing.

How much time and how many people are available to develop and test the model?   As model complexity increases, the development and test hours will increase as well.

What computing resources are available for the model?   A large model may consume significant amounts of memory, disk space, and CPU time. However, given the capabilities of current computers, this may not be a critical issue.

Will the model eventually be used in a hardware-in-the-loop (HIL) simulation?   This may place severe constraints on the execution time allowed for the model. Alternatively, a complex model may require high performance computing hardware for use in an HIL simulation, perhaps involving the use of multiple processors.

How can verification and validation be performed for the model implementation?
There must be reasonable ways of confirming that the model has been implemented correctly and that its behavior matches the system being modeled to an acceptable degree.

These issues should be addressed as part of planning for the simulation effort. The questions listed can be applied at the highest level of the entire system being simulated initially and again as the system is broken down into subsystems and individual components to be modeled. These questions are also useful in the development of additional models needed for a complete simulation, such as the gravitational field and solar pressure models in the communication satellite example above.

Although our focus is on the mathematical modeling of dynamic systems, note that the models of system components and the operational environment will not always contain dynamic behavior. For example, the motion of an aircraft in response to pilot control inputs is represented by dynamic equations. However, the atmospheric properties (air temperature, pressure, and density) at the aircraft's location are often modeled as a set of equations that depend only on the aircraft's altitude. No dynamic behavior is involved in this atmosphere model, only the determination of atmospheric attributes at a given aircraft altitude. The point here is that not all models that go into a simulation will necessarily include dynamic behavior.

2.3.1 **Level of Model Complexity**

The required level of complexity in a mathematical model can be determined by finding answers to the first two questions in the previous section, i.e., which effects to model and the level of modeling detail required. For most systems intricate enough to be worthy of simulation, a large number of effects can be identified that potentially have some bearing on system performance. The model developer must determine which of these effects are truly significant and which can be ignored. This is partially an economic decision because as more effects are added to a model, the amount of time and money needed to develop and validate the model will increase.

An example of limiting the number of effects modeled occurs in modeling the orbit of an earth satellite. In theory, the motion of the satellite will be perturbed by all of the massive bodies in the solar system and beyond. This set of bodies includes the earth, moon, sun, all the other planets, asteroids, distant stars, etc. In reality, the satellite motion is primarily influenced by a limited number of bodies, perhaps just the earth, moon, and sun. The developer can ignore the effects of the other bodies or may wish to treat them as a random disturbance, depending on the goals for the simulation. Selecting which bodies to model and which to ignore provides an answer to the first question.

Now to address the second question: the issue of model detail. A simple model for the gravitational field of the earth assumes that it is a perfect sphere and the gravitational field is uniform in all directions. The earth is actually nonspherical (it is slightly oblate) and this affects the gravitational field. Furthermore, the strength of the gravitational field varies at different locations due to local differences in the density of the earth. Thus, there are at least three levels of modeling detail for the earth gravitational field that could be selected: a perfect uniform sphere, an oblate sphere, and locally varying gravity. Each of these levels of model detail requires a different level of effort to implement and test, and each requires a different quantity and type of data that must be included in the model. Selecting which level of detail to use answers the second question.

One helpful approach when dealing with these issues is to begin with a relatively simple model containing a limited set of effects and a coarse level of model detail. Then, as the developer gains experience with the simulation, more effects and model details can be added as the need for them becomes clear. Often in the early stages of simulation development, it is not obvious which effects and model details are truly significant. If a large number of effects and model details are included in the initial design for the model, it may turn out that much effort has been wasted modeling things that turn out to be trivial in determining system performance.

If the software interfaces to each model are clearly and completely defined, it should be possible to replace these low fidelity models with higher fidelity versions without any significant changes in the rest of the simulation. Instead of replacing the original models, however, it may be more useful to maintain multiple levels of fidelity for particular models in the simulation simultaneously. This will allow the simulation user to select the desired level of fidelity of individual models as part of the simulation input data set. The availability of multiple model fidelity levels in a simulation allows the user to perform detailed modeling of particular effects or model details when needed. When this level of detail is not required, lower fidelity models can be used instead, which may reduce simulation execution time. Sometimes lower fidelity models execute at speeds orders of magnitude faster than higher fidelity versions. The ability to trade model detail for execution speed can help make the simulation a valuable tool for a variety of applications.

2.4 Modeling Methods

This section will discuss some techniques for developing the equations and data sets for a mathematical model. A model is "physics-based" if it is based on the equations of generally accepted physical laws. A spacecraft orbital model based on Newton's law of motion is an example of a physics-based model. Many systems have behavior that is too complex to represent in terms of the laws of physics. An example of this situation is the aerodynamic performance of a supersonic aircraft, which tends to be very nonlinear and difficult to represent using the equations of physics. In this case, the only reasonable approach for model development may be to measure the behavior of the system with a sub-scale model in a wind tunnel and use this data to create a set of interpolation tables. This approach leads to an "empirical" model.

2.4.1 Physics-Based Modeling: A Simple Pendulum Example

Figure 2.2 shows a pendulum suspended from a string of length l under the influence of gravitational acceleration g. The pendulum angular deflection with respect to the vertical is θ, given in radians. The mass of the pendulum bob is defined to be m. The goal for this model is to determine the period of oscillation of the pendulum as a function of the initial deflection angle θ_0, assuming that the initial velocity $\dot{\theta}_0$ is zero.

Figure 2.2 Simple pendulum.

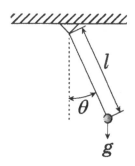

To determine the oscillation period, begin by considering which effects are significant. Look at the relevant physical effects and determine which ones to include in the model:

- Gravity must be modeled because the pendulum would not move without it.
- The mass of the pendulum bob must be modeled for the same reason.
- If we assume that the size of the bob is small in comparison to the length of the string, the bob can be modeled as a point mass. This simplifies the model significantly.

- If the mass of the string is much less than that of the bob, the mass of the string can be ignored.
- Friction within the string will be assumed to be a small effect over short time periods and will be ignored.
- The pendulum will be assumed to move slowly so that air resistance is not a significant factor over a short time period.

We know that a real pendulum will eventually slow down and stop due to friction in the string and air resistance. This is not the kind of behavior we are interested in, so we will modify our goal to be the determination of the oscillation period at the time motion is started. This assumes that the pendulum slows gradually and the oscillation period changes slowly.

We have made several simplifying assumptions that will ease the model development task. Next, apply the laws of physics to develop dynamic equations for the system. Only attempt to model the effects that were determined to be relevant in the previous analysis.

The component of gravitational force that affects the motion of the pendulum bob is in the direction perpendicular to the string. This force is defined in Equation 2.12. The gravitational force component parallel to the string will create tension in the string, but it will not affect the motion of the bob, so ignore it.

2.12 $F = -mg\sin\theta$

Note that the force F will always be acting to move the bob back towards the center position. Applying Newton's law $F = ma$ to the problem leads to Equation 2.13, where a is the tangential acceleration of the bob.

2.13 $a = -g\sin\theta$

The acceleration a is related to the angle θ by the equation $a = l\theta''$. This leads to the final dynamic equation of Equation 2.14.

2.14 $\theta'' = -\dfrac{g}{l}\sin\theta$

Note that this equation does not depend on the mass of the bob m, however it does depend on the assumptions listed previously. It is also a nonlinear differential equation because it contains the term $\sin\theta$. To completely determine a solution for this equation, the initial conditions of the system must be specified as shown in Equation 2.15. The parameter θ_0 in Equation 2.15 is the angle from which the bob is released at time zero with an initial velocity of zero. For this system, the possible values for θ_0 are assumed to lie in the range

$$[-\frac{\pi}{2}, \frac{\pi}{2}].$$

2.15 $\theta(0) = \theta_0$

$\theta'(0) = 0$

To make Equation 2.14 suitable for simulation, it must be transformed into a set of first-order differential equations using the procedure discussed in The Differential Equation Format on page 26. The resulting first-order equations and corresponding initial conditions are shown in Equation 2.16.

$$2.16 \quad \theta'_2 = -\frac{g}{l}\sin\theta_1$$

$$\theta'_1 = \theta_2$$
$$\theta_1(0) = \theta_0$$
$$\theta_2(0) = 0$$

Using the techniques of numerical integration (discussed in Chapter 3), we can solve these equations for various values of θ_0 and the oscillation period can be determined from examining the solutions.

Pendulum Simulation with the DSSL

Equation 2.16 represents a model of this dynamic system in differential equation format. With the use of the DSSL C++ routines, a complete simulation of this system is shown in Listing 2.1.

Listing 2.1 Pendulum.cpp

```cpp
// Pendulum simulation
#include <dssl.h>

#include <cstdio>
#include <cmath>

int main()
{
    // Define the state variables
    StateList state_list;
    State<> theta(&state_list), theta_dot(&state_list);

    // Integration step size and simulation end time
    const double step_time = 0.01, end_time = 10.0;

    // Set the initial conditions
    theta.ic = 0.5;
    theta_dot.ic = 0.0;
```

```
        state_list.Initialize(step_time);

        // Pendulum model parameters
        const double g = 9.81;
        const double L = 1.0;

        // Open an output file
        FILE* iov = fopen("pendulum.csv", "w");
        assert(iov);

        fprintf(iov, "Time, Theta\n");
        for(;;)
        {
            // Pendulum dynamic equations
            theta_dot.der = -(g/L) * sin(theta);
            theta.der = theta_dot;

            fprintf(iov, "%6.2lf, %9.6lf\n", state_list.Time(), double(theta));

            if (state_list.Time() >= end_time)
                break;

            state_list.Integrate();
        }

        fclose(iov);
        return 0;
}
```

This program must be compiled using the header files in the DSSL directory. You must also include the file StateList.cpp from that directory in the compilation to produce an executable image. After the program has finished executing, the file pendulum.csv will be available for analysis using a spreadsheet program such as Microsoft Excel.

Pendulum Simulation in Simulink

An equivalent model of the pendulum can be implemented in Simulink as shown in Figure 2.3. Parameters such as the simulation stop time must be set from a dialog box prior to starting a run. At the end of the run, the theta variable in the MATLAB workspace will contain the time history of the Theta1 Simulink block output. MATLAB data analysis and plotting commands can then be used to process and display the data.

Figure 2.3 Simulink pendulum model.

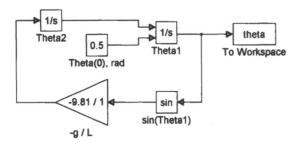

2.4.2 Linearization of Nonlinear Models

The technique of *linearization* is so common in engineering that it is worthwhile to examine some of the effects that can occur when it is used. The approach used in linearization is to identify a stable point or trajectory for a nonlinear system and model small variations about that point or trajectory using linear equations. It is possible to analyze the resulting model using a variety of mathematical methods suitable for use only with linear systems. To demonstrate the technique, this section will linearize the pendulum model from the previous section about the stable point at which the pendulum hangs straight down with zero velocity.

The nonlinear term in the pendulum model is the $\sin\theta$ term. If we make an assumption that the value of θ_0 is "small," Equation 2.14 can be modified with the approximation $\sin\theta \approx \theta$ (in radians). The limit for this approximation depends on the tolerable amount of error in the solution. This approximation results in Equation 2.17, which is now a linear differential equation that is solvable with standard calculus techniques. The solution to this equation, incorporating the initial conditions of Equation 2.15, is shown in Equation 2.18.

2.17 $\quad \ddot{\theta} = -\dfrac{g}{l}\,\theta$

2.18 $\quad \theta(t) = \theta_0 \cos\sqrt{\dfrac{g}{l}}\,t$

Equation 2.18 has an oscillation period of $2\pi\sqrt{\dfrac{l}{g}}$ seconds. Note that this period is independent of θ_0.

Our goal in solving this problem does not include the assumption of a small angle however, so we cannot employ this approximation. This example will show how the use of simplified, linear models in a simulation can produce unexpected and incorrect results when used inappropriately.

Figure 2.4 shows the results of numerically solving the nonlinear model of Equation 2.16 for values of θ_0 ranging from zero to 90 degrees and determining the oscillation period of each solution from the simulation output data. It also shows the oscillation period derived from the linear approximation to the solution, which is a constant for all θ_0. It is clear that as θ_0 approaches zero, the linear approximation becomes a good match to the nonlinear model. It is also clear that using the linearized model will result in significant errors if θ_0 is large.

Figure 2.4 Comparison of nonlinear and linear pendulum model oscillation periods.

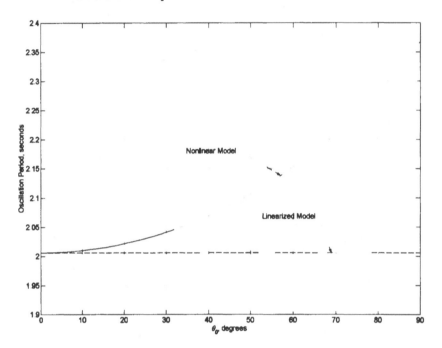

This example demonstrates the basic approach for developing a physics-based mathematical model of a dynamic system. Similar model development techniques are useful in other disciplines such as electronics and chemistry. These modeling techniques are applicable as long as the dynamic equations describing the system are well defined and the data values used in the equations are known with sufficient precision. In the pendulum example, the data values required were the gravitational acceleration g, the string length l, and the initial displacement θ_0. In addition, it is necessary to examine other data to verify that the assumptions used in the model development are reasonable — such as the assumption that the mass of the string is small relative to the mass of the bob.

Linear approximations of dynamic systems are used frequently in engineering, but their limitations should be well understood. Nonlinear system models are appropriate for use in simulation, and will result in more accurate results as compared to simplified linear models.

In situations where the dynamic equations or data values for a mathematical model are not known to a sufficient degree of precision, it is necessary to use alternative methods for model development. These techniques are discussed in the next section.

2.4.3 Empirical Modeling

Empirical modeling techniques use measured data from various types of experiments to develop a mathematical model of a system. In reality, all mathematical models are empirical to some degree. For example, the pendulum model in the previous section includes some experimentally determined constants. However, our interest in this section is on the development of models for systems with substantial dynamic behavior that is not readily modeled by known dynamic equations. The following sections present three empirical modeling techniques: table interpolation, system identification, and neural networks.

Table Interpolation

Table interpolation is a static modeling technique used to evaluate functions of the form shown in Equation 2.19. It is a static method because it does not permit the direct implementation of dynamic equations. However, table interpolation functions are useful in the construction of dynamic equations. For example, it is common to compute coefficients appearing in dynamic equations using table interpolation.

2.19 $y = f(x_1, x_2, x_3, \ldots)$

This approach is used when the function output must be determined experimentally. It is also applicable as a speed optimization technique if a lengthy computation (perhaps an iterative procedure) is required to evaluate the function. In that case, a table interpolation to estimate the result of the computation may execute many times faster than a direct computation.

The function inputs x_1, x_2, etc. can be any variable in the simulation — such as time, a state variable, or a constant. The number of function inputs is arbitrary, but in practical applications, it is usually five or less. As more inputs are added to the function, its memory requirements and execution time will increase. The output y depends only on the values of the function inputs at the time of evaluation.

An interpolation function with N inputs is evaluated with the use of an N-dimensional lookup table. Each input variable spans one dimension of the lookup table. For each table dimension, it is necessary to define a set of interpolation breakpoints which span the permissible range of the corresponding input variable. Each input variable can have a different number of interpolation breakpoints, and the breakpoints may be spaced equally across the span of the dimension or placed at arbitrary intervals.

A one-dimensional example of the data for a lookup table with eight equally-spaced breakpoints appears in Figure 2.5. The span of the input variable x is [0, 0.7]. If the input variable precisely matches the x location of one of the breakpoints, it is a simple matter to return the corresponding y value as the result of the function evaluation. If the input value falls between the breakpoints, an interpolation must be performed.

Figure 2.5 Example one-dimensional lookup table.

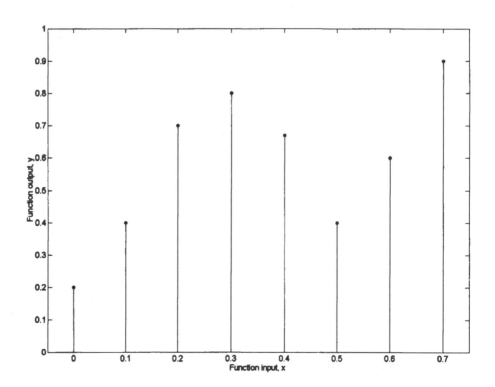

Many different techniques for performing interpolation exist that vary in computational complexity and smoothness of the interpolated function. Two methods that should satisfy most needs are: linear interpolation and cubic spline interpolation.

Linear Interpolation with Equally-Spaced Breakpoints

We can perform one-dimensional linear interpolation graphically by drawing straight lines between adjacent breakpoints as shown in Figure 2.6. The interpolated function is continuous and its derivative is discontinuous at the breakpoints.

Figure 2.6 Linear breakpoint interpolation.

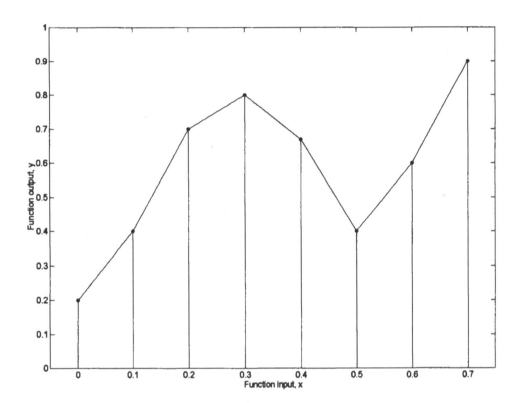

One-dimensional linear interpolation using equally-spaced breakpoints is performed with the following steps. Assume that there are N breakpoints with y coordinates stored in an array with indexes that begin at zero. The value of $x(0)$, the leftmost x coordinate, and Δx, the interval between x coordinates, must also be provided.

1. Ensure that the input variable x_{in} has a value greater than or equal to $x(0)$ and less than or equal to $x(0) + (N - 1)\Delta x$. A limit function can be applied, if that is appropriate. It is also possible to linearly extrapolate outside the table using the first (or last) two data points in the table to define a straight line. However, this approach may introduce significant errors if the extrapolation does not accurately model the behavior of the function outside the range of the table — do not consider it here. It may make more sense to issue an error message and abort the simulation run if the input variable is outside the valid input range of the table.

2. Determine the array index of the closest breakpoint with an x coordinate that is less than or equal to the function input value. For equally-spaced breakpoints, the lower breakpoint index is computed as shown in Equation 2.20. Note that L is truncated to an integer.

$$2.20 \quad L = \left\lfloor \frac{x_{in} - x(0)}{\Delta x} \right\rfloor$$

In Equation 2.20, L is the index of the lower of the two breakpoints that surround the input value x_{in}, $x(0)$ is the x coordinate of the first breakpoint in the array, and Δx is the x interval between breakpoints. Based on the range limits placed on x_{in} in step 1, L will be in the range $0 \le L < N - 1$.

3. Perform linear interpolation between the breakpoints with indices L and $L + 1$ as shown in Equation 2.21. A special case occurs when $L = N - 1$, which is when x_{in} is located at the last breakpoint in the array and the correct interpolation result is $y = y(N - 1)$. When this happens, $y(L + 1)$ is undefined, although it ends up being multiplied by zero. It is important to handle this case properly to avoid potential memory access faults and floating point problems.

$$2.21 \quad y = y(L) + [y(L + 1) - y(L)] \frac{x_{in} - x(L)}{\Delta x}$$

Linear Interpolation with Unequally-Spaced Breakpoints

If the x coordinates of the breakpoints are not equally spaced, it takes more work to determine which breakpoint interval contains the function input value. A general approach for locating the correct interval is the technique of bisection — an algorithm for performing an efficient search of an ordered list.

The bisection algorithm locates the breakpoint pair surrounding the function input value. Assume that the x and y breakpoint coordinates are stored in arrays of length N that are indexed starting at zero.

1. Ensure that the input variable x_{in} has a value greater than or equal to the first breakpoint in the table and less than or equal to the last breakpoint.

2. Define an index variable L and initialize it to zero. Define an index variable U and initialize it to $N - 1$. These lower and upper indexes bracket the entire list initially.

3. Repeat the following steps until the quantity $(U - L)$ is equal to one:

   (a) Set the current index i to be $\dfrac{U + L}{2}$, truncated to an integer.

   (b) If the breakpoint at index i is greater than the input x_{in}, set $U = i$. Otherwise, set $L = i$.

4. Upon exiting the loop in the previous step, L will contain the index of the lower breakpoint of the correct breakpoint interval.

5. Perform linear interpolation between the breakpoints at indices L and $L + 1$ as shown in Equation 2.22.

$$2.22 \quad y = y(L) + [y(L + 1) - y(L)] \frac{x_{in} - x(L)}{x(L + 1) - x(L)}$$

Although the bisection method is the most general technique for locating the correct breakpoint interval, it may be possible to eliminate this search much of the time. If the input value x changes slowly between evaluations of the function, the simple step of checking to see if the input is contained in the same breakpoint interval as the previous function evaluation will often eliminate the need for bisection. If the input is not in the same interval, bisection can then be performed.

Alternatively, as a next step, the breakpoint intervals immediately above and below the previously-used interval can be checked, and bisection performed if the input does not lie in those intervals. The technique of checking the previously-used breakpoint interval followed by checking the adjacent intervals (if necessary) can sometimes eliminate the use of bisection completely, except for the very first function evaluation. This efficiency is realized when the input variable does not change quickly enough to jump over a breakpoint interval between function evaluations. The drawback of this technique is that, when the assumption of a slowly changing input turns out to be incorrect, the function evaluation process will be a bit slower due to the additional checking that precedes bisection.

On average, the bisection algorithm requires approximately $\log_2 N$ iterations of the loop in step 3 of the algorithm, which is considerably more time consuming than the direct computation used to locate the breakpoint interval when equally-spaced breakpoints are used. The advantage of using unequally-spaced breakpoints is that it may be possible to adequately model a function with a much smaller table than would be required with equally-spaced breakpoints. The points can be closely spaced in regions where the function has rapid fluctuations and they can be more widely spaced in regions where the function is relatively smooth. When using equally-spaced breakpoints, the points must be spaced closely enough to accommodate the most rapid fluctuations in the function even if these fluctuations only occurs over a small part of the input variable's span.

An example will clarify this point. We will use table interpolation to evaluate the function $y = \cos(x^4)$ over the input span [0,2] and compare the required table size for equally-spaced and unequally-spaced breakpoints. Require that the maximum interpolation error magnitude be no greater than 0.05 at any location along the curve.

Figure 2.7 shows the result of selecting unequally-spaced breakpoints to evaluate this function. The breakpoints were carefully selected to limit the error magnitude to the required 0.05 at any location between them. The breakpoints at both ends of the input range must always be included. Note how the breakpoints are widely spaced in the lower x values and are closely spaced as the function varies more rapidly in the higher x values. Twenty-one breakpoints are required in this case.

Figure 2.7 Unequally-spaced breakpoint interpolation of $y = \cos(x^4)$.

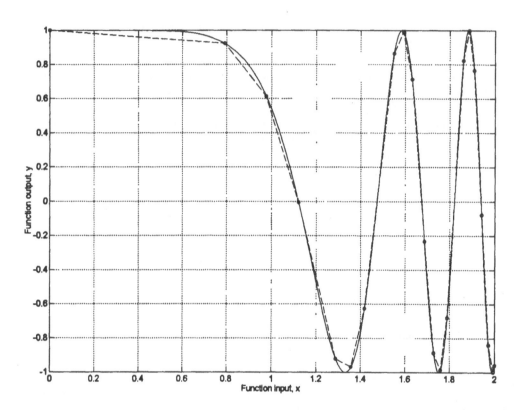

If equally-spaced breakpoints are used instead, it is necessary to use a breakpoint interval of 0.02 in order to limit the approximation error between breakpoints to 0.05 as shown in Figure 2.8. This requires 101 total breakpoints — a factor of 4.8 more points than are required in the unequally-spaced breakpoint implementation of this function.

Figure 2.8   Equally-spaced breakpoint interpolation of $y = \cos(x^4)$.

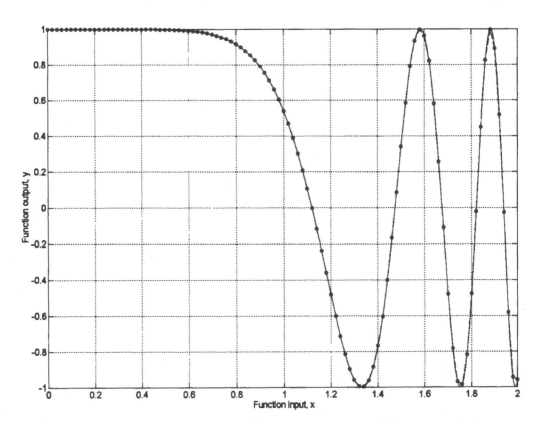

Figure 2.9 shows the interpolation error for both the unequally-spaced breakpoints of Figure 2.7 and the equally-spaced breakpoints of Figure 2.8. The error is distributed relatively evenly along the x axis for the case of unequal breakpoint spacing. In the equally-spaced breakpoint case, the error is very small for the lower part of the x range and grows larger as the function fluctuates more rapidly.

Figure 2.9 Interpolation error in Figure 2.7 and 2.8.

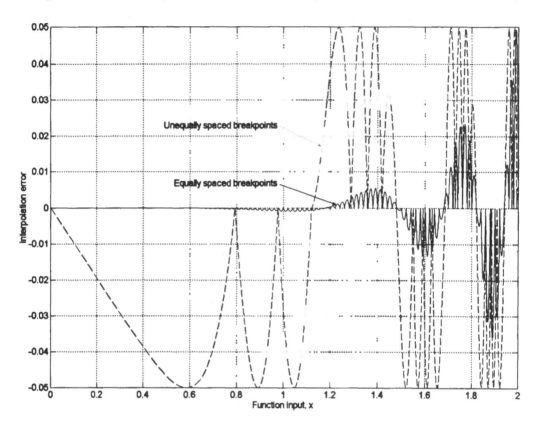

This example shows that, when using table interpolation, we must give some consideration to the choice between equally-spaced breakpoints versus unequally-spaced breakpoints. The selection of the appropriate type of breakpoint spacing depends on

- the characteristics of the function or data to be interpolated,
- the time available for function evaluation, and
- the memory available for table storage.

If unequally-spaced breakpoints are used, the locations of the breakpoints must be selected carefully to minimize the number of breakpoints required while simultaneously limiting the magnitude of the interpolation error. When equally-spaced breakpoints are used, one must choose the breakpoint interval to limit the maximum interpolation error to an acceptable value.

Cubic Spline Interpolation

A drawback of the linear interpolation method is that the derivative of the evaluated function is discontinuous at the breakpoints, as can be seen in Figure 2.6 (page 39). If a smoother interpolation function is required, cubic spline interpolation is an appropriate choice. Cubic spline interpolation uses a third-order polynomial to estimate the function value between breakpoints. Using this method, the estimating function, as well is its first and second derivatives, are continuous both between and at the breakpoints. In a sense, the cubic spline gives the smoothest interpolation possible through the breakpoints defining the function.

The costs of using cubic spline interpolation rather than linear interpolation are an increase in execution time and an increase in data memory required for a given number of breakpoints — as well as a significantly more complex algorithm. Each breakpoint interval requires the determination of four coefficients for the third-order interpolating polynomial, and this polynomial must be evaluated to determine the function output.

If the function to be approximated is somewhat smooth, it may be possible to use fewer breakpoints with cubic spline interpolation than would be needed with linear interpolation. This may mitigate the additional storage space required for the polynomial coefficients. Figure 2.10 shows the same set of interpolation breakpoints as Figure 2.5 with cubic spline interpolation used to estimate the function value between the breakpoints.

Figure 2.10 Cubic spline breakpoint interpolation.

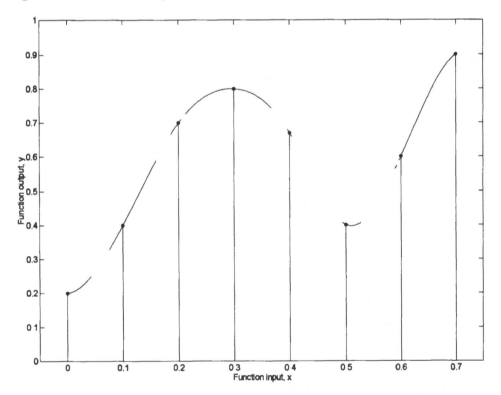

A simulation application of this algorithm should be broken into two steps. A preprocessing step during initialization determines the polynomial coefficients for each breakpoint interval. The resulting coefficient values are stored for use during simulation execution. During the simulation run, the function evaluation is carried out by first locating the breakpoint interval containing the input value (either equally-spaced or unequally-spaced breakpoints can be used) and evaluating the polynomial using the stored coefficients. An example of an algorithm for efficiently performing cubic spline interpolation with unequally-spaced breakpoints appears in [5].

Multidimensional Table Interpolation

The table interpolation examples presented in the previous sections were for functions that had only one input variable. The discussion now turns to interpolation methods for functions that have multiple inputs.

To define a multiple-input interpolation function, each input variable must have a set of breakpoints (either equally-spaced or unequally-spaced) associated with it. A function may have equally-spaced breakpoints for some input variables and unequally-spaced breakpoints for others. For each input, the breakpoint interval containing the current input must be located using the appropriate technique as described in "Linear Interpolation with Equally-Spaced Breakpoints" on page 38 and the following section "Linear Interpolation with Unequally-Spaced Breakpoints" on page 40. Using these breakpoints, a multidimensional interpolation must then be performed. It is possible to use linear interpolation for some input variables and cubic spline or other interpolation methods for other inputs, if that is appropriate.

Here's an example of a two-input function with equally-spaced breakpoints and linear interpolation for both input variables. It is straightforward to extend this example to three or more dimensions. Equations 2.23, 2.24, and 2.25 list the x and y axis breakpoint locations and the function values z at those locations. The table in Equation 2.25 is defined so that increasing values of x appear in the columns from left to right and increasing values of y are listed in the rows from top to bottom.

2.23 $\quad x=[3\ 4\ 5\ 6]$

2.24 $\quad y=[1.2\ 1.4\ 1.6\ 1.8]$

2.25 $\quad z = \begin{bmatrix} 0 & 0.1 & 0.3 & 0.3 \\ 0.1 & 0.3 & 0.5 & 0.4 \\ 0.1 & 0.5 & 0.6 & 0.7 \\ 0.2 & 0.5 & 0.6 & 0.9 \end{bmatrix}$

We will evaluate this function using linear interpolation. Assume that the correct breakpoint interval for each function input has already been located using the techniques mentioned previously. This example uses equally-spaced breakpoints, but the steps are identical for unequally-spaced breakpoints once the correct breakpoint interval has been determined for each input.

In Figure 2.11, the function inputs x and y define the point p, where we wish to evaluate the function output z. The four points defined by the intersection of the lines $x = x_1$, $x = x_2$, $y = y_1$, and $y = y_2$ represent the breakpoints that surround p (as defined in Equations 2.23, 2.24, and 2.25).

Two-dimensional interpolation must be performed in two steps.

1. The function z value is computed at the points p_1 and p_2 by performing linear interpolation along the x dimension.
2. The function z value at the point p is computed by performing linear interpolation between p_1 and p_2 along the y dimension.

Figure 2.11 Two-dimensional linear interpolation.

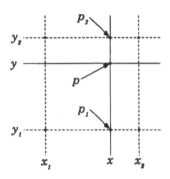

As a numerical example, let the input (x, y) pair be $(4.8, 1.55)$. Consulting Equations 2.23, 2.24, and 2.25, observe that $x_1 = 4$, $x_2 = 5$, $y_1 = 1.4$, $y_2 = 1.6$, $z(x_1, y_1) = 0.3$, $z(x_2, y_1) = 0.5$, $z(x_1, y_2) = 0.5$, and $z(x_2, y_2) = 0.6$.

First, compute the interpolated function values at p_1 and p_2 using the formulas shown in Equation 2.26. Numerical results for this example are shown in Equation 2.27.

$$2.26 \quad z(x,y_1) = z(x_1,y_1) + [z(x_2,y_1) - z(x_1,y_1)]\frac{x - x_1}{x_2 - x_2}$$

$$z(x,y_2) = z(x_1,y_2) + [z(x_2,y_2) - z(x_1,y_2)]\frac{x - x_1}{x_2 - x_1}$$

$$2.27 \quad z(x,y_1) = z(4.8,1.4)= 0.3 + [0.5 - 0.3]\frac{4.8 - 4}{5 - 4}= 0.46$$

$$z(x,y_2) = z(4.8,1.6)= 0.5 + [0.6 - 0.5]\frac{4.8 - 4}{5 - 4}= 0.58$$

Finally, perform linear interpolation between the two function values computed in Equation 2.26 along the y dimension as shown in Equation 2.28. The result is the interpolated value of the function output at the point p, with the numerical result for this example shown in Equation 2.29.

$$2.28 \quad z(x,y) = z(x,y_1) + [z(x,y_2) - z(x,y_1)]\frac{y - y_1}{y_2 - y_1}$$

2.29 $z(x,y) = 0.46 + [0.58 - 0.46]\dfrac{1.55 - 1.4}{1.6 - 1.4} = 0.55$

A plot of the function defined by Equations 2.23, 2.24, and 2.25 using linear interpolation appears in Figure 2.12. Note that the between-breakpoint surfaces resulting from the linear interpolation will not generally be flat. The only time an interpolation surface will be flat is when the four points at the corners of the surface all happen to lie in the same plane.

Figure 2.12 Two-dimensional function evaluation using linear interpolation.

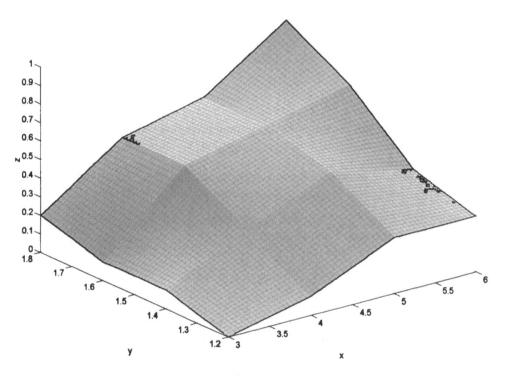

The function of Equations 2.23, 2.24, and 2.25 has been plotted using cubic spline interpolation in Figure 2.13. The resulting interpolated function is very smooth and passes through all the z values defined by the table of breakpoints. However, substantially more computation is required for multidimensional cubic spline interpolation. As was noted in the one-dimensional case, it may be possible to use fewer breakpoints if the interpolated function is smooth and maps well to the approximating polynomials used in cubic spline interpolation. The selection of the appropriate interpolation method depends on the requirements of the application.

It is possible to extend multidimensional interpolation to use any number of input variables. For example, with three inputs, linear interpolation is performed across a three dimensional box using the eight breakpoint values located at the box corners. In general, an

N-dimensional linear interpolation will require $2^N - 1$ one-dimensional interpolations to compute an output.

Figure 2.13 Two-dimensional function evaluation using cubic spline interpolation.

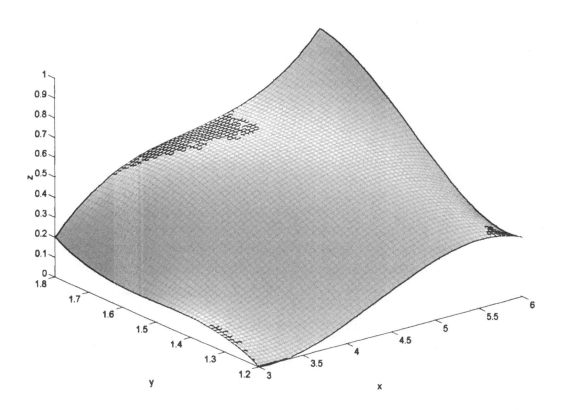

Linear function interpolation is a common tool in the simulation of complex dynamic systems. The selection of equally-spaced versus unequally-spaced breakpoints is a tradeoff between data table size and speed of function evaluation that depends on the characteristics of the data that represent the function. Linear interpolation is the standard method used with these tables due to the speed and simplicity of function evaluation. More complex interpolation techniques, such as the cubic spline method discussed here, are applicable when the requirements of a particular application dictate the use of a smoother approximating function.

Linear Interpolation with the DSSL

The DSSL library can perform linear interpolation for functions with any number of dimensions. Each function input can use either equally-spaced or unequally-spaced breakpoints. Equally-spaced breakpoints are the most computationally efficient. The unequally-spaced breakpoint algorithm employs the technique of first checking to see if the function input falls within the previous breakpoint interval, followed by testing the two surrounding intervals before resorting to bisection. Because of this, the use of unequally-spaced breakpoints may *not* result in significantly worse performance if the input function changes in sufficiently small steps between function interpolations.

Listing 2.2 shows a program that performs two-dimensional table interpolation with equally-spaced breakpoints along both axes. The output file created by this program was plotted in MATLAB to produce Figure 2.12.

Listing 2.2 `InterpTest.cpp`

```
// Two dimensional interpolation

#include <dssl.h>

#include <cstdio>
#include <cassert>

int main()
{
    // Define the equally-spaced breakpoints. The first argument is the
    // first breakpoint value; the second is the breakpoint separation.
    EqSpacedBkpt<4> x_bkpt(3, 1), y_bkpt(1.2, 0.2);

    // Define a two-dimensional interpolation function with the above bkpts
    LinearInterp<2> interp;
    interp.SetDimension(0, &x_bkpt);
    interp.SetDimension(1, &y_bkpt);

    const double data[] =
    {
        0.0, 0.1, 0.3, 0.3,
        0.1, 0.3, 0.5, 0.4,
        0.1, 0.5, 0.6, 0.7,
        0.2, 0.5, 0.6, 0.9
    };

    interp.SetupData(data);

    // Open a file for the output data
    FILE* iov = fopen("z.txt", "w");
```

```
    assert(iov);

    // Interpolate the function across the ranges of the X and Y breakpoints
    // and write the results to the output file
    for (int ix=0; ix<=60; ix++)
    {
        double x = 3 + 0.05 * ix; // Function X input
        x_bkpt(x);
        for (int iy=0; iy<=60; iy++)
        {
            double y = 1.2 + 0.01 * iy; // Function Y input
            y_bkpt(y);

            double z = interp(); // Function interpolation result
            fprintf(iov, " %lf", z);
        }

        fprintf(iov, "\n");
    }

    fclose(iov);
    return 0;
}
```

Linear Interpolation in Simulink

Simulink provides a one-dimensional table interpolation block as shown in Figure 2.14. This block takes two equal-length one-dimensional arrays as parameters: a monotonically increasing vector of x axis coordinates (which may be equally or unequally-spaced) and a vector of corresponding y values. If the block input is outside the range of the x array, the block performs extrapolation using the first or last two breakpoints. This block displays a graph of the function (compare to Figure 2.6).

Figure 2.14 Simulink one-dimensional interpolation.

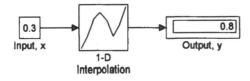

Simulink also has a two-dimensional interpolation block, shown in Figure 2.15. The parameters for this block are monotonically increasing arrays for the x and y axis breakpoints and the two-dimensional table of z values. The table must have the same number of columns as the number of x axis breakpoints and the same number of rows as the number of y axis breakpoints. If either input is outside the range of the corresponding set of breakpoints, the block extrapolates along that dimension. This block displays a graph of the table, with each table column drawn as a line.

Figure 2.15 Simulink two-dimensional interpolation.

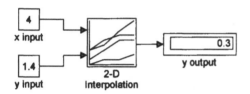

Simulink v4 provides additional blocks for performing interpolation along more than two dimensions. These newly-added blocks permit any number of function inputs and they support linear interpolation as well as cubic spline interpolation. The blocks allow the developer to select whether an out-of-range function input should result in limiting it to the valid range, extrapolating it, or halting the simulation with an error message.

System Identification

Another technique for developing models of dynamic systems is *system identification* [3]. To perform system identification, one or more test input data sequences and the measured output data sequences are required for the system being modeled. Typically, tests of a real world system must be designed and executed to generate this data. By applying a variety of system identification algorithms, it is possible to derive an estimate of the system transfer function from input to output. The resulting model is typically linear and time-invariant, so the developer must verify that this is an adequate representation of the system.

This book will not examine the details of algorithms for performing system identification. Simply note that, as was shown in "The s-plane Format" on page 23, it is a straightforward procedure to convert an s-domain transfer function resulting from system identification into an equivalent set of first-order differential equations suitable for implementation in a simulation.

The model resulting from system identification is a dynamic model, while table interpolation methods are static function evaluation techniques. System identification and table interpolation methods are similar in that they are based on the use of measured data rather than an assumed set of mathematical relations as was the case in physics-based modeling.

Neural Networks

Neural networks [6] provide a method for developing models from data using a method that is conceptually similar to system identification, but with a fundamentally different mathematical approach. A neural network is based on simple mathematical models of biological neurons — the fundamental cognitive units of the brain. This technique can be used to model highly nonlinear systems and phenomena that do not have an associated physics-based model.

A neural network functions as a static model, meaning that it processes a set of inputs to produce an output value during each evaluation. The actual processing occurs within the neurons. The neurons are interconnected through links, each of which has a weight associated with it. A weight controls the strength of the signal transmitted over its link. Each neuron has a set of these weighted signals connected to its input, which are summed and applied to the neuron activation function. The activation function determines the output signal of the neuron.

The "programming" of a neural network is contained in the connection pattern of the neurons, the type of activation function used within each neuron, and the learning algorithm used to set the connection weights between the neurons. The connection weights are set by an iterative procedure called *training* which applies a set of inputs to the network, evaluates the network output using the current weights, and compares the network output to the expected output. This comparison generates an error signal, which the learning algorithm uses to adjust the network connection weights to reduce the error. Training a neural network to perform a useful task may require applying thousands of training examples until the error for each example has been reduced to an acceptable level.

The training of a neural network is often a lengthy procedure, but once that step has been completed, the resulting model is fast and efficient. A simulation developer should consider the use of neural networks in simulation modeling when a complex, nonlinear system is to be modeled and the techniques presented earlier in this chapter cannot be used to develop a suitable model. One requirement for neural network model development is that a sufficiently large set of input-output training examples must be available to perform the training procedure.

2.5 Rigid Body Motion in Three-Dimensional Space

A model that describes the translational and rotational motion of one or more objects must express the motion of those objects with respect to a set of coordinate systems. It must be possible to determine the position, velocity, angular orientation, and rotational rate of each object in the different coordinate systems to perform system simulation. For example, when Newton's Law of motion is applied to determine the translational motion of an object, you must determine the direction of forces and moments acting on the object with respect to inertial (nonrotating and nonaccelerating) space. This may be difficult, because the forces and moments acting on the body are frequently defined in terms of a body-fixed coordinate system that accelerates and rotates with the object.

In an aircraft flight simulation, there are typically two primary coordinate systems [7]. One coordinate system is fixed to the body of the aircraft and moves with it in both translation and rotation. This coordinate system has its origin at the aircraft center of mass and is called the body-fixed coordinate system. The other originates on the surface of the earth at a defined location and is called the earth-fixed coordinate system. The relations between these coordinate systems define the aircraft position, velocity, *Euler angles* (roll, pitch, and yaw angles), and rotation rates.

In many cases, the effects of the rotation of the earth and its curvature are negligible, which allows the earth to be modeled as flat and nonrotating. Under these assumptions, the earth-fixed coordinate system is an inertial system, which allows the direct application of Newton's Law of motion. If the rotation of the earth is not negligible for a particular application, a more complex model defines an inertial coordinate system with its origin at the center of the earth. In this model, the earth-fixed coordinate system also has its origin at the earth center and rotates with respect to the inertial coordinate system. The motion of the aircraft is defined relative to the rotating earth coordinate system, and the equations of motion must be applied with reference to the inertial coordinate system. Although this level of modeling detail is sometimes necessary, we will not consider such complex cases.

2.5.1 Two-Dimensional Motion

Let's first examine the relatively simple case of a body that moves in a two-dimensional plane and rotates about the axis perpendicular to the plane. Figure 2.16 shows the relationship between the body-fixed coordinate system (x_b, y_b) and the (assumed inertial) earth-fixed coordinate system (x_e, y_e).

Figure 2.16 Coordinate systems for two dimensional motion.

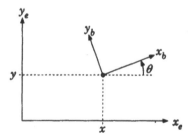

If we assume that the body mass m and its rotational inertia I are constant, the differential equations that describe the translational and rotational motion of the body in terms of the forces and the rotational moment in the body-fixed axes are shown in Equation 2.30. In these equations, F_x and F_y are the instantaneous forces acting on the body along the x_b and y_b axes, and M is the instantaneous rotational moment acting in the direction of the angle θ as shown in Figure 2.16. Equation 2.30 describes the position and orientation of the body in inertial space given the forces and moment acting on it in body-fixed coordinates at each instant in time. To completely specify the motion of the body, Equation 2.30 requires the forces F_x and F_y and the moment M as functions of time over the integration interval, as well as six initial conditions specifying $x(0)$, $x'(0)$, $y(0)$, $y'(0)$, $\theta(0)$, and $\theta'(0)$.

2.30 $x'' = \dfrac{[F_x\cos\theta - F_y\sin\theta]}{m}$

$\quad\ \ y'' = \dfrac{[F_x\sin\theta + F_y\cos\theta]}{m}$

$\quad\ \ \theta'' = \dfrac{M}{I}$

These equations of motion can be represented more clearly with the use of vector-matrix notation. The differential equations in Equation 2.30 can be rewritten as shown in Equation 2.31, where the position vector $P = [x\ y]^T$ and the force vector $F = [F_x\ F_y]^T$. The superscript T indicates matrix or vector transposition.

2.31 $P'' = \begin{bmatrix} \cos\theta & -\sin\theta \\ \sin\theta & \cos\theta \end{bmatrix}\dfrac{F}{m} = \mathbf{C}(\theta)^T\dfrac{F}{m}$

The matrix $\mathbf{C}(\theta)$ in Equation 2.31 is called a *direction cosine matrix*. It is an orthonormal matrix, which means that

$\quad\ \ \mathbf{C}(\theta)^{-1} = \mathbf{C}(\theta)^T$

for any value of θ. In other words, the matrix inverse of $\mathbf{C}(\theta)$ is equal to its transpose.

When a vector in earth-fixed coordinates is premultiplied by $\mathbf{C}(\theta)$, the result will be a vector in body-fixed coordinates, except for the difference in origin location. Using the orthonormality of $\mathbf{C}(\theta)$, you can transform a vector in body-fixed coordinates to earth-fixed coordinates (except for the difference in origin location) by premultiplying it by

$\quad\ \ \mathbf{C}(\theta)^T.$

These relationships are shown in Equation 2.32, where $\mathbf{X}_b$ is an arbitrary vector in body-fixed coordinates and $\mathbf{X}_e$ is the equivalent (except for the difference in origin location) vector in earth-fixed coordinates.

2.32 $\mathbf{X}_b = \mathbf{C}(\theta)\mathbf{X}_e$

$\quad\ \ \mathbf{X}_e = \mathbf{C}(\theta)^T\mathbf{X}_b$

2.5.2 Three-Dimensional Motion

When the motion of a body extends to three degrees of freedom in both translation and rotation, the dynamic equations become somewhat more complicated. However, the additional effort is worthwhile because this method of simulating the motion of a body accurately models the translational and rotational motion of rigid bodies in three-dimensional space. This approach is called "six degrees of freedom motion simulation," often shortened to "6DOF" simulation. I will present two methods for solving the 6DOF rotational equations of motion in a simulation, but first I'll clarify some issues regarding the coordinate systems.

The coordinate systems used here will always be orthogonal, meaning that the three coordinate axes are at right angles to each other. Our coordinate systems will also be right-handed, which means that an angular rotation has a positive sign when it occurs in a clockwise direction as viewed along the positive direction of the axis of rotation. In addition, in a right-handed coordinate system the z axis will be in the direction of the vector cross product between the x and y axes. In terms of unit-length vectors along each axis, $u_z = u_x \times u_y$ in a right-handed coordinate system. Figure 2.17 shows a positive rotation through the angle ψ from the (x_1, y_1, z_1) coordinate system to the (x_2, y_2, z_2) coordinate system, where the z_1 and z_2 axes are identical. Both of these coordinate systems are right-handed and orthogonal.

Figure 2.17 Positive rotation about the z axis.

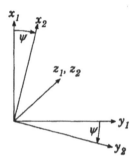

Next, we will examine the transformation of a vector in a given initial coordinate system through angular rotations about the three axes in a particular sequence. By performing these three rotations, we can place the transformed coordinate system in any desired orientation. The steps are: rotate about the z_1 axis, then about the y_2 axis, and finish with a rotation about the x_3 axis.

In matrix-vector form, the transformation of a vector from the (x_1, y_1, z_1) coordinate system to the (x_2, y_2, z_2) coordinate system is as shown in Equation 2.33.

$$2.33 \quad X_2 = \begin{bmatrix} \cos\psi & \sin\psi & 0 \\ -\sin\psi & \cos\psi & 0 \\ 0 & 0 & 1 \end{bmatrix} X_1 = C_z(\psi)X_1$$

In Equation 2.33, the vector X_1 is an arbitrary vector in the (x_1, y_1, z_1)coordinate system, X_2 is the same vector in the (x_2, y_2, z_2) coordinate system, and $C_z(\psi)$ is the direction cosine matrix that performs this coordinate transformation. The subscript z indicates the axis of rotation and the parameter ψ indicates the angle of rotation. Similarly, the next rotation through the angle θ about the y_2 axis is shown in Equation 2.34. The result of this transformation is the vector X_3.

$$2.34 \quad X_3 = \begin{bmatrix} \cos\theta & 0 & -\sin\theta \\ 0 & 1 & 0 \\ \sin\theta & 0 & \cos\theta \end{bmatrix} X_2 = C_y(\theta)X_2$$

The final rotation through the angle ϕ about the x_3 axis is shown in Equation 2.35. The vector $\mathbf{X}_4$ is the result after the full three axis coordinate transformation.

$$2.35 \quad \mathbf{X}_4 = \begin{bmatrix} 1 & 0 & 0 \\ 0 & \cos\phi & \sin\phi \\ 0 & -\sin\phi & \cos\phi \end{bmatrix} \mathbf{X}_3 = \mathbf{C}_x(\phi)\mathbf{X}$$

The complete transformation from the (x_1, y_1, z_1) coordinate system to the (x_4, y_4, z_4) coordinate system appears in Equation 2.36, where the three single axis direction cosine matrices are applied in sequence using matrix multiplication.

$$2.36 \quad \mathbf{X}_4 = \begin{bmatrix} 1 & 0 & 0 \\ 0 & \cos\phi & \sin\phi \\ 0 & -\sin\phi & \cos\phi \end{bmatrix} \begin{bmatrix} \cos\theta & 0 & -\sin\theta \\ 0 & 1 & 0 \\ \sin\theta & 0 & \cos\theta \end{bmatrix} \begin{bmatrix} \cos\psi & \sin\psi & 0 \\ -\sin\psi & \cos\psi & 0 \\ 0 & 0 & 1 \end{bmatrix} \mathbf{X}_1 = \mathbf{C}_x(\phi)\mathbf{C}_y(\theta)\mathbf{C}_z(\psi)\mathbf{X}_1$$

Equation 2.37 shows the result of multiplying out the matrices in Equation 2.36. We will call this matrix the $\mathbf{C}_{zyx}(\psi, \theta, \phi)$ matrix to indicate the sequence of axes used for rotations and the angle of rotation about each axis. Note that matrix multiplication is not generally commutative, so changing the order of the axes for the rotations produces a different (and incorrect) result. Because of this, it is critical to perform the axis rotations in the correct order.

$$2.37 \quad \mathbf{X}_4 = \begin{bmatrix} \cos\theta\cos\psi & \cos\theta\sin\psi & -\sin\theta \\ \sin\phi\sin\theta\cos\psi - \cos\phi\sin\psi & \sin\phi\sin\theta\sin\psi + \cos\phi\cos\psi & \sin\phi\cos\theta \\ \cos\phi\sin\theta\cos\psi + \sin\phi\sin\psi & \cos\phi\sin\theta\sin\psi - \sin\phi\cos\psi & \cos\phi\cos\theta \end{bmatrix} \mathbf{X}_1$$

$$= \mathbf{C}_{zyx}(\psi, \theta, \phi)\mathbf{X}_1$$

The orthonormality of the direction cosine matrix is maintained through the complete three axis rotation. Because of this, the direction cosine matrix for performing the reverse transform from the $\mathbf{X}_4$ vector to the $\mathbf{X}_1$ vector is the transpose of the $\mathbf{C}_{zyx}(\psi, \theta, \phi)$ matrix, which produces the $\mathbf{C}_{xyz}(-\phi, -\theta, -\psi)$ matrix. This matrix performs angular rotations of the opposite sign in the reverse axis order in comparison to the $\mathbf{C}_{zyx}(\psi, \theta, \phi)$ matrix.

When simulating the motion of a rigid body, we sometimes wish to transform vectors from earth-fixed coordinates to body-fixed coordinates. Define the vector $\mathbf{X}_1$ to be in earth-fixed coordinates and identify it as $\mathbf{X}_e$. The equivalent vector $\mathbf{X}_4$ in body-fixed coordinates will be called $\mathbf{X}_b$. The relations between these vectors are shown in Equation 2.38.

$$2.38 \quad \mathbf{X}_b = \mathbf{C}_{zyx}(\psi, \theta, \phi)\mathbf{X}_e$$

$$\mathbf{X}_e = \mathbf{C}_{zyx}(\psi, \theta, \phi)^T\mathbf{X}_b = \mathbf{C}_{xyz}(-\phi, -\theta, -\psi)\mathbf{X}_b$$

Equation 2.38 demonstrates how to transform vectors from earth-fixed coordinates to body-fixed coordinates and vice versa. We can use these relations to develop the 6DOF translational equation of motion. Define the instantaneous force acting on the body center of mass in body-fixed coordinates to be the vector

$$F_b = \begin{bmatrix} F_{b_x} & F_{b_y} & F_{b_z} \end{bmatrix}^T.$$

Equation 2.39 is the translational equation of motion, where P_e is the position of the body in earth-fixed coordinates and m is the instantaneous mass of the body. Using the methods described in Chapter 3, we integrate Equation 2.39 numerically to determine the body position and velocity over time.

2.39 $\quad P''_e = C_{zyx}(\psi, \theta, \phi)^T$

Equation 2.39 requires the three angles ϕ, θ, and ψ which are the roll, pitch, and yaw Euler angles. To determine these angles for a body that is undergoing angular accelerations, we must solve the rotational equation of motion. Let's now define this equation and examine approaches for solving it numerically.

The first step in the solution of the rotational equation of motion is to determine the angular rates of the body given the moments acting on it about its center of mass. This solution depends on the moments of inertia and the products of inertia for the body, which are defined in Equation 2.40 — where dm represents a differential element of the body mass at the location (x, y, z) in body-fixed coordinates. These integrations must be performed over the entire body mass. Here, as is often the case, one may assume that the moments and products of inertia of the body are constant — in other words, that the body is rigid.

2.40 $\quad I_{xx} = \int_m (y^2 + z^2) dm$

$I_{yy} = \int_m (x^2 + z^2) dm$

$I_{zz} = \int_m (x^2 + y^2) dm$

$I_{xy} = \int_m xy\, dm$

$I_{xz} = \int_m xz\, dm$

$I_{yz} = \int_m yz\, dm$

Next, place the moments and products of inertia into a matrix called the inertia tensor shown in Equation 2.41.

$$2.41 \quad I = \begin{bmatrix} I_{xx} & -I_{xy} & -I_{xz} \\ -I_{xy} & I_{yy} & -I_{yz} \\ -I_{xz} & -I_{yz} & I_{zz} \end{bmatrix}$$

The differential equation that defines the angular rates in body-fixed coordinates is shown in Equation 2.42, where $\Omega = [p \ q \ r]^T$ is the rotation rate vector and $M = [m_x \ m_y \ m_z]^T$ is the moment vector acting about the body's center of mass, all in body-fixed coordinates.

$$2.42 \quad \dot{\Omega} = I^{-1}(M - \Omega \times (I\Omega))$$

Equation 2.42 is integrated numerically to compute the body rotation rate vector over time. The initial condition associated with this equation is the body rotation rate at the start of the simulation run.

Now that we know the body rotation rate, the next step is to determine the angular orientation resulting from these rotation rates, usually as the *Euler angles* ϕ, θ, and ψ. There are two commonly used techniques for performing this computation in 6DOF simulations: Euler angle integration and quaternion integration. Euler angle integration is conceptually simpler, but it will run into numerical problems if the pitch angle θ approaches 90 degrees in magnitude where a singularity occurs in the equations. *Quaternion* integration is more mathematically complex, but this approach does not have any difficulty when θ passes through 90 degrees in magnitude.

Euler Angle Integration

Assume that the body rotation rate vector Ω is available from the solution of Equation 2.42. Then, relate the time derivatives of the Euler angles to the body-fixed rotation rates using Equation 2.43 [7]. The initial conditions associated with these equations are the initial Euler angles of the body.

$$2.43 \quad \begin{bmatrix} \dot{\phi} \\ \dot{\theta} \\ \dot{\psi} \end{bmatrix} = \begin{bmatrix} 1 & \sin\phi\tan\theta & \cos\phi\tan\theta \\ 0 & \cos\phi & -\sin\phi \\ 0 & \sin\phi\sec\theta & \cos\phi\sec\theta \end{bmatrix} \Omega$$

We can integrate Equation 2.43 numerically during simulation which — along with Equation 2.42 — gives the complete solution for the rotational motion of the body given the moments acting about its center of gravity in body-fixed coordinates. Using these results, we compute the $C_{zyx}(\psi, \theta, \phi)^T$ matrix as shown in Equation 2.37 (page 57) and use it in the solution of the translational equation of motion shown in Equation 2.39.

The numerical difficulty in Equation 2.43 occurs when the angle θ approaches 90 degrees in magnitude because the magnitude of the $\sec\theta$ terms in the last row of the matrix approaches infinity. If the simulation application will never have θ approach ± 90 degrees, Equation 2.43 is appropriate for the solution of the equations of rotational motion. An example where this assumption may be valid is in the flight simulation of a transport aircraft, where θ would never be expected to exceed, say, 40 degrees in magnitude.

Quaternion Integration

On the other hand, if any arbitrary value of θ must be accommodated in the simulation, it is necessary to use an alternative approach to determine the body orientation relative to earth-fixed axes. The use of quaternion integration is the preferred technique in this situation. A quaternion is a four-element vector

$$\mathbf{b} = \begin{bmatrix} b_1 & b_2 & b_3 & b_4 \end{bmatrix}^T$$

that can be thought of as a four-component complex number. Use a quaternion to maintain the relationship between the body-fixed and earth-fixed coordinate systems.

The values of the quaternion elements must be initialized from the initial values of the body Euler angles. The initial earth-fixed to body-fixed direction cosine matrix $\mathbf{C}_{zyx}(\psi, \theta, \phi)$ is computed as shown in Equation 2.37. In this section, call this initial direction cosine matrix $\mathbf{C}$ and select individual elements from it with the notation $\mathbf{C}_{rc}$ where r and c identify the row and column of a particular matrix element. Using this notation, $\mathbf{C}_{11}$ is the first element in the first row.

Initialize the elements of the quaternion. First, initialize the last quaternion element as shown in Equation 2.44.

2.44 $$b_4 = \frac{1}{2}\sqrt{1 + C_{11} + C_{22} + C_{33}}$$

Then, initialize the remaining quaternion elements as shown in Equation 2.45.

2.45 $$b_1 = \frac{1}{4b_4}(C_{12} - C_{21})$$

$$b_2 = \frac{1}{4b_4}(C_{31} - C_{13})$$

$$b_3 = \frac{1}{4b_4}(C_{23} - C_{32})$$

There is a potential problem if the computed value of b_4 happens to be zero, which results in division by zero in Equation 2.45. The file RigidBody.cpp on the companion disk contains some variations on Equations 2.44 and 2.45 that accommodate this situation and correctly initialize the quaternion from any arbitrary initial direction cosine matrix.

The differential equation that relates the change in the quaternion parameters to the rotation rate in body-fixed axes is shown in Equation 2.46, where

$$\Omega = [pqr]^T$$

as before.

$$2.46 \quad \dot{b} = \frac{1}{2} \begin{bmatrix} -b_4 & -b_3 & -b_2 \\ -b_3 & b_4 & b_1 \\ b_2 & b_1 & -b_4 \\ b_1 & -b_2 & b_3 \end{bmatrix} \Omega$$

To correctly model the relationship between the two coordinate systems, the magnitude of the quaternion vector must equal one. Floating point roundoff errors and integration errors accumulate over time and cause the magnitude of the vector to change slowly. To ensure accurate results, we must correct this error. As a first step in performing this correction, compute an error term as shown in Equation 2.47.

$$2.47 \quad e_b = 1 - \|b\|^2 = 1 - (b_1{}^2 + b_2{}^2 + b_3{}^2 + b_4{}^2)$$

Then use the error term as a correction to modify Equation 2.47 as shown in Equation 2.48. This equation is solved numerically to determine the quaternion vector during the simulation run.

$$2.48 \quad \dot{b} = \frac{1}{2} \left\{ \begin{bmatrix} -b_4 & -b_3 & -b_2 \\ -b_3 & b_4 & b_1 \\ b_2 & b_1 & -b_4 \\ b_1 & -b_2 & b_3 \end{bmatrix} \Omega + e_b b \right\}$$

Given the current quaternion vector **b**, compute the direction cosine matrix

$$C_{zyx}(\psi, \theta, \phi)$$

using the following method [8]. Here, the identifier C will represent $C_{zyx}(\psi, \theta, \phi)$ and we will use the same row and column subscript notation as before. The equations for computing the direction cosine matrix elements are shown in Equation 2.49.

$$2.49 \quad C_{11} = b_1 b_1 - b_2 b_2 - b_3 b_3 + b_4 b_4$$

$$C_{12} = 2(b_1 b_2 + b_3 b_4)$$

$$C_{13} = 2(b_2 b_4 - b_1 b_3)$$

$$C_{21} = 2(b_3 b_4 - b_1 b_2)$$

$$C_{22} = b_1 b_1 - b_2 b_2 + b_3 b_3 - b_4 b_4$$

$$C_{23} = 2(b_2 b_3 + b_1 b_4)$$

$$C_{31} = 2(b_1 b_3 + b_2 b_4)$$

$$C_{32} = 2(b_2 b_3 - b_1 b_4)$$

$$C_{33} = b_1 b_1 + b_2 b_2 - b_3 b_3 - b_4 b_4$$

Compute the Euler angles from the elements of **C** as shown in Equation 2.50.

2.50 $\phi = \arctan 2[C_{12}, C_{11}]$

$\theta = \arctan 2[-C_{13}, \sqrt{C^2_{23} + C^2_{33}}]$

$\psi = \arctan 2[C_{23}, C_{33}]$

In summary, to determine the body orientation relative to earth-fixed axes using quaternions, first initialize the quaternion vector **b** from the initial direction cosine matrix using Equation 2.44 and Equation 2.45. Update the quaternion during simulation execution by numerically integrating Equation 2.48. Use the current state of the quaternion to compute the direction cosine matrix $C_{zyx}(\psi, \theta, \phi)$ via Equation 2.49 and the three Euler angles using Equation 2.50. Finally, use the direction cosine matrix to integrate the translational equation of motion in Equation 2.39 (page 58).

Although the quaternion computation is more complicated than Euler angle integration, it is the preferred method for solving the rotational equations of motion if the numerical difficulty of Euler angle integration is a potential problem.

Three-Dimensional Motion Simulation with the DSSL

The DSSL C++ library provides routines that implement the equations given previously for simulating three-dimensional motion of rigid bodies. Listing 2.3 is a simulation of the motion of a projectile fired from a gun with a rifled barrel. For a short time while in the barrel, the projectile accelerates along the x body-fixed axis while simultaneously experiencing an angular acceleration that spins it about the x body-fixed axis. After the projectile leaves the barrel, no further acceleration is modeled.

Listing 2.3 RigidBodyTest.cpp

```
#include "RigidBody.h"


StateList state_list;
RigidBody body(&state_list);


int main()
{
    // All states will be initialized to zero
    Vector<3> pos_ic, vel_ic, euler_ic, body_rate_ic;
```

```
body.Initialize(pos_ic, vel_ic, euler_ic, body_rate_ic);

const double step_time = 0.001, end_time = 1.0;

state_list.Initialize(step_time);

printf("Time, Px, Py, Pz, Vx, Vy, Vz, Phi, Theta, Psi, P, Q, R\n");
for(;;)
{
    // Set all accelerations to zero for now
    Vector<3> translational_accel, angular_accel;

    if (state_list.Time() <= 0.01) // If still in the barrel, accelerate
    {
        translational_accel[0] = 10000.0;
        angular_accel[0] = 1000.0;
    }

    body.Compute(translational_accel, angular_accel);

    // Print state information
    printf("%lf", state_list.Time());
    for (int i=0; i<3; i++) printf(",%lf", body.GetPos()[i]);
    for (i=0; i<3; i++) printf(",%lf", body.GetVel()[i]);
    for (i=0; i<3; i++) printf(",%lf", body.GetEuler()[i]);
    for (i=0; i<3; i++) printf(",%lf", body.GetBodyRate()[i]);
    printf("\n");

    if (state_list.Time() >= end_time)
        break;

    state_list.Integrate();
}

return 0;
}
```

Three-Dimensional Motion Simulation in Simulink

Simulink v4 provides several new blocks for solving the rotational equation of motion using the quaternion integration and Euler angle integration techniques. Additional blocks perform conversions between a direction cosine matrix, a set of Euler angles, and a quaternion vector. These new blocks enable the implementation of a full 6DOF simulation with a reasonable amount of effort.

2.6 Stochastic Systems

A system that always responds identically to the same set of initial conditions and control input signals during multiple test runs is deterministic. If there is some variation in the system behavior from run to run — even though all initial conditions and control inputs remain the same — the system behavior is described as stochastic, or random. An example of stochastic behavior is an aircraft flying with a predefined sequence of control inputs. Wind gusts affect the flight path differently on each attempt, so although we model the aircraft deterministically, the wind model in this case is stochastic. If any part of a mathematical model is stochastic, we describe the model itself as stochastic.

In addition to external random disturbances such as wind gusts, there may be randomness associated with the system itself. Manufacturing tolerances may produce variations from unit to unit in parameters that affect the performance of the system. We model these random variations in the parameters of the system and its operational environment in a stochastic manner.

First, consider the case where a single number is required to specify a random effect that we wish to model. The example we will use is the misalignment of a system component due to manufacturing tolerances. The alignment is specified as an angle, α. To meet specifications, this angle must lie in the range from α_{min} to α_{max} and is equally likely to have any value in this range. Absolute limits on α are possible because we will assume that the system would not pass manufacturing tests if the angular limits were exceeded.

We use a *probability density function* (PDF) [9] to describe the *random variable* α. Figure 2.18 shows the PDF for α as described, where the angles $\alpha_{min} = 1.9$ degrees and $\alpha_{max} = 2.1$ degrees. This random variable is typically described in terms of a tolerance such as 2.0±0.1 degrees.

It is a property of any PDF that the function $f(\alpha)$ is nonnegative for all α. In this example, $f(\alpha) = 0$ for $\alpha > 1.9$ and for $\alpha > 2.1$ In addition, the integral of the PDF over the entire x axis always equals one as shown in Equation 2.51.

$$2.51 \quad \int_{-\infty}^{\infty} f(\alpha)d\alpha = 1$$

For any PDF, the probability that the angle α lies between two angles α_1 and α_2 (where $\alpha_2 \geq \alpha_1$) is shown in Equation 2.52.

$$2.52 \quad P(\alpha_1 \leq \alpha \leq \alpha_2) = \int_{\alpha_1}^{\alpha_2} f(\alpha)d\alpha$$

The uniform PDF is appropriate when all points over the possible range of values for a random variable appear to be equally likely. Programming languages and simulation development tools usually provide a uniform pseudorandom number generator that produces numbers over some range. A pseudorandom number generator that produces outputs over the range (0, 1) can be used as shown in Equation 2.53 to generate values from the distribution shown in Figure 2.18. In Equation 2.53, random() represents a call to the system random number generator routine that returns a value between 0 and 1.

Figure 2.18 Uniform probability density function.

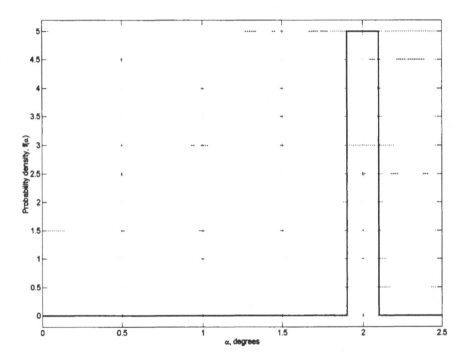

$$2.53 \quad x = \alpha_{min} + (\alpha_{max} - \alpha_{min})\, \text{random}()$$

One should always be cautious using system-supplied pseudorandom numbers because they are frequently of poor quality. One potential problem with these generators is that the first output value after the generator is seeded may not appear very random, i.e., it might always be a very small number. Another problem that sometimes occurs is that individual bits in the output may exhibit non-random behavior such as toggling between 0 and 1 with each call to the generator. It is a good idea to test a system pseudorandom number generator thoroughly before using it in a critical simulation application.

If the system-supplied pseudorandom number generator fails to satisfy your requirements, or if you have other needs such as cross-platform portability, you may want to develop your own uniform pseudorandom number generator routine. Some examples are provided in [10].

Another PDF that is commonly used is the normal (also known as Gaussian) distribution. This PDF is defined by Equation 2.54 where μ is the mean and σ is the standard deviation of the distribution. The normal PDF is used in situations where the total error is assumed to be the sum of a large number of independent errors.

2.54 $\quad f(x) = \dfrac{1}{\sqrt{2\pi\sigma^2}} e^{-\left[\dfrac{(x-\mu)^2}{2\sigma^2}\right]}$

Figure 2.19 shows a normal distribution of a random variable with a mean μ of 2 and standard deviation σ of 0.1. Compare this distribution to the uniform distribution shown in Figure 2.18.

Figure 2.19 Normal probability density function.

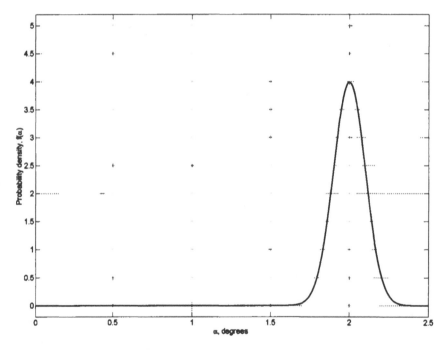

Pseudorandom number generators with non-uniform PDFs such as the normal distribution are not available in some simulation development environments. If this is the case, it will be necessary to transform the output of a uniform pseudorandom number generator into the desired PDF. An efficient technique for performing the transformation from a uniform PDF to a normal PDF is the Box-Muller method [11].

So far, we have looked at techniques for generating single pseudorandom samples from a given PDF. A *random process* is a sequence of random variables over time. An example of a random process is the sequence of additive noise values that appear in the output of an analog-to-digital converter that performs conversions at regular time intervals.

A simple type of random process is an uncorrelated sequence that generates a new sample from the appropriate PDF at each time step. This model is useful for simulating the additive noise of the analog-to-digital converter.

A more complex random process involves the use of filtered noise, where, for example, the power spectrum of the noise is assumed to be uniform up to a cutoff frequency and zero at all higher frequencies. An example application of filtered noise is a model of the noise in the output of a communication receiver. This random process could be simulated by constructing a lowpass digital filter (perhaps designed with the Remez technique [12]) and using an uncorrelated random sequence as the filter input. The resulting filter output approximates the desired bandlimited noise spectrum.

When simulating a stochastic system, each simulation output affected by one or more random inputs will generate a probability distribution over a number of runs. The technique of *Monte Carlo simulation* is used to determine the probability distributions of simulation outputs. A Monte Carlo simulation consists of a large number of simulation runs performed under identical conditions, except that each run uses a *different* pseudorandom sequence for each random parameter or process in each run. The various sequences of pseudorandom numbers generate performance variations that involve combinations of random behaviors. The more simulation runs performed in a Monte Carlo set, the more accurate the probability distribution of the simulation outputs will be. However, the time available for performing simulation runs often limits the number of runs in Monte Carlo sets to less than a statistically ideal amount. The results of Monte Carlo testing that contain limited numbers of runs should be examined critically to ferret out anomalies resulting from the limited data set size.

Random Numbers in the DSSL

The example program in Listing 2.4 generates one million uniformly-distributed random numbers over the range (0,1) and counts how many of the numbers fall into each of one thousand equal-width bins. It then generates one hundred thousand normally-distributed random numbers with zero mean and unit variance and computes their sample mean and variance.

Listing 2.4 RandomTest.cpp

```
// Program for testing random numbers

#include <dssl.h>

int main()
{
    Random r;
    const int n_bin = 1000;
    int bin[n_bin];
    for (int i=0; i<n_bin; i++)
        bin[i] = 0;
```

```
    for (i=0; i<1000000; i++)
    {
        double val = r.Uniform();
        int j = int(val*n_bin);
        assert(0 <= j && j < n_bin);
        bin[j]++;
    }

    printf("Bin, Count\n");
    for (i=0; i<n_bin; i++)
        printf("%4d, %d\n", i, bin[i]);

    const int n_gauss = 100000;
    double g[n_gauss], sum = 0;
    for (i=0; i<n_gauss; i++)
    {
        g[i] = r.Normal();
        sum += g[i];
    }

    double mean = sum / n_gauss;

    double dev_sq = 0;
    for (i=0; i<n_gauss; i++)
        dev_sq += pow(g[i]-mean, 2);

    double sigma = sqrt(dev_sq/n_gauss);

    printf("Mean: %lf; Sigma: %lf\n", mean, sigma);

    return 0;
}
```

Random Numbers in Simulink

Simulink provides blocks for generating both uniformly- and normally-distributed pseudo-random numbers. When using the uniformly-distributed pseudorandom generator, the user must specify the minimum and maximum values of the output interval as well as the seed to use for the generator. When using the normally-distributed pseudorandom generator, the user must specify the distribution mean, variance, and the generator seed. For a given seed, each generator will produce an identical sequence of pseudorandom values during each simulation run.

Figure 2.20 Simulink uniform random number generator block.

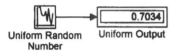

Uniform Random   Uniform Output
Number

Figure 2.21 Simulink normal random number generator block.

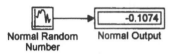

Normal Random   Normal Output
Number

Exercises[1]

*1. Indicate if each of the following systems is a dynamic system:

(a) A spacecraft coasting through deep space (gravitational effects are not significant).

(b) A logic circuit consisting of ideal boolean AND, OR, and NOT gates.

(c) A filter circuit consisting of resistors and capacitors.

(d) An automotive suspension system consisting of the frame, wheels, springs, and shock absorbers.

*2. Write the following differential equation as a system of first-order equations:

$$x''' = ax'' + bx' + cx + d$$

*3. Show how Equation 2.14 (page 32) is changed if wind resistance is included. The angular acceleration due to wind resistance is modeled as a constant C multiplied by the square of the bob velocity, acting in the direction opposite to the velocity.

4. Using the results of Exercise 3, add the effect of a steady wind to the model. The wind is modeled as moving with constant velocity v_w from left to right in the system shown in Figure 2.2 (page 31).

5. Verify that Equation 2.18 (page 35) is the solution of Equation 2.17.

6. Given a function $y = f(x)$ with x breakpoints {0, 0.2, 0.5, 0.7, 0.9} and y values at the breakpoints {0, 1.2, 2.1, 4.3, 3.9}, estimate the value of the function using linear interpolation at x values of 0.1, 0.2, and 0.55.

---

1. Answers are provided for those exercises with an asterisk in Appendix A, page 293.

*7. Given a function $z = f(x, y)$ with x breakpoints {0.5, 0.8, 1.5, 1.7}, y breakpoints {0, 1.4, 2.5, 4.7}, and z values at the breakpoints as shown below, where the x breakpoints are in increasing order across the columns to the right and the y breakpoints are in increasing order down the rows, estimate the value of the function using linear interpolation at (x, y) input value pairs of (0.8, 2.6), (0.7, 2) and (0.7, 0.9).

$$z = \begin{bmatrix} 0.2 & 0.3 & 0.6 & 0.5 \\ 0.3 & 0.4 & 0.3 & 0.5 \\ 0.5 & 0.7 & 0.4 & 0.7 \\ 0.6 & 0.9 & 0.7 & 0.9 \end{bmatrix}$$

8. Given the function $y = \cos(x^4)$, develop an algorithm for selecting linear interpolation breakpoints over the interval $0 \le x \le 2$ so that the maximum interpolation error is minimized. Use the minimum number of breakpoints possible and limit the interpolation to 0.05 across given range of x. Use your algorithm to select a set of breakpoints and compare your results with Figure 2.7 (page 42).

9. Derive the equations of motion for the inverted pendulum shown in ExerciseFigure 2.1 in terms of the cart position x relative to a fixed point on the ground and the pendulum angle from the vertical θ. The cart has mass m_c, the pendulum bob has mass m_b and is supported by a stiff shaft of length l, and the gravitational acceleration is g. The masses of the pendulum shaft and cart wheels are negligible. Wind resistance and friction in the pendulum pivot and in the wheel motion can also be ignored. $f(t)$ is an arbitrary external force applied to the cart in the x direction.

ExerciseFigure 2.1   Inverted pendulum.

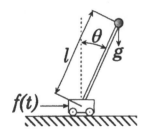

References

[1] Franklin, Gene F., J. David Powell, and Abbas Emami-Naeini, *Feedback Control of Dynamic Systems*. Reading, MA: Addison Wesley, 1986.

[2] Churchill, Ruel V., *Operational Mathematics*, Boston, MA: McGraw-Hill, 1972.

[3]   Juang, Jer-Nan, *Applied System Identification*. Upper Saddle River, NJ: Prentice-Hall, 1993.

[4]   Oppenheim, Alan V., and Ronald W. Schafer, *Discrete-Time Signal Processing*. Englewood Cliffs, NJ: Prentice Hall, 1989.

[5]   Press, William H., Saul A. Teukolsky, William T. Vetterling, and Brian P. Flannery, *Numerical Recipes in C: The Art of Scientific Computing*. Cambridge, England: Cambridge University Press, 1992, §3.3.

[6]   Beale, R., and T. Jackson, *Neural Computing: An Introduction*. Bristol, England: Adam Hilger, 1990.

[7]   Roskam, Jan, *Airplane Flight Dynamics and Automatic Flight Controls*. Lawrence, KS: Roskam Aviation and Engineering Corporation, 1979.

[8]   Farrell, Jay A., and Matthew Barth, *The Global Positioning System & Inertial Navigation*. New York, NY: McGraw-Hill, 1999, §2.4.2.

[9]   Papoulis, Athanasios, *Probability, Random Variables, and Stochastic Process*. New York, NY: McGraw-Hill, 1991.

[10]   Press, William H., Saul A. Teukolsky, William T. Vetterling, and Brian P. Flannery, *Numerical Recipes in C: The Art of Scientific Computing*. Cambridge, England: Cambridge University Press, 1992, §7.1.

[11]   Ibid., §7.2.

[12]   Ledin, Jim, *Digital Filtering and Oversampling*. Dr. Dobb's Journal, April, 2000.

Chapter 3

Non-Real-Time Simulation

3.1 Introduction

This chapter discusses the issues involved in combining a set of mathematical models to produce a complete simulation of a dynamic system. Using the techniques of Chapter 2, one begins by constructing models of suitable fidelity that describe the components of the system and its interactions with the environment and then assembles a system simulation from these models and from other elements — such as numerical integration algorithms.

A *simulation* is defined as a set of models executing over time [1]. A simulation begins execution by initializing the values of state variables and any parameters associated with its models. As the run executes over a span of simulated time, the simulation evaluates the model dynamic equations and performs state variable integration. In addition to these tasks, the simulation provides a user interface that allows the operator to specify initial conditions and model parameters and to control its execution. The user interface must also enable the selection of variables for display and storage as the simulation executes.

The techniques and numerical algorithms required for implementing a dynamic system simulation that produce valid, accurate results need to be examined. This chapter will focus primarily on *non-real-time simulation*. Chapter 4 covers the issues specific to *real-time simulation*. Before getting into the details of simulation algorithms, I will first discuss the characteristics of a good simulation user interface, some concerns to address in combining a disparate group of models into a unified simulation, and the topic of configuration management in simulation development.

3.2 The User Interface

The user interface for a simulation is usually a set of graphical dialogs, a command line environment, or a combination of these methods. The capabilities provided by a simulation user interface typically include:

The ability to display and modify model parameters and initial conditions. An example of a model parameter is the pendulum string length l in the example of Section 2.5.1 (page 54). An example of an initial condition is the initial deflection angle of the pendulum, θ_0.

Starting and stopping simulation runs. Once the model parameters and initial conditions have been set, the user starts a simulation run. The simulation will usually contain one or more stopping conditions, such as an end time. It is also helpful if the user interface lets the user pause a simulation run at any time, examine and possibly modify simulation variables, and then continue the run.

Immediate data displays. Graphs and numerical displays of data that are updated while the simulation runs provide immediate feedback on the behavior of the simulation. By monitoring this data, the user can identify and abort runs when the setup happens to be incorrect. Another use for the information provided by immediate displays is planning for upcoming simulation runs.

Identification of simulation data to be saved for later analysis. This involves selecting which variables are to be saved and the frequency at which they will be sampled and stored during simulation execution. Some variables only need to be saved one time per run, such as parameters that remain constant or variables that are computed just before the run terminates.

The DSSL C++ simulation library provided with this book includes a very limited subset of these user interface features. When desired, the simulation developer must implement most of them using the C++ language. The example simulations contain little in the way of user interface features — the source code editor serves as the interface for setting model parameters. It would require a great deal of work to add a general purpose command-line or graphical user interface that provides all of the features discussed.

Simulink provides all of the user interface capabilities in a dialog-based format. To change model parameters, the user double-clicks on a block diagram element and edits the parameter values in a dialog box. Simulation runs can be started and stopped by pressing graphical buttons at the top of the block diagram. Variable values can be displayed numerically on the block diagram or plotted in graphical "scopes" during simulation execution. It is also possible to sample variables at a regular rate and save the samples to the MATLAB workspace or to a disk file during simulation runs.

3.3 Model Issues

The models used in a simulation must be mutually compatible so that signals flow between them with the proper units and timing. Each model must also be compatible with the configuration of the simulation environment so that differential and difference equation updates occur properly. These issues must be addressed carefully when using a model in a simulation environment for which it was not originally developed.

A potential source of errors is mismatched units (e.g., feet versus meters) between the output of one model and the input of another model. Another possible problem is coordinate system mismatches between models. Errors of these types are particularly likely to occur if different people develop the various models and a rigorous definition of the interface between the models has not been specified. To guard against errors of these types, it is important to perform thorough testing during the process of integrating new models into a simulation.

3.4 Configuration Management

Configuration management is a basic software development process that should ideally be implemented before simulation development begins. The more complex a simulation project, and the more critical its results are to project success, the more important it is to have an effective approach for software configuration management. Configuration management addresses issues such as

- maintaining the integrity of source files during simulation development,
- specifying criteria for releasing a simulation version, and
- maintaining the ability to revert to a previous simulation version should the need arise.

Reasonably priced (and even free) software version control tools are available that can make the configuration management process robust and relatively easy. Some examples of these tools are Microsoft Visual Source Safe, GNU RCS, Rational Clear Case®, and MKS Source Integrity Professional™. In a well-planned simulation project, we implement a software version control system from the beginning of the development phase. If development is already underway and a configuration management tool is not currently in use, it is still feasible to install and begin using such a tool. In this situation, the integration of the tool into the development process will tend to be a bit more disruptive to the ongoing work than if it had been used from the start. The decision to begin using one of these tools mid-project sometimes occurs as the result of a serious problem, such as the inability to answer the question, "What changes did you make that caused the simulation to produce these results?"

Software version control tools usually operate under a check-out/check-in model and individual files have the read-only attribute when checked in. The situation becomes more complex when multiple developers are working with the same group of files and want to check out the same file. The various version control tools have different ways of dealing with this situation. Some allow multiple developers to check out the same file, while others only allow a file to be checked out to one user at a time. When more than one person has the same file checked out, there must a way to merge the changes made by both developers when the copies of the file are checked back in. This may require manual intervention if there are conflicting changes made by the different developers. Often, informal discussions between developers can avoid this difficulty through agreements of who will check out and make changes to particular files during a given time period.

After the changes to implement a specific feature or fix have passed initial developer tests, the files should be checked in so other developers will have access to the updated files. Developers should avoid leaving a group of files checked out for an extended period (e.g., while away on vacation) as this may make the files unavailable to others for modification.

A useful approach to configuration management is to maintain a "development" copy of the simulation under the control of a software version control system and another "released" copy of the simulation. The released copy is used to perform system testing and to generate critical simulation results. Use the development copy of the simulation to develop and test simulation improvements and bug fixes. When all testing for an iteration of simulation development has completed successfully, the development version undergoes the release process to become the new released version. The mechanics of the release process involve labeling all the current versions of the files under version control (using a feature of the version control software) with an identifier that indicates the new version being released, as well as copying the development simulation version into the release location.

By placing version control system labels on all current file versions, it is possible to identify which versions went into a particular simulation build at any time in the future. This step allows the reconstruction of past versions of the simulation should the need arise. This capability is useful, for example, when a test produces different results using a new simulation version in comparison to a previous version. The question then becomes whether the change in results is due to the simulation differences or perhaps due to changes in the embedded system under test (in an HIL simulation environment). If it is easy to restore the previous simulation version, one can determine what casued the variations. A good software version control tool should make the process of restoring a previous simulation version relatively straightforward. After testing with the restored version has completed, it should be simple to return to the latest versions of the source files.

As a final point, it is always necessary to maintain an adequate set of backup copies of the simulation software. Because the simulation is not released as part of a product, there is sometimes a tendency to avoid using the same degree of rigor in performing backups for embedded code. This can turn out to be a serious mistake if a disk crash causes the loss of a significant amount of simulation code and no backup copy exists.

In summary, it is critical to maintain adequate software configuration control from the beginning of a simulation project and to make regular backups of simulation software. Any of the many available software version control tools can make this task relatively easy for the simulation developers, system administrators, and project managers.

3.5 Integration Algorithms

Numerical algorithms can be used to solve systems of ordinary differential equations approximately. Assume that the behavior of a continuous dynamic system is modeled by a set of coupled first-order differential equations as discussed in the section "The Differential Equation Format" on page 26. A system of order q with m inputs is shown in Equation 3.1, where each x is a state variable and each u is an input signal.

3.1 $$\frac{d_{x_k}}{dt} = (fx_1, x_2, ..., x_q, u_1(t), u_2(t), ..., u_m(t)), k = 1, 2, ..., q$$

These equations are frequently nonlinear, which makes their analytic solution difficult or impossible. Write the differential equations of Equation 3.1 in vector form as shown in Equation 3.2, where x is a vector of q state variables and u is a vector of m input signals. As shown in "The Differential Equation Format" section in Chapter 2, an arbitrary differential equation containing second (or higher) derivatives usually can be transformed into an equivalent set of first-order equations in this format.

3.2 $\quad \dfrac{dx}{dt} = f(x, u(t))$

In simulating continuous systems on a digital computer, we advance time in small, discrete steps, and solve the dynamic equations approximately at each step using a numerical integration algorithm. Given a time step size h, the solution after a single integration step from $t = nh$ to $t = (n + 1)h$ (where n is the integer step number) is shown in Equation 3.3.

3.3 $\quad \mathbf{x}((n + 1)h) = \mathbf{x}(nh) + \displaystyle\int_{nh}^{(n+1)h} f(\mathbf{x}, \mathbf{u}(t))dt$

Due to the nonlinearity of the function f, the integral term in Equation 3.3 normally cannot be evaluated directly. Instead, we use a numerical integration algorithm in the form of a difference equation to estimate the integral over each time step. In the sections that follow, some commonly used integration algorithms will be discussed that take varying approaches to estimating the exact solution of Equation 3.3.

3.5.1 Euler Integration Algorithms

The simplest algorithm for performing numerical integration arises from the definition of the derivative as shown in Equation 3.4.

3.4 $\quad \dfrac{d\mathbf{x}}{dt} \equiv \lim_{h \to 0} \dfrac{\mathbf{x}(t + h) - \mathbf{x}(t)}{h}$

If the value of h is sufficiently small, we can make the approximation of Equation 3.5.

3.5 $\quad \dfrac{\mathbf{x}(t + h) - \mathbf{x}(t)}{h} \approx f(\mathbf{x}, \mathbf{u}(t))$

In terms of sampling times, with the subscript n indicating $t = nh$ and with a hatted variable indicating an approximate solution, we now have the formula of Equation 3.6.

3.6 $\quad \hat{\mathbf{x}}_{n+1} = \hat{\mathbf{x}}_n + hf(\mathbf{x}_n, \mathbf{u}_n)$

Equation 3.6 is the forward Euler integration algorithm. This is a first-order integration method, which means that it contains the function f evaluated at one point in time. It is also an explicit method because it does not use states or inputs from future values of n. This algorithm is shown graphically in Figure 3.1 where the crosshatched area is the approximation of the integral over the step between $t = nh$ and $t = (n + 1)h$.

Figure 3.1 Forward Euler integration.

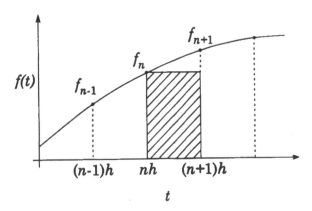

Alternatively, one can use a backward difference to approximate the derivative as shown in Equation 3.7.

3.7 $\quad \dfrac{\mathbf{x}(t) - \mathbf{x}(t-h)}{h} \approx f(\mathbf{x}, \mathbf{u}, (t))$

This results in the difference equation shown in Equation 3.8, which is the backward Euler integration algorithm.

3.8 $\quad \hat{\mathbf{x}}_{n+1} = \hat{\mathbf{x}}_n + hf(\hat{\mathbf{x}}_{n+1}, \mathbf{u}_{n+1})$

The backward Euler integration algorithm is a first-order implicit method. The algorithm is implicit because the state $\hat{\mathbf{x}}_{n+1}$ is a function of itself. Implicit algorithms require additional computation to solve for $\hat{\mathbf{x}}_{n+1}$, which commonly takes the form of an iterative technique such as the Newton-Raphson algorithm [2]. Implicit algorithms have advantages in terms of accuracy and numerical stability over explicit methods. However, the drawbacks of implicit methods are the additional computation requirements and their inappropriateness for real-time applications. These methods are not suitable for real-time use for two reasons:

1. The execution time required for the iterative solution of $\hat{\mathbf{x}}_{n+1}$ is unpredictable.

2. Input values from future times are required in the form of $\mathbf{u}_{n+1}$, which are not available at time step n when the integration must be performed.

The backward Euler integration algorithm is shown in Figure 3.2.

Figure 3.2   Backward Euler integration algorithm.

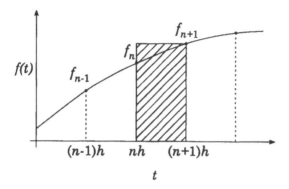

The Euler integration algorithms are both first-order methods, meaning that they have poor accuracy when compared to the higher order methods discussed in the following sections. For this reason, they are seldom used in practical simulation work.

3.5.2 Higher Order Implicit Integration Algorithms

We can improve the estimate of the area over the interval between $t = nh$ and $t = (n + 1)h$ by using the average of the values of f_n and f_{n+1}. This results in the trapezoidal algorithm, shown in Figure 3.3.

Figure 3.3   Trapezoidal integration.

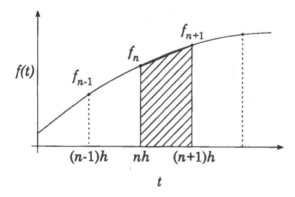

The formula for the trapezoidal algorithm is shown in Equation 3.9.

3.9 $$\hat{x}_{n+1} = \hat{x}_n + \frac{h}{2}\{f(\hat{x}_n, u_n) + f(\hat{x}_{n+1}, u_{n+1})\}$$

This is a second-order implicit method that can be viewed as a combination of the forward and backward Euler algorithms. Because it is a second-order method, it has better accuracy than either of the Euler methods. This is intuitively clear from comparing Figure 3.3 to Figures 3.1 and 3.2.

The trapezoidal method uses a straight line to interpolate between the points f_n and f_{n+1}. Higher order polynomials can be used to increase the accuracy of this interpolation. If a parabola is defined that passes through the three points f_{n-1}, f_n, and f_{n+1}, the result is the integration algorithm of Equation 3.10, the third-order implicit algorithm.

3.10 $\quad \hat{x}_{n+1} = \hat{x}_n + \dfrac{h}{12}\{-f(\hat{x}_{n-1}, u_{n-1}) + 8f(\hat{x}_n, u_n) + 5f(\hat{x}_{n+1}, u_{n+1})\}$

Finally, define a cubic polynomial that passes through the four points: f_{n-2}, f_{n-1}, f_n, and f_{n+1}. This leads to the fourth-order implicit algorithm of Equation 3.11.

3.11 $\qquad \hat{x}_{n+1} = \hat{x}_n + \dfrac{h}{24}\{f(\hat{x}_{n-2}, u_{n-2}) - 5f(\hat{x}_{n-1}, u_{n-1}) + 19f(\hat{x}_n, u_n)$

$\qquad\qquad + 9f(\hat{x}_{n+1}, u_{n+1})\}$

The higher order implicit methods all have the same advantages as the backward Euler algorithm, including better accuracy and numerical stability. These are multiple-step methods — they use the value of the function f from more than one time step. Only one new evaluation of f is required at each step. However, like the backward Euler algorithm, they are not appropriate for real-time simulation applications because they have an indeterminate execution time and they require the use of inputs from future times. In the next section, these algorithms will be modified to make them explicit and therefore suitable for use in real-time simulation.

3.5.3 Adams-Bashforth Integration Algorithms

The Adams-Bashforth integration algorithms are members of a family of explicit multiple-step methods that includes the forward Euler algorithm. These algorithms are derived from the implicit methods of the previous section using extrapolation to make them explicit.

We can develop an explicit variation of the trapezoidal algorithm by forming an estimate of f_{n+1} that is a linear extrapolation from the points f_{n-1} and f_n. This method is the second-order Adams-Bashforth algorithm, and is shown graphically in Figure 3.4.

The formula for the second-order Adams-Bashforth algorithm is shown in Equation 3.12.

3.12 $\quad \hat{x}_{n+1} = \hat{x}_n + \dfrac{h}{2}\{3f(\hat{x}_n, u_n) - f(\hat{x}_{n-1}, u_{n-1})\}$

This is a second-order explicit algorithm. Its accuracy and stability are not as good as those of the trapezoidal algorithm, but it has determinate execution time and does not require inputs from future times. The second-order Adams-Bashforth algorithm is a popular integration algorithm for use in both real-time and non-real-time simulation applications.

Figure 3.4 Adams-Bashforth second-order integration.

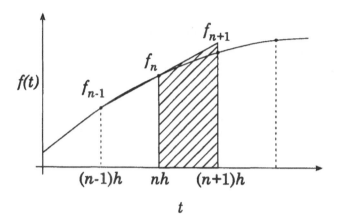

We can create variations of the third- and fourth-order implicit algorithms of the previous section by extrapolating the polynomials to estimate f_{n+1}. Passing a parabola through the points f_{n-2}, f_{n-1}, and f_n and extrapolating to estimate f_{n+1} produces the integration algorithm of Equation 3.13, the third-order Adams-Bashforth integration algorithm.

$$3.13 \quad \hat{x}_{n+1} = \hat{x}_n + \frac{h}{12}\{5f(\hat{x}_{n-2}, \mathbf{u}_{n-2}) - 16f(\hat{x}_{n-1}, \mathbf{u}_{n-1}) + 23f(\hat{x}_n, \mathbf{u}_n)\}$$

Passing a cubic polynomial through the points f_{n-3}, f_{n-2}, f_{n-1}, and f_n and extrapolating to estimate f_{n+1} produces the integration algorithm of Equation 3.14, the fourth-order Adams-Bashforth integration algorithm.

$$3.14 \quad \hat{x}_{n+1} = \hat{x}_n + \frac{h}{24}\{-9f(\hat{x}_{n-3}, \mathbf{u}_{n-3}) + 37f(\hat{x}_{n-2}, \mathbf{u}_{n-2}) - 59f(\hat{x}_{n-1}, \mathbf{u}_{n-1})$$
$$+ 55f(\hat{x}_n, \mathbf{u}_n)\}$$

The use of implicit algorithms higher than second order and Adams-Bashforth algorithms higher than first order presents a problem during the first few simulation frames because the necessary previous values of f have not yet been defined. The solution to this problem is to use lower-order algorithms during the initial integration steps until enough past values of f are available for the high-order algorithm. For example, if the second-order Adams-Bashforth algorithm is used, take the first integration step using the forward Euler algorithm. This will provide a value for f_{n-1} to use in the second-order algorithm on the subsequent step.

The Adams-Bashforth algorithms are explicit methods that use inputs only from current and past times, so they are appropriate and popular for use in real-time simulation applications. These algorithms are multiple-step methods that require only one new evaluation of f at each step. However, they perform extrapolation, which can lead to transient errors if there are discontinuities in the function f. In the next section, Runge-Kutta algorithms will be examined, which do not experience transient errors in the presence of discontinuities because they avoid extrapolation.

3.5.4 Runge-Kutta Integration Algorithms

The Runge-Kutta algorithms are based on the concept of approximating the exact solution of a differential equation with a number of terms from its Taylor series expansion. Second-, third-, and fourth-order Runge-Kutta algorithms will be considered in this section.

We can develop an explicit second-order algorithm by breaking the integration step into two equal intervals. First, perform a forward Euler step to the midpoint and then use the resulting estimate of the state at the midpoint to perform a forward Euler step across the entire interval. This is known as the *modified Euler-Cauchy algorithm*, which is one member of the family of second-order Runge-Kutta algorithms. The steps in this algorithm are shown in Equation 3.15.

3.15 $\hat{x}_{n+1/2} = \hat{x}_n + \dfrac{h}{2} f(\hat{x}_n, u_n)$

$\hat{x}_{n+1} = \hat{x}_n + hf(\hat{x}_{n+1/2}, u_{n+1/2})$

Breaking the integration interval into three steps leads to the third-order Runge-Kutta integration algorithm. This method first uses forward Euler integration to compute an estimate of f at one-third of the frame. This estimate is used to compute an estimate of f at two-thirds of the frame. The algorithm then uses these estimates to compute an overall average derivative for the frame as shown in Equation 3.16.

3.16 $\hat{x}_{n+1} = \hat{x}_n + \dfrac{h}{4}\{f_n + 3\hat{f}_{n+2/3}\}$

Equation 3.17 shows the substep calculations required for a step of Equation 3.16.

3.17 $f_n = f(\hat{x}_n, u_n)$

$\hat{f}_{n+1/3} = f\left(\hat{x}_n + \dfrac{h}{3}f_n, u_{n+1/3}\right)$

$\hat{f}_{n+2/3} = f\left(\hat{x}_n + \dfrac{2h}{3}\hat{f}_{n+1/3}, u_{n+2/3}\right)$

Fourth-order Runge-Kutta integration breaks the integration interval into four substeps and forms an average of the derivative over the full interval as shown in Equation 3.18.

3.18 $\hat{x}_{n+1} = \hat{x}_n + \dfrac{h}{6}\{f_n + 2\hat{f}_{n+1/2} + 2\bar{f}_{n+1/2} + \hat{f}_{n+1}\}$

Equation 3.19 shows the substep calculations required for a step of Equation 3.18.

3.19 $\quad f_n = f(\hat{x}_n, u_n)$

$$\hat{f}_{n+1/2} = f\left(\hat{x}_n + \frac{h}{2}f_n, u_{n+1/2}\right)$$

$$\bar{f}_{n+1/2} = f\left(\hat{x}_n + \frac{h}{2}\hat{f}_n, u_{n+1/2}\right)$$

$$\hat{f}_{n+1} = f(\hat{x}_n + h\bar{f}_{n+1/2}, u_{n+1})$$

The fourth-order Runge-Kutta algorithm is popular for non-real-time simulations, but it is not appropriate for use in real-time simulation applications because it requires inputs from future times. To see why this is the case, assume that the four derivative evaluations must occur at equally-spaced times and that the input vector u contains real-time inputs from hardware. Under these conditions, the evaluation of $\hat{f}_{n+1/2}$ requires an input vector from a future time because it must be evaluated at $t = (n + 1/4)h$, but it requires an input vector from $t = (n + 1/2)h$. Similarly, $\hat{f}_{n+1}$ must be evaluated at $t = (n + 3/4)h$, but it requires an input vector from $t = (n + 1)h$. The second- and third-order Runge-Kutta algorithms do not share this difficulty and are appropriate for use in real-time simulation.

The Runge-Kutta algorithms are single-step methods that avoid using the value of the function f from previous steps. This leads to some computational inefficiency because potentially useful information from previous steps is ignored. On the other hand, Runge-Kutta algorithms can usually take larger step sizes than the implicit and Adams-Bashforth methods discussed previously. When f contains discontinuities, the Runge-Kutta algorithms avoid the transient errors that occur when using the Adams-Bashforth methods because extrapolation is not used.

3.5.5 Variable Step Size Integration Algorithms

The discussion of integration algorithms to this point has assumed the use of fixed-time step sizes which the user must select prior to performing a simulation run. An alternative approach is to dynamically adjust the time step size as the simulation is running. This technique relies on the assumption that it is possible to estimate the integration error during execution and increase or decrease the integration step size to keep the error within prescribed bounds. Integration algorithms that employ this concept are called *variable-step algorithms*.

When using a variable-step integration algorithm, the time required for a simulation to execute depends on the dynamic activity of the simulated system. During periods when the state variables are changing slowly, the time step size becomes larger and simulated time passes more swiftly. During transients or other conditions when the states change rapidly, the time step size decreases and simulated time passes more slowly. Variable-step algorithms require additional computation to estimate the integration error and to adjust the time step size. In many cases, a simulation that uses a variable-step integration algorithm will execute in much less time in comparison to a fixed-step algorithm however, assuming similar integration error is tolerable in both cases.

The variable-step algorithms are not appropriate for use in real-time applications because real-time simulations must normally perform I/O operations at regular intervals. In general, real-time applications *only* use fixed-step integration algorithms.

Variable-step algorithms will not be discussed in this book. The implementation of these algorithms can be quite complex. An example of a variable-step implementation of the fourth-order Runge-Kutta method appears in [3]. Dynamic system simulation tools such as Simulink provide a variety of integration algorithms, including several of the variable-step variety. The DSSL library provided on the CD-ROM contains only fixed-step explicit integration algorithms from the Adams-Bashforth and Runge-Kutta families.

3.5.6 Integration Errors

Because the difference equations that implement numerical integration algorithms necessarily produce approximations to the exact solution given in Equation 3.3 (page 77), each step of an integration algorithm will introduce some error into the estimated solution. The error that occurs in a single integration algorithm step arises from two sources: *roundoff error* and *truncation error*.

Roundoff Errors

A roundoff error is the result of a computation using finite-precision rational numbers (such as the floating-point numbers used by computers) to approximate infinite-precision real numbers. The amount of roundoff error in a particular computation depends on the number and type of arithmetic operations performed, as well as the precision of the floating-point representation used. Given a specific floating-point format and sequence of arithmetic operations, the only way to reduce roundoff error is by increasing the precision of the number representation used in the computation. This can be done by switching from a single precision floating-point format to double precision, for example. Single precision floating-point numbers usually have about seven decimal digits of precision, while double precision floating point numbers have about fifteen decimal digits of precision. The drawbacks to using double precision are that the variables take up twice as much space in memory and more processor time may be required to perform the computations.

For dynamic simulation of practical systems, the use of single precision floating point (rather than double precision) may introduce significant roundoff error into the solution of the dynamic equations. The severity of this problem depends on

- the form of the dynamic equations,
- the integration algorithm in use,
- the integration time step size, and
- the length of the simulation run.

As a rule, when performing numerical integration, it is preferable to use double precision in the integration algorithms whenever possible. The additional memory and processing time required by double precision are rarely significant costs in comparison to the benefits of increased simulation accuracy.

Truncation Errors

The second source of integration algorithm error, truncation error, is the error that results from a single integration step if the roundoff error is zero. In other words, it's the error if the integration step were executed on a computer with infinite numerical precision. The name "truncation error" is derived from the error introduced by truncating the Taylor series approximation of a function to a finite number of terms. The Runge-Kutta integration algorithms discussed previously are based on a truncated Taylor series approximation.

Truncation errors will be discussed in terms of the first-order linear system shown in Equation 3.20, where x, x_0, and λ may be complex numbers.

3.20 $x' = \lambda x, \quad x(0) = x_0$

The exact solution to Equation 3.20 is shown in Equation 3.21, where λ must have a negative real part if the system is to be stable.

3.21 $x(t) = x_0 e^{\lambda t}$

If forward Euler integration is used to estimate the solution of Equation 3.20, the resulting difference equation appears in Equation 3.22.

3.22 $\hat{x}_{n+1} = \hat{x}_n + h\lambda \hat{x}_n$

This solution can be expressed in the form of the recursion of Equation 3.23.

3.23 $\hat{x}_{n+1} = (1 + h\lambda)\hat{x}_n = x_0(1 + h\lambda)^n$

We can place this result into the form of Equation 3.24.

3.24 $\hat{x}_n = x_0 e^{\bar{\lambda} h n}$

In Equation 3.24, the term $\bar{\lambda}$ is defined as shown in Equation 3.25.

3.25 $\bar{\lambda} = \dfrac{1}{h}\log(1 + h\lambda)$

In Equation 3.25, $\bar{\lambda}$ is the characteristic root of a discrete-time system consisting of the first-order differential equation combined with the integration algorithm. $\bar{\lambda}$ needs to be as close as possible to λ so that the response of the digital system in Equation 3.24 is a good approximation of the continuous system given by Equation 3.21. Assuming that $|h\lambda| \ll 1$, which must be true if the simulation is to have good accuracy, one can approximate the term $\log(1 + x)$ by retaining only the first two terms in the expansion

$$\log(1 + x) = x - \frac{x^2}{2} + \frac{x^3}{3} - \frac{x^4}{4} + \ldots .$$

Using this approximation, express the error in $\bar{\lambda}$ as a fraction of λ with the expression of Equation 3.26.

3.26 $\quad \varepsilon_\lambda = \dfrac{\bar{\lambda} - \lambda}{\lambda} \cong -\dfrac{1}{2} h\lambda, \quad |h\lambda| \ll 1$

This result applies only to the forward Euler integration algorithm. We can compute the fractional error in $\bar{\lambda}$ for the other integration algorithms discussed as well. These errors will all have the form of Equation 3.27, where the constant α depends on the particular integration algorithm and k is the order of the integration algorithm.

3.27 $\quad \varepsilon_\lambda = \alpha(h\lambda)^k, \quad |h\lambda| \ll 1$

In the case of a multiple-step integration algorithm, the computation of the fractional error in $\bar{\lambda}$ assumes that the previous state values used in the algorithm are exact. Equation 3.27 indicates that the truncation error can be reduced by reducing the step size h, by increasing the integration algorithm order k, or by selecting an integration algorithm with a smaller magnitude of α. Reducing the integration time step size can reduce the truncation error to an arbitrarily small level. However, doing this will also increase the execution time for the simulation while increasing the roundoff error in the solution.

Increasing the order of the integration algorithm also reduces the truncation error, but this approach has drawbacks as well. A higher-order integration algorithm will require additional execution time, but in most cases, the primary drawback is that the possibility of numerical instability increases. The numerical stability of integration algorithms will be examined in Section 3.5.7 (page 91).

Tables 3.1 through 3.3 list the values of the algorithm order k and error coefficient α for the integration algorithms discussed previously [4]. From an examination of these tables, we see that the implicit methods have smaller magnitudes for α than Adams-Bashforth methods of the same order, except when $k = 1$. The superior performance of the implicit methods is a result of the "feedback" inherent in their design.

Table 3.1   Implicit integration algorithm order and error parameters.

Implicit Methods	k	α
Backward Euler	1	1/2
Trapezoidal	2	1/12
Implicit Third Order	3	1/24
Implicit Fourth Order	4	19/620

Table 3.2   Adams-Bashforth integration algorithm order and error parameters.

Adams-Bashforth Methods	k	α
Forward Euler	1	−1/2
Adams-Bashforth Second Order	2	−5/12
Adams-Bashforth Third Order	3	−3/8
Adams-Bashforth Fourth Order	4	−251/720

Table 3.3   Runge-Kutta integration algorithm order and error parameters.

Runge-Kutta Methods	k	α
Runge-Kutta Second Order	2	−1/6
Runge-Kutta Third Order	3	−1/24
Runge-Kutta Fourth Order	4	−1/120

The Runge-Kutta second- through fourth-order methods have much smaller error coefficients than the Adams-Bashforth methods. However, recall that each step of the Runge-Kutta methods require k evaluations of the derivative function while the Adams-Bashforth methods only require a single evaluation. To compare the errors between the Adams-Bashforth and Runge-Kutta second-order algorithms based on an equal number of derivative evaluations, double the step size for the Runge-Kutta method. If one replaces h with $2h$ in Equation 3.27, for the case of the second-order Runge-Kutta method, the result is an error coefficient that is four times larger, with a value of −2/3. Under these conditions, the magnitude of the second-order Runge-Kutta error is 8/5 as large as the error of the second-order Adams-Bashforth method. A similar calculation shows that the magnitude of the error coefficient for third-order Runge-Kutta is 3 times larger than that of the third-order Adams-Bashforth method when the number of derivative evaluations are taken into account. Finally, the magnitude of the error coefficient for fourth-order Runge-Kutta is (256/120) / (251/720) or 6.12 times larger than that of the fourth-order Adams-Bashforth methods when the number of derivative evaluations are taken into account.

From this analysis, we conclude that with a fixed number of derivative function evaluations, the Adams-Bashforth methods will give superior error performance in comparison to the Runge-Kutta methods. The implicit methods have better performance than the explicit methods, but the implicit methods are only usable in non-real-time circumstances where their indeterminate execution time is acceptable.

Another way to gain a feel for the effects of truncation error is by examining the impulse responses of the different algorithms. To generate the impulse response for an integration algorithm, set the function f_n to zero everywhere except over the integration step at $n = 0$, where $f_0 = 1$. Figure 3.5 shows the responses of the implicit algorithms of first- through fourth-order to impulse inputs along with the ideal (continuous-time) response of an integrator to an impulse, which is a step function at $n = 0$.

Figure 3.5   Implicit integration algorithm impulse responses.

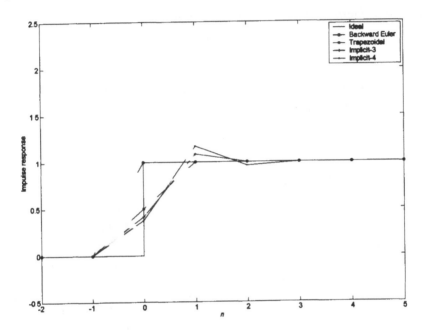

Figure 3.6 shows the impulse response of the Adams-Bashforth first- through fourth-order algorithms, (which includes the forward Euler method) along with the ideal impulse response of an integrator.

Figure 3.6   Adams-Bashforth integration algorithm impulse responses.

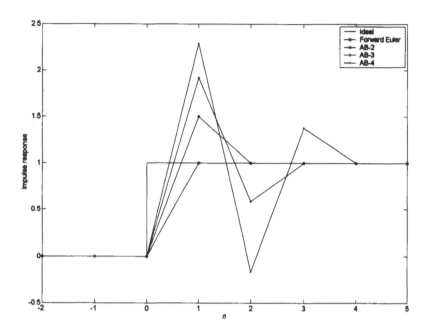

Note that the magnitude of the errors in Figure 3.6 is larger than in Figure 3.5 and that there is a larger time lag in the response of the Adams-Bashforth algorithms due to the use of extrapolation. From Figure 3.6, it also is clear that the higher-order Adams-Bashforth algorithms have larger transient errors when driven by an impulse input.

The impulse responses for the second- through fourth-order Runge-Kutta algorithms are shown in Figure 3.7. Note the complete lack of transient errors, which is due to the single-step nature of these algorithms.

Figure 3.7 Runge-Kutta integration algorithm impulse responses.

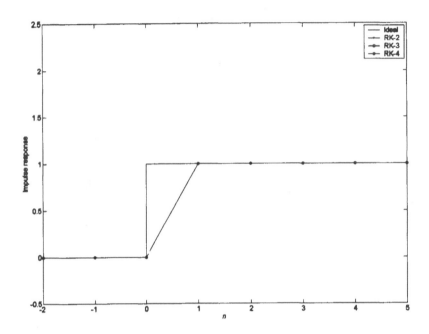

Figures 3.5–3.7, stressed that the Runge-Kutta methods have better transient performance than the Adams-Bashforth and implicit methods when the input function is discontinuous. We can conclude that if the input function is continuous, the implicit or Adams-Bashforth methods provide the best performance, depending on which is suitable for the application. If the input function is discontinuous, the Runge-Kutta methods provide superior transient response to the discontinuities. In all cases, higher order algorithms will provide lower truncation error for a given time step size.

As the integration algorithm executes over a large number of steps, the roundoff and truncation errors accumulate to form the global integration error. There is no direct method for determining the magnitude of global integration error for a general nonlinear simulation other than by solving the dynamic equations analytically and comparing the solutions to the simulation results. Because analytical solution of the equations is rarely possible for a nonlinear dynamic system, we must use indirect methods to estimate the global errors.

A simple method to estimate the amount of global error in a simulation due to truncation error is to perform two simulation runs in the following manner. In the first run, select an integration time step size and in the second, use a time step size half of the value used in the first run. Then compare the results of the two simulation runs and if they have good agreement, the first (longer) step size is probably adequate. If they do not match closely, it is likely because there is a significant amount of global integration error when the longer time step is used. If this is the case, the first integration step size should be reduced and the process repeated until the solution does not change significantly when the step size is halved.

If repeated application of this procedure does not lead to smaller errors as the time step size is reduced, the global error may be due to roundoff effects rather than truncation error. If this is the case, decreasing the integration time step size will actually cause the global error to grow. However, if the simulation uses double precision floating-point numbers, roundoff error will rarely be significant unless a very large number of integration steps are performed.

3.5.7 Integration Algorithm Stability

Numerical instability occurs when roundoff and truncation errors — which may be very small during initial integration steps — grow without bound over a number of steps. This occurs when the time step size is too large, causing the difference equations used to estimate the solution of the dynamic equations to become unstable. For the Adams-Bashforth and implicit methods, higher order integration algorithms tend to reach the point of instability with smaller time step sizes than lower order algorithms. For the Runge-Kutta algorithms, the reverse is true [4]. The improved stability of the higher-order Runge-Kutta algorithms is a consequence of breaking the integration step up into multiple substeps. The implicit integration algorithms have better stability characteristics than the explicit algorithms due to their implicit nature, which can be viewed as a form of feedback.

The characteristics of the dynamic system also influence the stability of the simulation. In the discussion here, assume that it is possible to linearize a nonlinear simulated system about an equilibrium point. Given this assumption, integration algorithm stability is achievable as long as the dynamic system being simulated is stable in the vicinity of the equilibrium point and the time step size is sufficiently small.

Numerical stability will be discussed in terms of the linear first-order dynamic system discussed previously in Equation 3.20 (page 85), with the exact solution as given in Equation 3.21. The value of the constant λ will be set to 1 and the effect of various integration time step sizes on the numerical integration results will be examined. Figure 3.8 shows the solutions of Equation 3.20 using the forward Euler method of Equation 3.6 (page 77) with six different values of the time step h.

Figure 3.8(a)	$h = 0.01$	shows good accuracy
Figure 3.8(b)	$h = 0.5$	there is significant error, though the trend of the solution is still in reasonable agreement with the exact solution
Figure 3.8(c)	$h = 1$	the solution goes to zero after one step and stays there, which is clearly inaccurate, though stable
Figure 3.8(d)	$h = 1.9$	the solution is a damped, stable oscillation
Figure 3.8(e)	$h = 2$	the solution is an undamped oscillation with constant amplitude
Figure 3.8(f)	$h = 2.1$	the solution is an oscillation with growing magnitude, which represents an unstable system

Values of h larger than 2.1 will produce oscillations with magnitudes that grow at faster rates.

Figure 3.8 Forward Euler integration using various time step sizes.

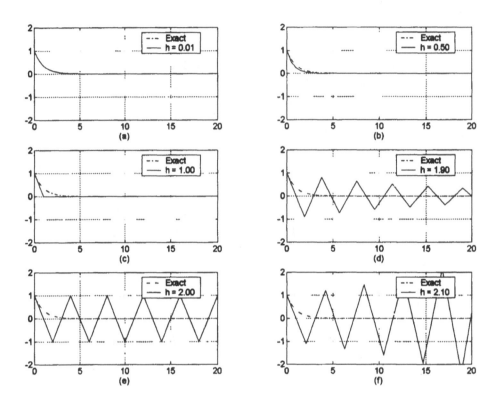

For this simulation using the forward Euler integration method, any value of the time step size h greater than 2 produces a numerically unstable solution. Notice in Figure 3.8 that by the time h has increased to the point of instability, any concept of accuracy in the solution has long been lost. This will be the case in situations where the solutions of the dynamic equations all have response times that do not vary by more than a few orders of magnitude. Dynamic equations with response times that lie within a few orders of magnitude of each other are called *non-stiff systems*. When numerically solving non-stiff systems, the primary concern is to maintain accuracy in the integration algorithm and numerical stability tends not to be an issue. The other case, *stiff systems*, consists of dynamic equations with time constants that vary over several orders of magnitude. Stiff systems are the topic of the next section.

A mathematical development of the various integration algorithm stability limits will not be presented here. For more information related to this area see [2] and [4]. Instead, the following statements regarding numerical stability issues are provided:

1. If the dynamic system being simulated is non-stiff, accuracy considerations will tend to dictate the integration time step size selection. Stability will not be a concern.

2. When performing non-real-time simulation, the use of implicit integration algorithms will provide better accuracy and stability characteristics for a given time step size than explicit

algorithms. This is at the expense of additional computations required by the implicit methods due to the need for iterative solution.

3.5.8 Stiff Systems

A system may include both fast-moving and slow-moving dynamics, which are represented by the time constants of the system model. The stiffness of a system is characterized as the ratio of its longest time constant to its shortest time constant. A system is stiff if this ratio is roughly three orders of magnitude or higher. When simulating stiff systems, carefully select the integration method to ensure that the solution remains numerically stable and produces accurate results while executing with reasonable efficiency.

Consider the open-loop dynamic system represented by the Simulink model shown in Figure 3.9. This system consists of a first-order actuator controlling a first-order plant. In this example, the actuator has a time constant of one millisecond and the plant has a time constant of one second.

Figure 3.9   Example of a moderately stiff dynamic system.

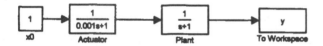

This system input is a unit step. The solution at the plant output is given by Equation 3.28.

$$3.28 \quad y(t) = 1 + \frac{1}{999}[e^{-1000t} - 1000e^{-t}]$$

If the system of Figure 3.9 is simulated using the forward Euler integration method and a step time of 1.9 milliseconds for a period of 10 seconds, the peak magnitude of the integration error is about 0.001. If the step time is increased to slightly more than 2 milliseconds, the simulation becomes numerically unstable and the truncation error grows without bound. The point of this example is that even in the case of mild stiffness, there is little degradation of simulation accuracy before instability occurs.

Many real-world dynamic systems have several orders of magnitude more stiffness than in the example of Figure 3.9. To simulate these very stiff systems with an arbitrarily selected integration algorithm, it may be necessary to take extremely small time steps to accommodate the shortest system time constant. This is inefficient because the system components with longer time constants do not require the same small integration steps needed to simulate the fast components. In fact, if a very small time step is used for the slow-moving components, the accuracy of the overall simulation may suffer due to the roundoff error that accumulates over the large number of integration steps required.

Two approaches for simulating stiff systems will be discussed. The first approach is to select an integration algorithm that works well in the presence of stiffness. For non-real-time simulation applications, many integration algorithms are available that work well with stiff systems. The implicit algorithms described previously, for example, have good performance in the presence of stiffness. The Gear algorithms [2] are another family of implicit algorithms that are intended primarily for the simulation of stiff systems. By using integration algorithms with good performance in the presence of stiffness, it is possible to maintain simulation accuracy and stability while taking much larger time steps than would be possible with other algorithms such as Adams-Bashforth or Runge-Kutta.

A second approach to the simulation of stiff systems involves the use of *multiframing*. Multiframe simulations break the simulation into multiple pieces that execute at different frame rates. The *frame rate* is the inverse of the integration step time and is expressed in frames per second. In the example of Figure 3.9, we could run the actuator simulation with a 0.1 millisecond step time (10,000 frames per second) and the plant simulation with a 0.1 second step time (10 frames per second). This technique is suitable for real-time applications as well as for non-real-time simulations.

The multiframe method adds complexity because any values from the slower frame rate subsystem that are used as inputs by the fast frame rate subsystem must be extrapolated or interpolated. Extrapolation must be used to estimate the value of any algebraic slow frame output at these intermediate frames. Interpolation can be used for state variables from the slow frame rate because the state $\hat{x}_{n+1}$ is available each time the integration algorithm executes. There will also be some difficulty in performing real-time I/O at regular intervals if the various frame rates are running on a single processor. These issues will be covered in detail in Chapter 4.

Of these two approaches to simulating stiff systems, only the multiframing method is applicable for real-time applications. This is due to the unsuitability of implicit integration algorithms in situations where real-time I/O is required. In non-real-time simulations, it is usually easiest to employ an integration algorithm with good performance in the presence of stiffness, which avoids the difficulties associated with multiframing. Simulation tools such as Simulink typically provide a variety of fixed-step and variable-step integration methods, some of which are ideal for stiff systems.

3.5.9 Combined Discrete-Continuous Systems

A dynamic system modeled with both difference and differential equations is called a combined discrete-continuous system, or simply a *combined system*. Combined systems present special challenges for simulation because the integration time step required for the simulation of the continuous system components often varies from the time step of the discrete subsystem. In addition, the inputs from the discrete components to the continuous components may appear as discontinuous signals, which limits the selection of integration algorithms.

Figure 3.10 shows a common situation where a continuous plant is controlled by a digital system. The digital controller operates at a fixed update rate and receives its input from the plant via an analog-to-digital converter (ADC), which samples and quantizes the analog signal. The output from the digital controller is sent to a digital-to-analog converter (DAC), which converts the output signal to a voltage and holds it at a constant value until it is updated on the next frame.

Figure 3.10 Example of a combined discrete-continuous system.

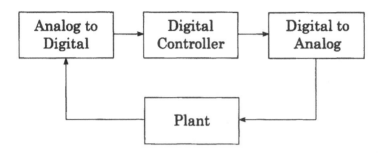

The quantization of the ADC and DAC depends on the number of bits of resolution each device provides. For example, a 12-bit ADC has 2^{12} = 2,048 equally-spaced steps over its input range. During each update, the ADC selects the nearest quantization level to the continuous input value and provides the numerical value of that quantization level to the digital controller. The DAC accepts a numerical value and outputs a voltage level associated with that value.

In the most general situation — where the integration time step for the continuous plant simulation differs from the controller update interval — the simulation must use the multiframe technique. For an accurate simulation, the plant model normally requires a smaller integration time step than the controller update interval. When using a fixed-step integration algorithm, the simplest approach is to make the integration step size an integer submultiple of the controller update interval.

When the inputs from the slower rate system (the digital controller) to the faster rate system (the plant model) are digital-to-analog converter outputs, no extrapolation is required because the signals remain constant between updates.

Combined systems are an important application area for dynamic system simulation. Embedded system developers often use simulation as a tool in the design, development, and testing of complex dynamic systems where an analog plant is controlled by an embedded digital controller.

3.6 Initial Conditions, Driving Signals, and Stopping Conditions

Before simulation execution can begin, all of the system initial conditions must be specified. These initial values include the starting position and velocity of moving objects, actuator positions, fuel tank levels, and charges on the capacitors in a circuit. In general, each first-order differential or difference equation has an initial condition associated with it. In a typical simulation, the user defines some of the initial conditions by setting input variables and other initial conditions are computed during the initialization phase of simulation execution.

Once initialization has completed and the simulation enters its dynamic loop, inputs must be provided to drive the behavior of the simulated system. For an automobile simulation, this set of signals might include the throttle, steering wheel, and brake inputs as well as environmental parameters such as wind gusts and road conditions. These inputs may be provided from predefined data sets, or by a simulation of driver and environment behavior, or perhaps by a person operating a training simulator in real time in conjunction with an environmental simulation. The selection of the source for this information depends on the goals of the simulation project.

There will be conditions that cause an executing simulation to stop. A simulation may stop after the completion of a predefined length of simulated time, or in response to a user pressing a "halt" button in a dialog box. The decision to stop may be the result of a more complex computation, such as ending an air-to-air missile flight simulation after the missile has intercepted its target. Some simulations may have no stopping condition at all, such as a simulation that runs in parallel with an actual system. An example of this situation is a simulation of a nuclear power plant that runs in parallel with the plant itself.

This section has presented some of the factors a simulation designer must address to produce a useful simulation of a complex system. If the designer handles these issues well, the simulation will be easy to use and will have limited opportunities for user error that lead to invalid results. In addition, with careful design of the interface between the driving signals and the rest of the simulation, it may be possible to readily adapt the simulation to different applications such as an HIL simulation or an operator training simulator.

3.7 Data Collection and Storage

It is easy to develop a simulation that generates a staggering amount of data. This occurs when the simulation runs for a long time while saving a large set of variables at a high sampling rate. While the resulting data can provide a great deal of insight into the behavior of the simulated system, it results in a rapid consumption of disk space. For a simulation that will be used regularly over a project life cycle, steps must be taken to limit the quantity of data produced and to store that data in a way that makes it easy to retrieve and analyze.

The first step toward limiting the amount of data generated by a simulation is to select to capture only those variables that are necessary for later analysis. Often, it is possible to capture intermediate values and later use a data analysis tool to manipulate these values to compute final results. For example, if three-dimensional position components of two bodies in space are captured, it is not necessary to also capture the distance between those bodies as a separate variable. During later analysis, compute the distance between the bodies using the components of their positions.

The second step in limiting simulation output data is to only collect time history data at the minimum required sampling interval. In many cases, this minimal interval will cover a large number of integration steps. Of course, the fine step-by-step detail of the simulated system behavior will be lost, but this loss must be weighed against the reduction in data storage space.

There may also be conditions that indicate the transition of the system between slowly varying, steady-state behavior to periods of high activity. Use these conditions to change the data capture interval dynamically so that during steady-state operation, the capture interval is relatively large and during high activity periods the interval is reduced. An example of this situation is a guided missile simulation that transitions to terminal guidance after a lengthy midcourse flight segment. During the midcourse segment, parameters vary slowly and a relatively large capture interval is appropriate. After transition to terminal guidance, the system exhibits variations that are more rapid and a smaller capture interval is required.

We will identify two different categories to indicate the value that we place on the output data from our simulation runs. The first category contains runs where we are only interested in looking at the results immediately and then wish to discard the data. This category contains, for example, the simulation runs performed during development as debugging checkouts of new models, or for verifying proper simulation operation after powering up the system. This category is easy to deal with because each new run can simply overwrite the output data from the previous run.

The second category of simulation output data includes the results of simulation runs that are of lasting significance. Data from simulation validation runs and data used for making important project decisions fall into this category. This type of simulation output data requires careful handling to ensure that the results are clearly identified and can be readily located at a later time — even after they have been archived to offline media. Data in this category may be retained for a long period, perhaps for the entire life cycle of the project. A plan must be in place to ensure the proper performance of these data identification and archiving tasks.

A procedure for saving the simulation initial conditions and any user-selectable parameter settings that are active during these critical simulation runs will need to be employed. In addition, full configuration information must be saved that identifies the simulation software versions used as well as any hardware items used.

Meeting the requirements for critical data storage in a user-friendly, cost-effective manner involves some manual activities as well as some automated processes. Configuration management has already been explored and we can assume that there is some form of configuration identification associated with the simulation software and any relevant hardware at any given time. There are several possible ways to associate this configuration information with the output data from a simulation run. For example, the simulation may read the current software and hardware configuration identifiers from a disk file and store them as part of the simulation output data. Another possibility is to simply use the data file timestamp applied by the file system to determine the date and time of the run, which can then be compared to the dates and times of configuration changes. Many other possibilities exist; whatever method is closer must minimize the possibility of errors and the amount of work required by the simulation developers and users.

There are several methods available for identifying the data stored during critical simulation runs. One approach is to store an integer value in a disk file (beginning with, say, 1) and use this number as part of the simulation output data filename. After saving the output data for each critical run using the current value of this run number, increment the number and overwrite the contents of the run number disk file with the new value. This will assign each simulation run a different, increasing integer value. The result of this approach is a unique identifying number for each critical output data set. The run number provides a key for accessing all the results from a particular run.

The remaining category of data to be saved for each critical run includes the initial conditions and other parameter settings used during that run. Depending on the simulation environment in use, this may be simple or impossible to automate. The simulation operator must use some means to record any important information that cannot be stored automatically. This data can be saved in handwritten form in a logbook or it may be typed into a word processor document as the simulation runs are executing.

Regardless of the details of the methods used, the important thing to remember is that sufficient information must be stored in a form that permits later analysis and repetition of the run. This means that the users must be able to determine the value of *every* parameter that went into a critical run from the information stored. If this is not possible, it may be necessary to perform potentially costly repetition of simulation runs, which diminishes the credibility and perceived value of the simulation effort. This type of problem can be avoided if adequate configuration management and data collection procedures are prepared and then scrupulously adhered to during simulation development and use.

Exercises[1]

1. For the problem $x' = -x$, $x(0) = 1$ the forward Euler method is unstable for $h > 2$. Find the maximum stable value of h for this problem using the trapezoidal, Adams-Bashforth second-order, and Runge-Kutta second-order algorithms.

*2. Convert the system in Figure 3.9 (page 93) into a second-order differential equation, including the initial conditions. Verify that Equation 3.28 (page 93) is the solution for this differential equation with a unit step input and zero initial conditions.

3. Implement a simulation of the system in Figure 3.9 using the DSSL library. Include an evaluation of Equation 3.28 (page 93) in the simulation and subtract its result from the plant output to determine the integration error. Try all of the available second-order integration algorithms and find the one that completes 10 seconds of simulation time with the largest time step while never exceeding an error magnitude of 1.0e–6.

4. Implement the system in Figure 3.9 in Simulink. Include Equation 3.28 in the simulation and subtract its result from the plant output to compute the integration error. Try all of the available variable-step integration algorithms and find the one that completes 10 seconds of simulation time fastest while never exceeding an error magnitude of 1.0e–6.

Hint: Write a MATLAB command file that uses the `sim` command to run the simulation and uses the `tic` and `toc` commands to measure the simulation execution time.

---

5. Using the simulation developed in Exercise 4, try all of the Simulink fixed-step integration algorithms and find the one that completes 10 seconds of simulation time fastest while never exceeding an error magnitude of 1.0e–6. Compare the time required to run this simulation to the time required for the fastest variable-step method found in Exercise 4.

6. Develop a simple command-line driven user interface in C++ for use with a simulation that supports the commands `get` var, `set` var = value, `go`, `halt`, `wait`, and `@filename`. In these commands, var is a global simulation variable name, value is a numeric value, and filename is the name of a text file containing a series of these commands. The `get` and `set` commands are used to display and modify simulation variables. The `go` command starts a simulation, the `halt` command stops it, and the `wait` command prevents any

---

1. Answers are provided for those exercises with an asterisk in Appendix A, page 294.

more commands from executing until the simulation has halted. Note that the implementation of the `halt` and `wait` commands may require a multithreaded implementation.

7. Implement the user interface you developed in Exercise 6 in a simulation that uses the DSSL library to solve the problem $x' = \lambda x$, $x(0) = x_0$. Include user-modifiable variables to select the integration algorithm, the time step size, the simulation end time, and the values of λ and x_0. Also, compute the exact solution and the integration error. Have the simulation write the values of the current time, the state estimate $\hat{x}$, and the integration error at each integration step to a file in a suitable format and plot this data using a spreadsheet or other software.

8. The Lorenz equations are a set of first-order nonlinear differential equations related to weather prediction that demonstrate chaotic behavior. The equations are:

$$x' = \sigma(y - x)$$
$$y' = \rho x - y - xz$$
$$z' = xy - \beta z$$

where $\sigma = 10$, $\beta = 8/3$, and $\rho = 28$. Implement this system of equations in a simulation and select an appropriate fixed-step integration algorithm and step size. Use the initial conditions $x(0) = y(0) = z(0) = 5$. Run the simulation for 20 seconds and make a plot of y vs. x. Verify the accuracy of the integration algorithm and time step that you selected by halving the time step and demonstrating that the solution does not change significantly.

9. Develop a simulation of a combined system of the form shown in Figure 3.10 (page 95) where the plant is the system $\theta'' = u$ and the ADCs and DAC are 8-bit devices with a full-scale range of ± 1. The digital controller implements the difference equation $u_{n+1} = -3\theta_n - 4\theta'_n$ where θ_n and θ'_n are sampled and quantized values. The controller update interval is 0.1 second. The initial plant output is $\theta(0) = 1$ and all other initial conditions are all zero. Select an appropriate fixed-step integration algorithm for the plant model and simulate the system for 10 seconds with an integration time step selected so that the peak error magnitude of the plant output lies in the range $(0.0005, 0.001)$.

Hint: To generate an "exact" solution for use in computing the error, perform a simulation run with a very small (but not too small) integration step size.

---

*10. Develop a simulation of a home heating system consisting of a furnace and thermostat modeled with the equation

$$T' = K(t)[C(t) + (T_o - T)]$$

where T is the temperature at the thermostat and T_o is the outside temperature. All temperatures are in degrees Celsius. $K(t)$ represents the temperature change time constant and $C(t)$ is the steady state inside-outside temperature difference, which both change when the furnace turns off or on. When the furnace is off, $K(t) = 8 \times 10^{-5}$/sec and $C(t) = 0°$. When the furnace is on, $K(t) = 5 \times 10^{-4}$/sec and $C(t) = 40°$. The thermostat is a switch with hysteresis that turns on when the measured temperature drops below 20° and turns off when the measured temperature rises above 22°. The initial conditions are $T_o = 0°$, $T = 18°$ and the furnace is off. Using an appropriate fixed-step integration algorithm, simulate the system for one hour with a step time selected so that the peak magnitude of the error in the simulated temperature lies in the range (0.01, 0.02). How many times does the furnace switch on during the hour of operation?

11. Extend the simulation of the previous problem to allow specification of the outside temperature T_o using a table of temperatures equally spaced in time. Use the following data to compute T_o:

Time	Outside Temperature (°C)
Noon	12
4 PM	10
8 PM	5
Midnight	–6
4 AM	–8
8 AM	–3
Noon	5

(a) Use linear interpolation to compute the outside temperature and accurately simulate the system for 24 hours.

(b) Repeat part (a) using a smoother interpolation method such as cubic spline interpolation. Comment on the differences in the results of parts (a) and (b).

References

[1] Defense Modeling and Simulation Office, *DoD Modeling and Simulation Glossary*. Alexandria, VA: U.S. Department of Defense, 1997.

[2] Parker, T.S., and L.O. Chua, *Practical Numerical Algorithms for Chaotic Systems*. New York, NY: Springer-Verlag, 1989.

[3] Press, William H., Saul A. Teukolsky, William T. Vetterling, and Brian P. Flannery, *Numerical Recipes in C: The Art of Scientific Computing*. Cambridge, England: Cambridge University Press, 1992, §16.2.

[4]   Howe, R.M., *Dynamics of Real Time Digital Simulation*. Ann Arbor, MI: Applied Dynamics International, 1987.

Chapter 4

HIL Simulation

4.1 Introduction

Chapter 3 discussed general dynamic system simulation techniques, many of which are applicable to both non-real-time simulations and real-time simulations. This chapter focuses on issues that are specific to real-time, hardware-in-the-loop (HIL) simulation. An HIL simulation incorporates some of the actual embedded system hardware into a larger system simulation. It supports a variety of application areas such as system-level testing during early product development, embedded software verification, and operator training. The HIL simulation approach is particularly valuable because it provides a controlled environment in which significant parts of the actual system hardware and software operate under realistic conditions.

One incentive for HIL simulation system testing is that it may be quite expensive to perform testing of the actual system. For example, an aircraft flight control system requires expensive and potentially dangerous flight operations to perform full system testing. As an alternative to flight testing, one could build a realistic simulation of the behavior of the aircraft and its environment and integrate the actual flight control system hardware and software into this simulation. This would allow the system tests performed to be in a laboratory environment on the ground — typically a much quicker and cheaper way to produce the desired results.

HIL simulation testing can be performed before a full prototype of the system has been built. This allows system hardware and software development to proceed in parallel while enabling software integration in the HIL simulation. Without the availability of the HIL simulation, the integration effort cannot begin until prototype hardware becomes available. This might occur late in the development cycle and may require the integration of a large body of software with the prototype hardware. Large hardware/software integration efforts late in the development cycle are difficult tasks that frequently lead to serious project delays, cost explosions, and sometimes to outright project failure. HIL simulation enables integration of the software and hardware at a much earlier stage in the development cycle, significantly reducing the risk related to these problems.

At the simplest level, the only embedded system hardware needed to perform HIL simulation is the embedded CPU and its I/O devices, which connect to a real-time simulation computer through complementary I/O devices. This setup can test the full range of behavior of the embedded software, assuming the real-time simulation of the remaining system elements and of the environment is sufficiently rich and realistic. The limited amount of embedded system hardware required for this simulation configuration means that software testing can begin early in the development process. A primary benefit of this early-phase HIL simulation is that by the time the embedded software first operates in the actual system, it will already have undergone a great deal of thorough testing in a realistic simulated environment.

Of course, the results of HIL simulation tests are only meaningful if the simulation accurately represents reality in all the test scenarios. The processes of simulation verification and validation, as discussed in detail in Chapter 7, are critical components in assessing simulation accuracy. Briefly, verification is the process of demonstrating that the simulation has been implemented according to its specifications, which is necessary in any software development project. Validation demonstrates that the simulation provides an accurate representation of reality for its intended purposes. Ideally, validation is performed by comparing the results of actual system tests in an operational environment with simulation results from equivalent test scenarios. This is not possible early in the product development cycle when prototype hardware is not yet available. During this early period, other approaches must be used to gain confidence in the validity of the HIL simulation, which will be discussed in Chapter 7. HIL simulation can significantly reduce, but not eliminate, the costs involved with full system tests; it is always necessary to perform some system testing in order to provide data for simulation validation.

An additional benefit of HIL simulation is that it is easy and safe to perform tests that would be prohibitively dangerous in an actual system test. In the example of the flight control system, a dangerous test scenario would be an engine failure during a landing approach. In addition, HIL simulations are useful for performing system regression testing in an efficient manner. Regression tests demonstrate that previously existing system functionality has not been affected by a change to the embedded system hardware or software. In an HIL simulation environment, it is often possible to automate significant portions of system regression tests and to quickly run through them after each significant change to the embedded system implementation. The ability to easily and rapidly perform regression testing allows it to happen frequently, leading to higher confidence in the quality of the embedded product.

A final benefit of HIL simulation is the speed with which we can produce results. It may take months to plan, set up, and execute a series of actual system tests. In comparison, it typically takes only take a few hours or days to perform the equivalent tasks in an HIL simulation. This is because the logistical and safety-related issues involved with testing a complex dynamic system can be avoided by using the HIL environment to perform the tests.

4.2 HIL Simulation Design

An HIL simulation is normally required to operate in real time so that it interacts properly with the embedded system hardware and software used. The simulation computer must support the interface signals and communication protocols used by the system hardware. In addition to the modeling and simulation issues discussed in Chapters 2 and 3, the simulation design must also address issues involved with interfacing the simulation to a set of input/output (I/O) devices operating in real time. Depending on the features of the simulation software environment and the complexity of the embedded system, this may result in a significant amount of effort devoted to the development of I/O device drivers and related low-level software.

In this chapter, we assume that the HIL simulation must operate in real time and that it must support a wide variety of different types of I/O signals. These characteristics will limit our choices for the type of computer system hardware and the simulation software environment. Because the embedded system hardware typically requires I/O at fixed time intervals, the HIL simulation will be restricted to the use of fixed-step integration algorithms suitable for real-time applications.

The requirement for precise I/O timing leads to the conclusion that, in most cases, a general-purpose operating system such as Windows or UNIX is not appropriate for real-time simulation. These operating system perform a variety of operations that have the potential to disrupt real-time software operations. Some examples of these disruptive operations include:

- Paging parts of a program memory image to disk in order to free up memory for other programs.
- Blocking program execution while higher priority system processes execute.
- Unacceptable latencies during interrupt processing.

Although workarounds may exist for some of these problems in a given operating system, in most situations, the preferred approach is to use a dedicated real-time software environment for HIL simulation. This environment may be provided by a real-time operating system (*RTOS*), or by a real-time kernel provided as part of a simulation development and execution tool. With such a real-time environment, a simulation can be developed that reliably executes at a rate of several thousand frames per second on modest computing hardware, assuming that the simulation is not too complex.

Another issue to address in developing an HIL simulation is the determination of which precise components of the embedded system to physically use in the simulation and which components to simulate. In many cases, the answer is obvious; other times, a variety of "cost-versus-test coverage" questions may need to be addressed to arrive at an answer. Often, it makes sense to design for a variety of HIL simulation configurations, making it possible to select either a software model or a hardware component for a particular simulation run.

For a product containing embedded computing resources, the most desirable system component to include in an HIL simulation is usually the embedded CPU. For simplicity, assume there is only a single CPU in the embedded system. In addition, I will use the term *CPU* broadly to encompass the microprocessor and related hardware such as RAM, ROM, and I/O interfaces. If interfaces between the simulation and the embedded CPU are provided that accurately mimic the operation of the embedded hardware, the embedded software can run on the CPU in the HIL simulation without modification. It is highly desirable to be able to run the unmodified embedded software in the HIL simulation because this approach provides the most meaningful results. If it were necessary to make special modifications to the embedded software to allow it to run in the HIL simulation, the confidence in the results of the simulation tests would be diminished.

In addition to the embedded CPU, it may make sense to include other embedded system components in the HIL simulation, such as sensors and actuators that interface to the embedded CPU. For each sensor and actuator in the system, a determination must be made whether it makes sense to include the physical item in the simulation or to simulate its operation in software. If sensor hardware is included in the simulation, a realistic input signal must be generated for it. Producing a simulated input signal may be simple, as in the case of a low-bandwidth analog signal. Alternatively, it may be an extremely complex task if the input signal has characteristics that make its generation difficult, as in the case of a scene viewed by a video camera.

Similarly, including an actuator in the simulation may be easy or it may require a great deal of work. A simple actuator would be a relay that turns a subsystem off and on, such as a furnace that is under the control of a thermostat. A more complex actuator example would be an electric motor that operates under widely varying load conditions. For this actuator, it will be necessary to develop additional hardware to apply load torque to the motor in a way that accurately models the dynamics of the system in its operational environment.

Figure 4.1 shows a generic embedded system including the plant, the embedded CPU, and a set of sensors and actuators that connect the plant to the CPU. The dotted line represents the boundary between the components of the system to be simulated in software and the embedded system hardware to be used in the HIL simulation. Each line that passes through the boundary represents an interface to be implemented between the embedded system hardware and the real-time simulation. In this example, sensors 1 and 3 and actuators 2 and 3 are simulated in software. The actual hardware is used for sensor 2 and actuator 1.

Figure 4.1 Example HIL simulation configuration.

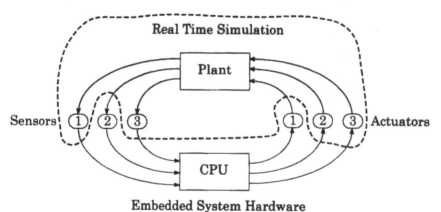

Embedded System Hardware

A drawing such as Figure 4.1 represents an HIL simulation conceptual design. The placement of the boundary between hardware and simulation software in this diagram affects the cost of the simulation development effort as well as the usefulness of the results produced. All parties involved in the embedded system development project should be aware of this design, as well as the costs and benefits that are expected to result from the specific configuration that was chosen.

For the remainder of this chapter, we assume that a digital, non-real-time simulation of the dynamic system is already available. An HIL simulation is to be implemented that includes the embedded CPU along with a selection of the embedded system sensors and actuators. The issues involved in converting a non-real-time simulation to real-time operation will be examined, as well as the types of problems that can be expected to occur in integrating embedded system hardware into the simulation.

4.3 Real-Time Simulation

An HIL simulation must normally execute as a real-time application. In some cases, it may be possible to slow down the real-time elements of the embedded system so that the simulation can run slower than real-time speed, but this is not the usual approach. Instead, the HIL simulation must typically operate as a hard real-time application, meaning that it must always meet its timing deadlines. In addition to meeting these deadlines, the simulation is required to read input devices, perform simulation computations, and write to output devices in a manner that accurately models the behavior of the simulated system. These I/O operations usually occur at a fixed rate which determines the required frame rate for the simulation.

As discussed in Chapter 3, the requirement to process real-time inputs at regular intervals limits the number of suitable integration algorithms. Only explicit fixed-step integration algorithms are appropriate for real-time HIL simulation. Several algorithms meet these requirements and are appropriate for use in real-time simulation. Of the integration algorithms discussed in Chapter 3, the Adams-Bashforth methods and the Runge-Kutta second and third order methods are suitable and are commonly used. The Adams-Bashforth algorithms are best for minimizing truncation error when the integrator input approximates a continuous signal. If the integrator input contains discontinuities, the Runge-Kutta methods may be more appropriate.

In addition to selecting an integration algorithm family, the algorithm order must be chosen. First-order methods have a large error coefficient as shown in Tables 3.1 through 3.3 (page 86), so try to avoid using them. The error coefficients for algorithms of order 2 through 4 decrease with higher order, implying that a higher algorithm order leads to lower truncation error. Higher order integration algorithms require additional computation, though this penalty is often negligible in comparison to the execution time of the other parts of the simulation. The greatest drawback of the higher order algorithms is that as the algorithm order increases, the potential for instability increases as well. For this reason, it is usually best to use a second-order algorithm, at least for initial simulation development. In most simulation development environments, it is easy to change the integration algorithm order. This allows experimentation to test the accuracy and stability of a variety of integration algorithms.

In an HIL simulation, issues relating to operating the embedded system hardware must be addressed carefully. For instance, we may need to apply power to the embedded hardware under the control of the simulation software. This is necessary in cases where system power-up involves the application of multiple power sources in a timed sequence. In simpler systems, it may be appropriate to apply power to the embedded hardware via manual switching.

With power applied to the embedded system, the simulation must perform any needed initialization and can then begin real-time operation. Before starting a simulation run, the simulation initializes the embedded system hardware to place it in a state that matches the initial conditions for the run. Then the simulation run begins executing, simultaneously starting the real-time operation of the embedded system hardware. If the embedded hardware contains moving parts, it may be necessary for the simulation software to continuously monitor the behavior of the embedded system and be prepared to perform a controlled shutdown if problems occur. This monitoring and shutdown is necessary in situations where it is possible to damage the embedded system hardware or other equipment, or where an out-of-control piece of hardware could become a safety hazard.

At the end of the simulation run, the embedded hardware needs to be shut down in a graceful manner. This may involve issues such as bringing moving parts to a stop and forcing a reset of the embedded processor. It may also be necessary to remove some or all of the power sources from the embedded hardware to minimize problems with overheating or wear of moving parts.

Interfacing embedded system hardware to a real-time simulation involves several issues in addition to the basic tasks of sensing simulation input signals and feeding simulation output signals to the embedded hardware. HIL simulation is often used with one-of-a-kind prototype embedded hardware and it is prudent to take extraordinary precautions to prevent damage or unnecessary wear to this valuable equipment. If damage occurs during a test that was foreseeable and preventable, project managers may conclude that the potential benefits of HIL simulation testing do not outweigh the risks to their prototype embedded hardware. It is crucial to anticipate and deal effectively with situations where damage to the embedded system or other hazards may occur.

4.4 HIL Simulation Implementation

The most straightforward approach to building up an HIL simulation is to start with a complete non-real-time simulation of the embedded system and its environment. This simulation may have only a single frame rate, or it may be a multiframe simulation with several different frame rates. To convert this simulation for HIL use, it is necessary to make the integration time steps align with real time. I/O devices that pass input signals from the embedded system hardware into the simulation at appropriate points must be incorporated, as well as I/O devices that send output signals from the simulation to the embedded hardware. Finally, we must bypass or at least neutralize the effects of the simulation models of the embedded hardware and software components that have been integrated into the simulation.

The HIL implementation of this simulation must be capable of running at real-time speed on the simulation computer without missing any timing deadlines. Sometimes the simulation is incapable of meeting the timing requirements, which means that steps must be taken to improve the simulation execution speed. Several possible reasons for an inability to meet frame time deadlines and ways to address each one will be discussed next.

4.4.1 Non-Real-Time Operations

There may be operations occurring as part of the non-real-time simulation that are inappropriate for use in a real-time simulation. These operations are suitable in non-real-time applications and they typically provide valuable services to the simulation. When converting a simulation to real-time use, we must identify inappropriate operations and provide alternative implementations that are preferable for real-time use. Some examples of inappropriate operations follow.

1. Reading or Writing Disk Files

This is not normally appropriate during simulation real-time execution because it introduces unacceptable delays when disk operations block awaiting completion. A real-time simulation should employ alternative techniques, such as reading data from files into memory during initialization, to improve real-time performance. Depending on the simulation execution environment, support may be available for non-blocking file I/O which may alleviate this problem. When reading from a file using non-blocking I/O calls, the read operation must be started some time before the data is actually required. It is important to allow enough time for the worst case I/O delay between the start of the read operation and the time the data is needed.

When writing data to disk during the simulation run, it is necessary to use a data capture technique that is compatible with real-time operation. An example of such a technique is storing the data in memory during the run and writing it to disk after the run completes. Non-blocking file write operations may be an appropriate alternative. Another approach that works in a prioritized multitasking environment is to use a lower priority task to perform file I/O during times when the high priority simulation tasks are idle.

Simulation software tools that support HIL simulation generally provide a suitable method for real-time data collection. If using such a tool, it is best to use the data collection tools it provides rather than writing to a file directly.

2. Dynamic Memory Allocation

Another operation that is not compatible with real-time operation is dynamic memory allocation. As a program runs for a long time and performs many memory allocation and free operations, the memory heap becomes fragmented. Fragmentation occurs when there are several blocks of memory allocated throughout the available memory space with holes between them where previously allocated blocks have been freed. Each memory allocation requests a block of some size, and the system must then locate a free chunk of memory of at least that size. This search will take some time to complete, and it may be lengthy if the memory pool has become fragmented and contains a large number of allocated blocks.

The way to avoid this problem is to perform all memory allocation during simulation initialization. Simulation models rarely require repeated memory allocation and free operations during execution, so this approach should not cause undue hardship.

3. Algorithms with Indeterminate Execution Time

Some numerical algorithms require a number of processing steps that varies depending on the input data. An algorithm that searches for the minimum value of a function over some interval is an example. Depending on the smoothness of the function, the search may require only a few steps or a large number of steps. This indeterminism is not appropriate in an HIL simulation if it creates a potential for missing timing deadlines.

There are several different approaches for resolving this type of problem. One solution is to create an interpolation function that provides an approximation of the algorithm behavior.

This approach can provide the needed speed and accuracy, although if the function is complex or has several inputs, it may require a large interpolation table.

Another approach is to use an alternative algorithm with deterministic execution time. In many cases, an algorithm is available with slower average execution time than the original algorithm, yet the deterministic version has better worst-case performance than the original. In a real-time application such as HIL simulation, the worst-case algorithm performance is usually all that concerns us.

Finally, it may be possible to combine the original algorithm with a more deterministic one to provide overall deterministic operation. In the example of the previous minimum-finding algorithm, it may work best to first use a deterministic algorithm to find an approximate solution. This could be something as simple as evaluating the function at equally-spaced points across its range and saving the location of the minimum function value. Then, use the original search algorithm to refine this result using a limited number of iterations. Although slower on average, this approach may be more appropriate for real-time use due to its predictability.

4.4.2 Short Integration Step Times

The integration step time used in the digital simulation may be shorter than necessary. This is because the effect of an unnecessarily short step time is usually just an increase in the execution time for non-real-time simulations. In a real-time simulation, a too short step time may result in missed timing deadlines.

The accuracy of the simulation generally improves with shorter step times, unless the step time is so short that the error due to roundoff becomes large compared to the integration truncation error. When double precision variables are used for integration algorithms, the step time must be extremely short before roundoff error becomes significant. Because an integration step time that is shorter than necessary seldom causes problems, digital simulations often use a step time that is shorter than required for reasonable simulation accuracy and numerical stability. If the real-time version of the simulation fails to meet timing deadlines, examine the integration step time and determine if it can be increased.

There are two possible approaches to use for this analysis. The first involves detailed examination of the simulation models to determine the longest acceptable step time for each model. The shortest of these individual step times is the longest acceptable simulation step time. If this analysis results in a longer step time than the current value, increase the step time to the new, larger value.

An alternative approach is to simply perform several simulation runs increasing the frame time slightly on each run. Continue with larger and larger frame times until unacceptable inaccuracy or instability occurs. Once this limiting step time has been found, decrease it a bit to move away from the boundary and then perform a set of simulation runs under various conditions and check the accuracy and stability of the results. This testing must stimulate all the modes of system dynamics across the range of expected system behavior. If these test runs produce results that are in acceptable agreement with the original, shorter frame time, the longer frame time should be suitable for use in the real-time simulation.

If one of the approaches above resulted in an increase in the integration step time, the simulation will require less computing power to run in real time. This reduction in computing requirements may allow the simulation to execute on the available computing hardware without missing any deadlines.

The discussion in this section has assumed that the simulation has a single frame time. It is frequently true that some parts of a system have much slower dynamics than other parts. If this is the case, it may be helpful to break a simulation that executes with only one frame time into two or more sub-simulations that execute with different frame times. This is the technique of multiframing, which will be discussed later in this chapter (see page 121). In a multiframe simulation, system components with slower dynamics have a larger integration step time than that of faster components. The multiframe approach reduces computing requirements because the simulation models do not execute at a higher rate than necessary.

4.4.3 Slow Model Algorithms

Sometimes the algorithms used in simulation models are deterministic, but just too slow to meet the real-time deadlines. If this is the case, it may be possible to substitute a different algorithm that executes faster while performing the same function.

An example of algorithm substitution is the situation where a one-dimensional unequally-spaced breakpoint function has an input that is known to monotonically increase at a slow rate. The standard approach used in unequally-spaced functions is to perform a search using bisection to locate the breakpoint interval containing the function input each time the function is evaluated. If the input is slowly increasing, avoid the search and simply check if the input is in the same interval as for the last evaluation, or if it has moved into the next breakpoint interval. This avoids the time required for the bisection while producing identical results — as long as the assumption about the input behavior is satisfied.

An alternative to algorithm substitution is the optimization of algorithm behavior. Using a tool such as a profiler, locate the places in an algorithm where significant parts of the execution time are spent. There are a variety of techniques that can improve the efficiency of the code execution. Some of these efficiency-enhancing techniques follow.

Loop unrolling   Rather than using a loop construct, code the instructions inside the loop as a series of in-line operations. This eliminates the overhead of performing the loop iteration checking and branching. An intermediate method of loop unrolling is to perform several steps during each loop rather than only one step. For instance, if four operations are performed each loop instead of one, the loop overhead per operation will be reduced by a factor of four. Loop unrolling is only useful when the operations contained in the loop are very simple and require execution time on the order of the time required for the loop overhead.

Moving invariant computations outside loops   Some values only need to be computed once for repeated use inside a loop. These computations should occur before entering the loop so that redundant evaluations are avoided. Similarly, some values only need to be computed one time per simulation run. Move these calculations to the initialization portion of the run, rather than performing them during each simulation frame. This optimization technique improves the simulation speed in each case where it is used. The speedup will depend on the complexity of the computation and the number of times its re-execution can be avoided.

Function inlining   Some languages, C++ in particular, permit the optional inlining of functions. Function inlining replaces each call to a function with the instructions in the body of the function. In the C language, this effect is achieved using preprocessor macros to expand a series of statements, permitting a tradeoff between the memory requirements of a program and its execution speed. The memory required for the program will usually increase when using this technique because each occurrence of a call to the inlined function will be replaced by the instructions in the function body. The speedup from inlining results from the avoidance of parameter passing and function call overhead. Inlining shows the greatest performance speedup when it used with functions that are short and occur inside loops.

The previous discussion implied that manual effort is needed to implement these optimization techniques. When using an optimizing compiler, most of the benefits of the loop-unrolling and invariant-code-motion methods can be achieved by adding switches to the compiler command line that select appropriate optimization levels. Even when using an optimizing compiler, it should never hurt (and may help) performance if these techniques are employed in the implementation of our simulation source code. However, overuse of these techniques can result in code that may have good performance, but is difficult to understand. It is important to strike a balance between source code optimization and maintainability.

4.4.4 Slow Simulation Processor

Sometimes the easiest and least expensive approach for speeding simulation execution is to simply purchase a faster real-time processor. If you buy a new processor that is identical to the older one in all respects other than clock rate, you can expect a speedup in model execution roughly proportional to the increase in clock frequency. This may be enough of an improvement to allow the simulation to execute in real time.

An alternative, more difficult, approach is to move from a one-processor system to a multiprocessor system. This will require a hardware platform with a capability for real-time multiprocessor operation such as the VME bus or the CompactPCI bus. In addition, it is necessary to break up the simulation software into suitably-sized chunks and provide interprocessor communication where needed. If N processors are used and the simulation is broken into N pieces with approximately equal execution times, the overall execution speedup should be about a factor of N. This assumes that the separate pieces of the simulation can execute in parallel (rather than sequentially) and the interprocessor communication overhead is small relative to the simulation software execution time.

The most difficult part of achieving this level of improvement is breaking the simulation into approximately equal size pieces that can run in parallel. Though it may be tough to implement, the multiprocessor approach is sometimes the only option for making a complex simulation capable of running in real time.

4.5 Analog I/O Error Sources

HIL simulations frequently interface with embedded hardware using analog I/O signals. Several potential sources of error are possible in such a configuration. In this section, these error sources will be discussed as well as some ways to prevent their occurrence or to minimize their effects when they are unavoidable.

Consider the system shown in Figure 4.2. This diagram represents an HIL simulation that uses actual controller hardware (which may be analog or digital internally) and the analog interfaces between this hardware and a real-time plant simulation. For the sake of simplicity, assume that the controller has one analog input and one analog output, and that the actual plant is a continuous system. In this figure, the box labeled "ADC" is an analog-to-digital converter and the box labeled "DAC" is a digital-to-analog converter.

Note that the ADC and DAC are part of the real-time simulation. In the real-world system, the actual analog plant replaces the set of elements contained in the "Real-Time Simulation" box in Figure 4.2. The dynamic behavior of the plant simulation differs from the behavior of the actual analog plant and these differences will now be addressed.

Figure 4.2 HIL simulation of an analog plant.

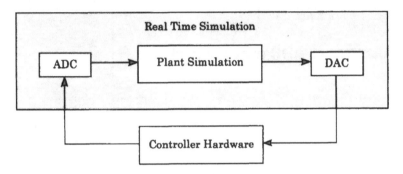

4.5.1 Aliasing

We begin by sampling the analog controller output signal at the input to the real-time simulation. The ADC must sample at a rate at high enough to capture all significant frequency components in the input signal. The *Nyquist sampling theorem* states that the sampling frequency of an ADC must be at least twice the highest frequency component of its input signal in order to permit accurate reconstruction of the input signal. Reconstruction in this sense means the ability to accurately convert the input signal back to an analog signal using a DAC.

Given an ADC with a sampling frequency f_s, the highest frequency in the input signal that can be reconstructed is one half of f_s, which is the Nyquist frequency f_N. This relationship is shown in Equation 4.1.

$$4.1 \quad f_N = \frac{f_s}{2}$$

If there are components in the input signal at frequencies higher than f_N, they will be aliased. *Aliasing* occurs when an input signal is sampled at a frequency that is too low. As a result, the frequency of the sampled signal is lower than the frequency of the input signal. To demonstrate this, we use a pure sinusoid as an input signal and feed it into an ADC with a sampling rate of f_s. Then we convert it back to an analog signal using a DAC as shown in Figure 4.3.

Figure 4.3 Aliasing demonstration setup.

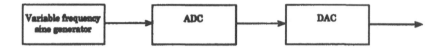

Using the setup in Figure 4.3 and varying the sine wave frequency from zero to f_s, the frequency of the signal measured at the output of the DAC will be as shown in Figure 4.4. In this figure, the frequencies are normalized so that $f_N = 1$.

Figure 4.4 Aliasing of ADC input signal.

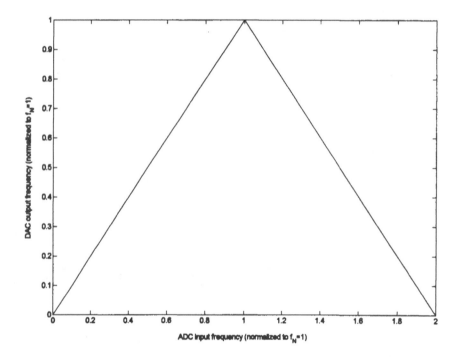

From Figure 4.4, notice that for input frequencies ranging from zero to f_N, the frequency of the output signal matches the frequency of the input signal. For input signal frequencies beyond f_N, however, the output signal is lower in frequency than the input signal. For an input signal with a frequency equal to the sampling rate f_N, the output of the DAC is at zero frequency, or a constant value.

Figure 4.5   Sampling a sine wave with frequency f_s.

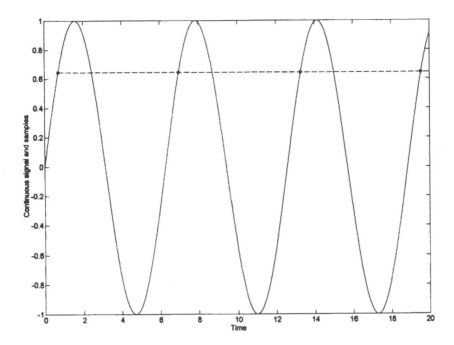

Figure 4.6 shows why this happens. The ADC takes one sample for each complete cycle of the input sine wave. This sample always occurs at the same phase of the sine wave, so the result is that the apparent measured signal is the dotted line — a constant value.

Aliasing is a bad thing in the context of system simulation, so steps must be taken to ensure that it does not occur. The two primary ways to prevent aliasing are 1) by ensuring that the ADC samples at a high enough frequency and 2) by filtering out unwanted signal components with frequencies greater than f_N.

In the first approach, we identify the minimum required ADC sampling frequency by determining the highest meaningful frequency component in the controller output signal. Using the Nyquist sampling theorem, the ADC sampling frequency must then be at least twice this frequency. Any lower sampling frequency would lead to aliasing, which corrupts the behavior of the simulation.

The second approach to avoiding aliasing is to lowpass-filter the controller output signal before performing the analog-to-digital conversion. The goal of this filter is to allow all frequencies below f_N to pass through unchanged and to eliminate all frequencies above f_N. This approach is useful if there is no clearly defined upper limit on frequency content for the controller output signal, or if there is high frequency noise on the ADC input signal. When using this approach, ensure that the ADC sampling frequency is high enough to capture all significant frequency components in the controller output signal. Also be sure to verify that the lowpass filter does not significantly alter the dynamic behavior of the system.

4.5.2 DAC Zero-Order Hold

In most HIL simulation applications, DAC output signals are updated once per simulation frame and hold the same value until they are updated on the next frame. The process of maintaining a constant DAC output value between updates is called a *zero-order hold*. Figure 4.6 shows an example of a continuous signal as the dotted line and its zero-order hold approximation as the stairstep waveform.

Figure 4.6   DAC zero-order hold.

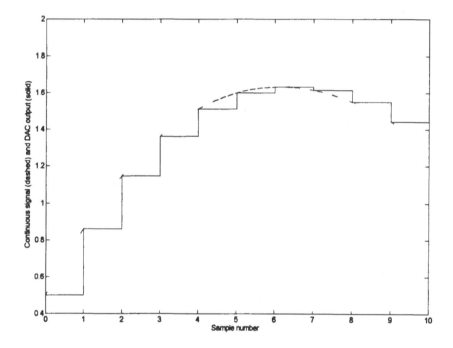

From the figure, we can see that the zero-order hold has the effect of introducing a time delay into its output that is, on average, equal to one-half of the sample period. It also has a characteristic stairstep appearance that is not typically expected as output from a continuous system. The stairstep appearance can be reduced or eliminated by lowpass-filtering the DAC output signal before passing it on to the controller. However, the insertion of a lowpass filter will increase the time delay between the desired and actual output signal even further.

The time delay due to the DAC zero-order hold a is significant difference between the HIL simulation and the actual plant. If care is not taken in analyzing and compensating for its effects, the HIL simulation behavior may vary considerably from actual system operation.

A simple way to reduce the effect of the DAC zero-order hold is to decrease the simulation frame time. Cutting the frame time in half will also cut the zero-order hold delay in half. This approach can reduce the effects of the zero-order hold to negligible levels, assuming sufficient computational resources are available, but will never eliminate it.

The average zero-order hold delay can be eliminated with the use of extrapolation. We can extrapolate the DAC output value one-half of the frame time forward in time using an appropriate extrapolation formula. Equation 4.2 is a first-order extrapolation formula that uses the current and prior values of the desired output signal. In this equation, x_n is the desired output signal and $\hat{x}_n$ is the extrapolated value output to the DAC.

$$4.2 \quad \hat{x}_n = x_n + \frac{x_n - x_{n-1}}{2}$$

Although it eliminates the average delay due to the zero-order hold, extrapolation will introduce some error into the DAC output signal. If the input to the extrapolation is assumed to be a sine wave with frequency ω, the formula of Equation 4.2 will generate a sine wave output with errors in both amplitude and phase. For the extrapolation to be reasonably accurate, the product ωh, where h is the integration step time, must be much less than one. If this is the case, the approximate fractional error in magnitude is given in Equation 4.3 and the approximate phase error appears in Equation 4.4 [3]. In Equation 4.3, A is the amplitude of the extrapolation input sinusoid, $\hat{A}$ is the amplitude of the output sinusoid, and ε_m is the magnitude error coefficient. In Equation 4.4, ε_a is the phase angle of the extrapolation output sinusoid relative to the input signal in radians.

$$4.3 \quad \varepsilon_m = \frac{\hat{A}}{A} - 1 = \frac{3}{8}(\omega h)^3 \,, \omega h <<1$$

$$4.4 \quad \varepsilon_a = -\frac{3}{12}(\omega h)^3 \,, \omega h <<1$$

Notice that the errors in magnitude and phase in these equations due to the extrapolation are both proportional to

$$(\omega h)^3.$$

These formulas are approximations that assume the product ωh is small. However, they do provide reasonable accuracy up to a value of $\omega h = 0.5$. The extrapolation formula of Equation 4.2 provides very good accuracy for low frequencies — though performance will degrade rapidly if the product ωh becomes too large. This rapid growth in error is a result of the cubic term in the error formulas.

If the derivative of the output signal is available, the extrapolation can be computed with increased accuracy. The derivative will be available if the output signal is a continuous state variable. In other cases, it may be possible to compute an exact or approximate value for the output signal derivative. Using the derivative, the extrapolation formula becomes:

$$4.5 \quad \hat{x}_n = x_n + \frac{h}{2}x'_n$$

The errors in magnitude and phase angle for a sinusoidal input to this extrapolation formula are shown in Equations 4.6 and 4.7 [3].

4.6 $\quad \varepsilon_m = \dfrac{\hat{A}}{A} - 1 = \dfrac{1}{8}(\omega h)^3$, $\omega h \ll 1$

4.7 $\quad \varepsilon_a = -\dfrac{1}{24}(\omega h)^3$, $\omega h \ll 1$

The error in magnitude for the extrapolation formula of Equation 4.5 is one-third that of Equation 4.2 (page 117). The phase error of Equation 4.5 is one-sixth that of Equation 4.2. Clearly, if the derivative of the output signal is available, Equation 4.5 is the preferable DAC extrapolation formula.

Equations 4.2 and 4.5 are first-order extrapolation formulas. It is possible to develop extrapolation formulas of second and higher order by fitting polynomials through previous samples of the desired output signal. If the derivative of the output signal is available, we can use extrapolation formulas that incorporate these derivative values to improve the accuracy. In general, increasing the order of the formula will reduce the extrapolation error, as will the use of the signal derivative. The cost of this improved accuracy is a more complex computation that requires additional effort to start up properly. For details on higher order extrapolation formulas, see [3].

To accurately simulate the analog plant in the configuration shown in Figure 4.2, we must avoid introducing artifacts into the performance of the simulated system. This requires that aliasing be prevented in the simulation ADC input signals and that errors due to the DAC zero-order hold are minimized. Both of these problems can be addressed at least partially by using a high enough sampling rate for the ADC and DAC. Use the additional techniques of ADC input signal filtering and DAC output signal extrapolation to further minimize the effects of these problems.

4.6 Computing Hardware and I/O Devices

In previous sections, only analog signals have been considered as simulation inputs and outputs. In the simulation of complex dynamic systems, several additional categories of I/O devices are commonly used. Some of the other signal types that appear frequently in dynamic embedded systems and, hence, HIL simulations are:

- Discrete digital (TTL, differential, etc.)
- Serial (RS-232, RS-422, etc.)
- Real-time data bus (MIL-STD-1553, CAN, ARINC-429, etc.)
- Instrumentation bus (IEEE-488, etc.)
- Network (Ethernet, etc.)
- Sensors with unique signal requirements (LVDT transducers, thermocouples, etc.)

These I/O devices, along with one or more simulation processors, must be installed in a computer system that provides adequate software and hardware support to enable real-time operation. The issue of software support for the I/O devices is critical. If a software driver for an I/O device is not available, the simulation developer will have to create one, which may involve a large amount of work.

The simulation computer must also have well-defined and repeatable real-time performance characteristics. A high performance simulation might require that the software update all the simulation models and perform I/O at precise intervals of a few hundred microseconds.

The simulation computer must provide system-level software that supports real-time computing and does not allow code execution to be blocked in inappropriate ways. Most general-purpose operating systems do not provide sufficient support of real-time features to be useful in anything other than a relatively low frame rate HIL simulation. Higher simulation frame rates may necessitate the use of a real-time operating system or a real-time simulation kernel on the simulation computer.

A summary of requirements for a high performance, real-time simulation computer system includes:

- Support for multiple high performance CPUs
- Support for hard real-time operations at a high frequency
- High data transfer rates between CPUs and I/O devices
- Support for a variety of I/O devices

In years past, specially designed, extremely expensive simulation computers were developed to meet these requirements. More recently, many HIL simulation developers have turned to the VME bus as the basis for their simulation computer systems. In the future, newer buses such as CompactPCI may provide a lower cost foundation for developers of real-time simulations.

For low budget HIL simulation projects, software environments are available for running real-time simulations on IBM PC-compatible computer hardware. PC-compatible computers contain expansion buses that support the ISA or PCI standards. The ISA bus standard dates to the original PC design and has lower data transfer rates and other limitations compared to the newer, faster PCI bus.

Many manufacturers provide I/O cards that plug into the PC's ISA or PCI bus slots. It is possible to develop a low cost, moderately high performance HIL simulation computer system that consists of a PC-compatible computer and a few I/O cards. With this approach, it is likely that the software tools purchased for simulation development will cost more than the system hardware elements. Chapter 9 will discuss some software products that enable the development of real-time simulations for PC-compatible computers.

4.7 HIL Simulation Software Structure

The simulation software contains sections of code to perform the tasks needed during real-time simulation. A diagram of the software flow of an HIL simulation is shown in Figure 4.7.

Figure 4.7   HIL simulation software flow.

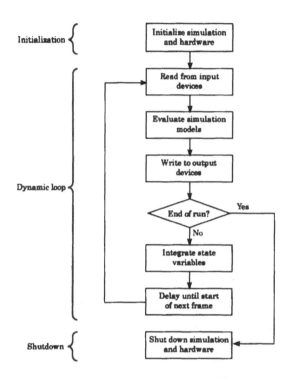

As seen in this flow diagram, the HIL simulation software consists of three main parts:
1. Initialization of the simulation software and external hardware.
2. A dynamic loop that includes I/O, simulation model evaluation, and state variable integration.
3. Shutdown of the simulation software and external hardware at the end of the run.

At the bottom of each pass through the dynamic loop, an interval timer must expire before execution of the next frame begins. The length of this interval is the simulation frame time. As discussed previously, the frame time must be short enough to maintain simulation model accuracy and integration algorithm numerical stability. It must also be short enough to minimize ADC aliasing and reduce the time delay due to the DAC zero-order hold to an acceptable level, assuming that the DAC output signals have not been extrapolated. At the same time, the frame time must be long enough to tolerate the worst-case time to complete all the calculations and I/O operations in the dynamic loop.

A shorter frame time requirement implies higher performance requirements for the simulation computer hardware. Alternatively, a shorter frame time may require simplification of the simulation models so that their calculations can complete in the available time. If the frame computations and I/O cannot complete in the available time, it may be possible to increase the frame time so that timing requirements can be met. However, as seen in Chapter 3, increasing the frame time causes the simulation accuracy to degrade. Further increases will eventually cause the numerical integration algorithm to become unstable.

When the simulation computer is unable to complete the computations of a frame before the timer interval expires, a *frame overrun* occurs. When this happens, the simulation is no longer functioning as a hard real-time system. The simulation developer should implement appropriate handling for frame overruns. At a minimum, the simulation should give some notification to the operator that an overrun has occurred. Beyond that, there are some choices on how to handle the situation.

Whether an overrun is a critical problem or not depends on how often it happens and its size. If the overrun happens only one time (or maybe a few times) during the simulation run, the effects are likely to be minimal — assuming that the length of time by which the execution of the frame exceeds the allowable frame time is small and that it catches up to real time on the next frame. A large, one-time frame overrun that requires several simulation frame periods for recovery will likely invalidate the simulation results for the rest of the run.

Frame overruns are an indication that the simulation has reached the limits of the computing hardware. Rather than live with frame overruns, it is preferable to take steps to eliminate them. Approaches that will achieve this goal include:

- Optimize the algorithms used in the simulation models to increase execution speed.
- Simplify one or more of the simulation models so that less execution time is required.
- Replace the simulation processor with one that is faster.
- Lengthen the simulation frame time (if this does not create other problems).
- Split the simulation across multiple processors running in parallel.
- Split the simulation into multiple frame rates that make better use of the available processor time.

The last option in this list is examined in the next section.

4.8 Multiframing

It is common for some subsystems in a simulation to have time constants that are significantly longer than those of other subsystems. When this occurs, it is possible to improve simulation performance by using the technique of *multiframing*. A multiframe simulation consists of multiple subsystem simulations that run at different frame rates. The frame times h_1, h_2, etc. are normally set at integer multiples of a common factor, the fastest frame time h_f. The simulation updates each subsystem at the times appropriate for its frame rate and the subsystems transfer data among themselves as needed.

Faster frame rate models that use output values from slower rate models must use interpolation or extrapolation techniques to compute input values appropriate for the current time. Without the use of interpolation or extrapolation, the inputs to the fast frame would appear as steps that change only when the slow frame updates them. For continuous signals, it is preferable to smooth the steps using interpolation or extrapolation. This is only needed for values that pass from a slow frame rate to a faster frame rate. Data values passed from a fast frame to a slower frame do not require interpolation or extrapolation because they are valid at the time the slow frame executes.

4.8.1 Multiframing in a Single Task with No Fast-Frame I/O

We will begin with a simulation that runs as a single task on a single processor and intend to modify this simulation to use two frame rates. Identify the fast frame time as h_f and the slow frame time as h_s. Call the ratio (h_s / h_f) the *frame ratio* and insist that it be an integer. In this example, the fast frame will execute four times for every slow frame, resulting in a frame ratio of four.

This multiframe simulation can be implemented by treating the slow frame rate as the "master" frame rate and executing one slow frame followed by four fast frames during each master frame. For this to work, it must be possible to execute one slow frame and four fast frames within each slow frame period. One way of doing this is shown in Figure 4.8. We use traces that are high to indicate that the frame is executing and low to indicate that the frame is idle. The slow frame begins execution at the left edge of the graph at time t_n, where the subscript is referenced to the slow frame.

Figure 4.8   Multiframing in a single task with no fast-frame I/O.

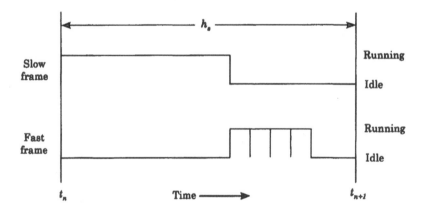

Figure 4.9 Extrapolation (left) and interpolation (right) of a data sequence.

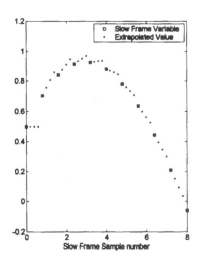 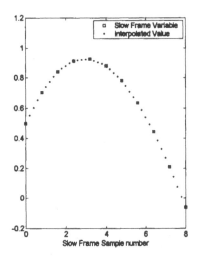

In this figure, notice that the slow frame executes once every h_s seconds, but the fast frame does not execute at regular intervals. Instead, the fast frame executes in bursts of four at intervals of h_s seconds. This arrangement is only acceptable if the fast frame does not perform any real-time I/O. For the moment, assume that this is the case.

Data must be passed between the fast and slow frames as required by the models within each frame. Passing data from the fast frame to the slow frame is easy: at the start of each slow frame execution, the variables in the fast frame have been updated to the same time as the current values of the slow frame variables. Simply make the fast frame variables available for use by the slow frame.

Passing data from the slow frame to the fast frame is a bit trickier. The slow frame updates its variables at t_n, t_{n+1}, etc., but the fast frame requires inputs at t_n, $t_{n+1/4}$, $t_{n+1/2}$, etc. Because the fractional frame values of the slow frame variables are not directly computed, we must estimate them using extrapolation or interpolation. State variables may be estimated using interpolation; extrapolation must be used for all other variables (which are called *algebraic variables*). The simulation should use interpolation whenever possible because it has superior error characteristics compared to extrapolation. This can be seen in Figure 4.9, which shows extrapolated and interpolated values of a data sequence with a frame ratio of four. Clearly, the interpolated sequence provides a better estimate of the slow frame variable values between updates.

It is possible to use interpolation for state variables because at the end of the slow frame execution at time t_n, the integration algorithm will have computed the values of the state variables for time t_{n+1}. The fast frame will require inputs at times t_n, $t_{n+1/4}$, $t_{n+1/2}$, and $t_{n+3/4}$. From this, note that it was not an arbitrary choice that the slow frame executes before the fast frame in Figure 4.9. The slow frame must execute before the fast frame to provide the latest values of the variables required by the fast frame.

At the start of the first fast frame execution, the slow frame state variable values at time t_{n+1} are available. Assuming that the previous state variable value from time t_n is saved, interpolate the remaining fast frame input values using Equation 4.8. In this equation, x represents a state variable passed from the slow frame to the fast frame and $\hat{x}$ is the result of the interpolation.

4.8 $$\hat{x}_{n+1/4} = x_n + \frac{1}{4}(x_{n+1} - x_n)$$

$$\hat{x}_{n+1/2} = x_n + \frac{1}{2}(x_{n+1} - x_n)$$

$$\hat{x}_{n+3/4} = x_n + \frac{3}{4}(x_{n+1} - x_n)$$

The simulation must use extrapolation to estimate algebraic variables, because after executing the step at time t_n, the algebraic variables will have values valid at time t_n. The extrapolation formulas for the fast frame steps appear in Equation 4.9. In this equation, y represents an algebraic variable passed from the slow frame to the fast frame and $\hat{y}$ is the result of the extrapolation.

4.9 $$\hat{y}_{n+1/4} = y_n + \frac{1}{4}(y_n - y_{n-1})$$

$$\hat{y}_{n+1/2} = y_n + \frac{1}{2}(y_n - y_{n-1})$$

$$\hat{y}_{n+3/4} = y_n + \frac{3}{4}(y_n - y_{n-1})$$

Perform the interpolation or extrapolation using methods of first order, as shown in Equations 4.8 and 4.9 or use higher order algorithms [3]. Higher order algorithms will provide greater accuracy at the expense of additional computation.

4.8.2 Multiframing in a Single Task with Fast-Frame I/O

If the fast frame performs real-time I/O, we must ensure that it executes at fixed intervals of h_f seconds. Simultaneously, the slow frame must execute at intervals of of h_s seconds. In a single-task environment, this means that the slow frame must be broken up into (h_s / h_f) subframes that each take roughly the same length of time to execute.

Figure 4.10 Multiframing in a single task with fast frame I/O.

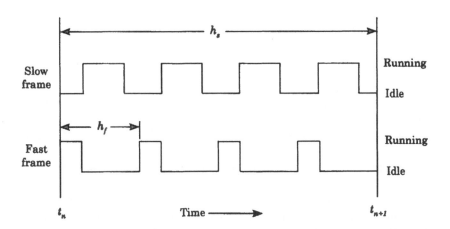

In Figure 4.10, note that by interspersing four fast frames with the four approximately equal-length subframes of the slow frame, both the fast frame and the slow frame execute at the correct real-time intervals. Synchronize the fast frame with the real-time clock so that it executes every h_f seconds. After the fast frame completes execution, immediately execute the next slow subframe. As long as the sum of the fast frame execution time and the following slow subframe execution time never exceeds h_f, this approach will work so that both frames execute at the proper intervals.

There are, however, some serious drawbacks to this approach. First, algebraic inputs to the fast frame will have to be extrapolated over a longer time period because the slow frame execution is not completed before starting the fast frames. The state variable inputs to the fast frame will also need to be extrapolated, rather than interpolated. The state variables can be extrapolated using the formulas shown in Equation 4.10.

4.10 $\hat{x}_{n+1/4} = x_n + \frac{1}{4}(x_n - x_{n-1})$

$\hat{x}_{n+1/2} = x_n + \frac{1}{2}(x_n - x_{n-1})$

$\hat{x}_{n+3/4} = x_n + \frac{3}{4}(x_n - x_{n-1})$

At the start of the fast frame execution at time t_n, the algebraic variables will have values valid at time t_{n-1}. This means that they must be extrapolated across the entire frame from t_{n-1} to t_n, plus the fractional frame between t_n and t_{n+1}. The formulas for this extrapolation are shown in Equation 4.11.

4.11 $\hat{y}_{n+1/4} = y_{n-1} + \frac{5}{4}(y_{n-1} - y_{n-2})$

$\hat{y}_{n+1/2} = y_{n-1} + \frac{3}{2}(y_{n-1} - y_{n-2})$

$\hat{y}_{n+3/4} = y_{n-1} + \frac{7}{4}(y_{n-1} - y_{n-2})$

This approach will introduce additional errors due to the need to use extrapolation rather than interpolation for the state variables and a longer extrapolation period for algebraic variables. However, this is a necessary tradeoff to allow real-time I/O in the fast frame of the simulation.

The second drawback to this multiframing approach is the need to split the slow frame into subframes that take approximately equal lengths of time to execute. This is rarely a simple thing to do. It may be necessary to perform a considerable amount of experimentation to find the proper points at which to stop execution for each subframe. Each time the slow frame execution is stopped and restarted, it is necessary to save and restore all the intermediate variable values for use in subsequent subframes.

We may need to repeat all the work that went into dividing the frame into subframes if the addition of enhancements to the simulation models results in frame overruns for one or more of the subframes. This approach is tedious and fragile in the sense that you may need to redo a large amount of work because of normal evolutionary changes in the simulation. The next section looks at an approach that avoids this particular problem.

4.8.3 Multiframing Using Multiple Tasks

If the simulation execution environment supports priority-based, preemptive multitasking or multithreading, this capability can be used to implement a multiframe simulation so that all frames perform I/O at regular intervals. The primary advantage of this approach over the one used in Section 4.8.2 is that there is no need to manually split the slow frame into the roughly equal length subframes. The multitasking scheduler takes care of this for us automatically. It is only necessary to schedule the execution of each frame at the desired intervals and to make sure that each frame does not exceed its allowed execution time.

The technique known as *Rate Monotonic Scheduling* (RMS) will ensure that all of the threads in the multiframe simulation execute at the correct times. RMS is a method for scheduling real-time tasks so that the deadlines of each task will always be met. The term "task" will be used to mean either a task or a thread. The mathematical basis of RMS has been rigorously developed and analyzed [4].

To use RMS, first identify the execution frequency of each task. In our real-time multiframe simulation application, this frequency will be the frame rate of the task. Assign the scheduling priority of the tasks so that the highest frequency task has the highest priority down to the lowest frequency task, which has the lowest priority. The assignment of priorities as a monotonic function of task execution rate is what gives RMS its name.

The execution time of each task cannot be so long that it causes itself or any lower priority tasks to miss deadlines. Upper bounds for the execution time of each task can be determined such that the entire system is guaranteed to not miss any deadlines as long as all tasks stay within their allotted execution time. Figure 4.11 shows our fast and slow simulation frames executing in an RMS environment. The slow frame and the fast frame both become ready to execute at time t_n. Because the fast frame has the higher priority, it will always execute when both tasks are ready to run. The fast frame completes its execution and then the slow frame executes until it is time for the fast frame to execute again. At that time, the fast frame executes and runs to completion. Then the slow frame continues from the point where it was blocked.

Figure 4.11 Multiframing in a multitasking environment with RMS.

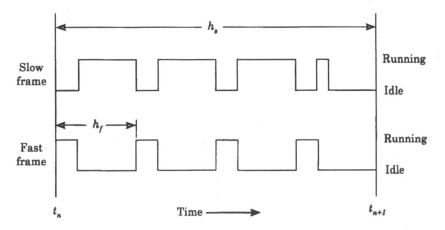

One drawback to this in comparison to the manual frame-splitting approach is that some additional overhead time is consumed by task switching. However, if the models in each frame are of significant complexity, the task-switch overhead will usually be small relative to the execution time of the frame.

Because the slow frame does not execute before the fast frame, it is necessary to extrapolate the algebraic variables and state variables passed from the slow frame to the fast frame using Equations 4.10 and 4.11. As in the single-task method of Section 4.8.2, this extrapolation will introduce some error into the fast frame computations. This is the price for the capability of performing real-time I/O in both the fast and slow frames.

So far, the assumption has been that the entire simulation is running on a single processor. As an alternative, run the different frames of a multiframe simulation might run on separate processors in the simulation computer. This provides the performance enhancement of parallel multiprocessing. The only significant drawback to multiprocessing, aside from the additional cost and system complexity, is the potential for slower I/O transfer rates for interprocessor communication compared to tasks in a single processor environment. However, similar to the task-switch overhead discussed previously, the interprocessor communication latency is often small relative to the execution time of the simulation models.

If a multiframe simulation is designed so that all inter-frame communication takes place through a carefully designed interface, it should be a fairly easy job to move each frame from one processor within the system to another. This enables load balancing across multiple processors as the models of a complex, high performance simulation evolve over time.

The examples of this section and the preceding sections have assumed only two frame rates. It is possible to have any number of frame rates in a multiframe simulation. A multiframe simulation with several frame rates that all perform real-time I/O is much easier to develop and maintain using the multitask approach rather than the single task, manual frame-splitting approach discussed in Section 4.8.2. If the faster frame rates do not need to perform real-time I/O, the single-task approach of Section 4.8.1 will provide the best performance in terms of minimizing extrapolation errors while avoiding the overhead of task-switching.

4.9 Integrating and Debugging HIL Simulations

Integrating an HIL simulation involves connecting the real-time simulation computer system to the embedded system hardware so that they function together properly. This is a major hurdle in the HIL simulation development process, and it can be the source of substantial delay and expense if not properly planned and executed.

In an HIL simulation of moderate to high complexity, there are usually several I/O signals of different types, such as analog, digital, serial bus, etc. During the integration phase, the simulation developer must verify the proper operation of each of these signals through a series of tests designed for this purpose. It is necessary for these tests to verify the following attributes for each I/O signal:

Basic connectivity The signal is connected to the right pin on the right connector of the embedded system and the cabling makes a good connection between the embedded system and the HIL simulation computer I/O device.

Correct interface impedance The connection between the embedded system and the HIL simulation computer must not distort the embedded system signals due to improper interface impedance.

Proper cable shielding The simulation computer interface must not introduce undesired noise into the embedded system, nor can it allow added noise to appear on inputs to the simulation computer.

Correct signal interpretation For an analog signal, this includes the scale factor and full-scale range of the signal. For digital signals, the signal interpretation involves the high- and low-voltage levels and the meaning of each level. Other signal types, such as serial data buses, will have more elaborate interpretations that must be obeyed by the simulation.

Integration tests begin at a pure hardware level to verify a) the correctness of the connections and b) that the I/O signals are undistorted and free of added noise. Verification of correct signal interpretation requires more elaborate testing involving software running on the embedded system and on the simulation computer. It is valuable to have special test software running on the embedded system and in the simulation computer that enables testing across the full range of I/O signals between the two systems. This I/O test software may be part of the system embedded software, or it may be a special software load used only for test purposes. Often, however, test software of this type is unavailable for the embedded system. In this situation, we must rely on ingenuity to devise tests that verify the proper interpretation of the signals between the embedded system and simulation computer.

It is critical that thorough testing is performed at the I/O signal level before continuing with the integration process because problems at the signal level can be very difficult to track down when the full simulation is running. For example, an ADC scale factor that is in error by a few percent will typically allow the system to operate reasonably well, yet some signals in the system will have values that are smaller or larger than expected. Because the effects of this error will propagate throughout the system, identification of the source of the problem can require a considerable amount of effort.

Once the I/O signals connecting the embedded system to the simulation computer have been verified to operate correctly, the next step is to integrate the real-time simulation with the embedded system. As discussed earlier, HIL simulation development began with a software-only simulation of the embedded system and its environment. The simulation was then modified to support real-time operation. A reasonable next step in the integration process is to implement a *ridealong mode*. In ridealong mode, the software-only simulation is run in real time and drives the embedded system hardware with the simulation output signals. We onitor the outputs of the embedded system to determine if it is operating correctly, but do not use them as inputs to the real-time simulation.

Figure 4.12 shows a schematic representation of the ridealong mode implementation. By changing the switch position, the test operator can select either the hardware or the simulated version of the controller as the input to the simulation. For integration purposes, testing shoule begin in ridealong mode. This mode allows a real-time simulation to run that already works correctly, while allowing us to observe the behavior of the embedded hardware when driven with the same inputs as the simulated controller.

Figure 4.12 HIL Simulation ridealong mode.

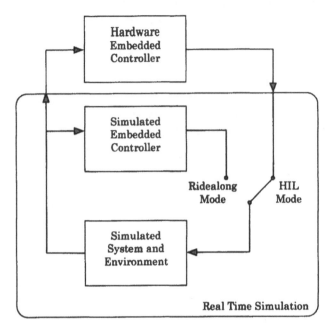

Of course, in ridealong mode, the hardware controller does not actually close its control loops because the simulation does not use the hardware controller outputs. The simulated controller will be an imperfect representation of the hardware controller, so expect the outputs of the hardware controller to diverge from those of the simulated controller at some rate. However, the tests should still give a very good idea of whether or not the embedded controller is operating correctly in this environment. We can make overlay plots of the outputs of the hardware controller with those of the simulated controller and expect to see a good match, at least for some period of time. An upper bound on the rate of divergence between the hardware and simulated controllers can also be estimated and checked during ridealong mode testing.

If errors such as incorrect signs or scale factors on analog signals have slipped through previous testing, they should be immediately obvious in the overlay plots that result from ridealong mode testing. With these plots, we can directly verify the proper behavior of the hardware controller output signals and indirectly verify the correct operation of the hardware controller input signals.

With the successful completion of ridealong mode testing, closed loop operation can now be performed using the embedded controller hardware to drive the real-time simulation. Flipping the software switch in Figure 4.12 to "HIL Mode" enables closed loop operation. Because a careful, gradual approach has been used to reach this point in the integration process, there is a high probability that the closed loop simulation will work correctly on the first attempt. If this approach had not been used, the first attempt at closed loop operation would likely result in immediate loss of control by the hardware controller due to errors in the interface signals or in their software interpretation. Identifying the sources of these problems in a closed loop environment is extremely tricky because the effects of the problems immediately propagate throughout the system.

Ridealong mode can be used in other situations in addition to the integration process. On occasion, subtle hardware or software problems may cause the HIL simulation to exhibit erroneous behavior. As discussed previously, the closed loop nature of the simulation environment can make tracking down the source of the problem quite difficult. The ability to use ridealong mode as a tool in these situations greatly simplifies the debugging process. In effect, ridealong mode opens up the closed control loop and allows detailed observation of the embedded controller operation without the need for special test software on the controller.

4.10 When to Use HIL Simulation

HIL simulation is a valuable technique that has been in use for decades in the development and testing of complex systems such as missiles, aircraft, and spacecraft. With the availability of low cost, high performance simulation computers and I/O devices, the advantages of HIL simulation can be realized by a much broader range of system developers. With a properly designed and implemented HIL simulation, products can be developed faster and tested more thoroughly at a cost that may be considerably less than the cost of using traditional system test methods.

An HIL simulation is a cost-effective and technically valid approach in any of the following situations:

- When the cost of an operational system test failure may be unacceptably high — such as when testing aircraft, missiles, and satellites.
- When the cost of developing and operating the HIL simulation can be saved through reductions in the number of system operational tests. For example, this may be the case with an automotive antilock brake control system that must be tested under a wide variety of driver input and road surface conditions.
- When it is necessary to be able to duplicate test conditions precisely. This allows one to perform comprehensive regression testing as changes are made to the embedded system during its development.
- When it would be valuable to perform development testing on system component prototypes. This allows us to thoroughly test subsystems (such as an embedded CPU) in an HIL environment before a full system prototype has even been constructed.

The decision to use HIL simulation in a project development effort should not be taken lightly. The design, development, and ongoing operation of an HIL simulation will require the dedication of significant resources for a long period of time. The embedded product development project will also have to include in its plans the requirements to provide hardware, software, and technical support for HIL simulation development and operation.

However, even with these costs, HIL simulation is frequently used in the development of complex, dynamic embedded systems. The benefits of HIL simulation can outweigh its costs while enabling a faster time to market for the embedded product. Another advantage is that the final product will have undergone more thorough testing than if HIL simulation had not been used. Ongoing maintenance and upgrade issues will be less of a concern if there is an HIL environment available for isolating and fixing problems and for testing system enhancements.

Exercises

1. The system of ExerciseFigure 4.1 was examined in Chapter 3, Section 3.5.8 (Stiff Systems). Implement a multiframe simulation of this system so that the actuator and plant models run at different frame rates and each integration step time is as large as possible. Using the DSSL library, build a multiframe simulation that contains two StateList variables with different integration step times. Implement the single-task multiframing method of Section 4.8.1 using a nested loop structure. In the outer loop, compute the slow frame derivatives and call the slow frame the StateList.Integrate method. In the inner loop, compute the fast frame derivatives (using extrapolation or interpolation as needed) and call the fast frame the StateList.Integrate method. Use forward Euler integration with step times as large as possible so that the magnitude of the error in the response does not exceed 0.001. Assume that all initial conditions are zero.

ExerciseFigure 4.1 Moderately stiff system.

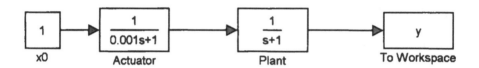

2. The system shown in ExerciseFigure 4.2 is a continuous plant with a continuous controller. Build an HIL simulation that uses the controller hardware with a simulated plant. The controller hardware performs the functions of the summing junction and the Compensator block in the figure. Use the DSSL library with the forward Euler integration method. Determine the largest integration step size for the plant simulation that has a peak error magnitude in the unit step response of no more than 0.001. Assume that all initial conditions are zero.

Hint: The controller remains a continuous system — you only wish to digitally simulate the plant. Approximate this in a software-only simulation by using multiframing with a controller frame rate that is 10 to 100 times that of the plant.

ExerciseFigure 4.2 Continuous plant with continuous controller.

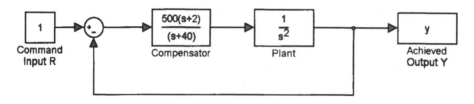

3. Add an antialias filter to the plant model input of Exercise 2. Using a filter design package of your choice, design a continuous analog eighth order lowpass Butterworth filter with a cutoff frequency of one-half the plant model frame rate. For example, in MATLAB, the command to design this filter with a cutoff frequency of 100 Hz is [B,A]=butter(8,100*2*pi,'s'), where B and A are the numerator and denominator polynomial coefficients of the s-domain filter transfer function. Add the filter between the compensator and the plant so that it runs at the compensator frame rate. Determine the error in the step response with this configuration. If necessary, change the plant integration step time (and the filter cutoff frequency) from the results of Exercise 2 so that the peak error magnitude in the step response is just under 0.001.

4. Modify the system of Exercise 3 to replace the constant command input with a sine wave generator that updates its output at the plant model frame rate. Run the simulation using sine wave frequencies of $\frac{1}{4h}$, $\frac{1}{2h}$, $\frac{3}{4h}$, and $\frac{1}{h}$ in Hertz, where h is the plant model frame time. Perform this procedure both with and without the antialias filter of Exercise 3 installed. Plot the output signal y for each of the runs. Comment on the differences between the pairs of plots at the same sine wave frequency with and without the antialias filter installed.

References

[1] Leveson, Nancy G., *Safeware: System Safety and Computers*. Reading, MA: Addison Wesley Longman, 1995.

[2] Glasow, Priscilla. A. (Editor), *Department of Defense Verification, Validation and Accreditation (VV&A) Recommended Practices Guide*. Washington, DC: U.S. Department of Defense, 1996.

[3] Howe, R. M., *Dynamics of Real-Time Digital Simulation*. Ann Arbor, MI: Applied Dynamics International, 1987.

[4] Sha, L., Mark H. Klein, and John B. Goodenough, *Rate Monotonic Analysis for Real-Time Systems* (CMU/SEI-91-TR-6). Pittsburgh, PA: Software Engineering Institute, Carnegie Mellon University, 1991.

Chapter 5

Distributed Simulation

5.1 Introduction

A *distributed simulation* of a dynamic system consists of a group of component or subsystem simulations that communicate across a network during execution. The individual simulations may run on a single computer system or they may run on computers that are separated by large distances. All of the simulations run in parallel and pass data among themselves as needed over the network. The techniques of distributed simulation are applicable to both non-real-time simulations and to real-time simulation applications.

For non-real-time simulation applications, a primary benefit of distributed simulation is the execution speedup that results from running on multiple processors in parallel. This assumes that the additional overhead required by the network communication is small in comparison to the execution time saved by running the component simulations in parallel. In a non-real-time application, there should be no difference in the results of the distributed simulation when compared to the results of an equivalent system simulation that runs as a single process on one computer. To achieve this result, there can be no errors or lost data packets during network communication and the simulations must always maintain proper time synchronization among themselves. Although the issues involved are nontrivial, it is possible to satisfy these requirements with the use of appropriate communication methods. These techniques will be discussed later in this chapter.

In real-time simulation applications, we can also achieve the execution speedup benefits of running the subsystem simulations in parallel. Models can be implemented that are more complex and realistic and, consequently, require more execution time when multiple processors are running simultaneously. One low-cost way to implement a distributed simulation that operates in this manner uses multiple PC computers connected on a local area network. To operate as a hard real-time simulation, the PCs in this system must run a suitable real-time kernel or operating system and the network traffic must be limited to avoid communication bottlenecks. In a sense, this configuration is similar to a multiprocessor computer system such as a VME chassis containing several processors. The primary difference are that network cabling and software is used for communication among the processors rather than data transfers across a VME chassis backplane. Data transfers across a network are typically slower than across a backplane, but with the use of low-cost 100 megabit-per-second network hardware, the speed difference may be negligible.

Another significant benefit of distributed simulation for real-time applications is the ability to connect multiple HIL simulations into a larger distributed simulation, even if the HIL simulations are located a great distance from each other. An example is an aircraft development effort where there is an HIL simulation of the engine control system and a separate one for the aircraft flight control system. These simulations may be located at sites that are thousands of miles apart. Using distributed simulation techniques, these two HIL simulations can be connected into a larger simulation that allows them to interact in real time under a variety of flight conditions. The ability to integrate the two subsystems into a larger system simulation early in the product development process provides powerful feedback into the development effort that leads to higher product quality and faster time-to-market.

The use of distributed simulation in real-time applications leads to a considerably different set of requirements for network communication performance in comparison to non-real-time simulation applications. In non-real-time simulations, the correctness and completeness of the communication are the primary concerns. Meeting these requirements implies the use of communication techniques such as acknowledging the receipt of data and retransmission of data packets that are lost or corrupted while traveling across the network. These techniques cause delays in simulation execution whenever there is a problem with a data packet. In the non-real-time environment, these added delays are not significant and do not cause problems related to the correctness of the simulation execution.

In a real-time simulation application — although communication must still be correct and complete — we have the new requirement that each data transfer must take a limited amount of time to finish. The requirements for correctness, completeness, and speed are in conflict with each other, so there must be compromises. Typically, the data packets sent across the network are updates to the values of a set of variables describing the state of the transmitting simulation. If one of these packets is lost, and the high reliability communication techniques are being used, we will detect the packet loss and retransmit it. The process of error detection and packet retransmission takes some length of time to complete. There is a small chance that the retransmitted packet will also have a problem of some kind, requiring another error detection and retransmission cycle.

In a non-real-time distributed simulation, we insist that the packets arrive at the receiving simulation in the order in which they are sent by the transmitting simulation. If a packet is lost, the transmitting simulation may continue to send updates even as the retransmission of the lost packet is in progress. When this happens, the receiving simulation may have one or more updates of the data values queued for delivery to the simulation that must wait for the arrival of the retransmitted packet. Although this approach is acceptable for a non-real-time simulation, the idea of holding up delivery of fresh data while older, stale data is retransmitted is completely inappropriate for a real-time simulation.

When a network data packet is lost in a real-time distributed simulation, it is usually preferable to immediately use the packet that was transmitted following the lost packet and ignore the missing packet. Simulations operating in this mode must be prepared for the possibility that a small percentage of the data sent on the network will not arrive at its destination. This leads to the requirement that updates be transmitted at a sufficiently high rate so that if a small number of them are lost, the overall performance of the system simulation is not affected adversely.

There is a possibility that two or more sequential update packets will be lost before they arrive at their destination simulation. A distributed simulation to detect this situation and perhaps issue an error message or abort the run if it occurs. When using networking technologies — particularly over large distances — we accept the fact that there will be occasional communication disruptions. A disruption may be of a momentary nature or it may last for an extended length of time. In the case of a momentary problem, such as the loss of a single data packet, the simulation should continue with minimal degradation. When extended disruptions occur, the distributed simulation should detect the problem and respond appropriately.

This chapter will cover techniques that enable the distribution of a dynamic system simulation across a communication network. Low-level communication protocols used in networks will be discussed and as well as ways to maximize network performance. Some higher-level application programming interfaces suitable for distributed simulation will also be examined.

5.2 TCP/IP

TCP/IP is a family of communication protocols that enable high-level networking activities such as serving web pages, file transfer, login to remote computer systems, and email. TCP/IP also provides protocols used in low-level communication activities, such as transferring packets of data from an application program on one computer on a network to an application on another computer. The TCP/IP protocols form the foundation for communication within local area networks and across the Internet.

TCP/IP stands for Transmission Control Protocol/Internet Protocol. TCP and IP are two of the primary protocols in the TCP/IP family. IP is a low-level protocol with the job of delivering data from a source computer to a destination computer. TCP is a higher-level communication protocol that adds reliability features and delivers data packets in the proper order to the correct application on the destination computer.

For our purposes, the TCP/IP architecture is organized as shown in Figure 5.1. The top box in the figure represents the application program — the only part of this architecture that most software developers work with directly. The remaining boxes represent the TCP/IP networking software and hardware that will be considered as part of the computer and its operating system.

Figure 5.1   TCP/IP architecture.

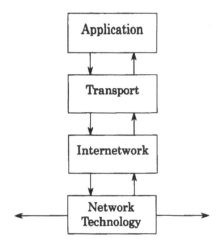

As shown in Figure 5.1, the application communicates directly with the transport layer protocol. The transport layer is responsible for delivering data sent by an application to the correct application on the destination computer. This layer may also provide reliability features in the form of error detection and data retransmission. Reliability is an optional feature for transport-level protocols, and, as discussed, its use can do more harm than good for some applications such as real-time simulation. The two primary transport protocols provided by TCP/IP are TCP, a reliable protocol, and UDP (User Datagram Protocol), an unreliable protocol. These will be discussed in more detail later.

The transport layer communicates with the internetwork layer, which is responsible for delivering data across the network to the correct computer system. The primary internetwork protocol for TCP/IP is IP. On a local network of directly-connected computers, the job of the internetwork protocol is relatively simple and essentially consists of placing the data on the network so the destination system can receive it. On a larger network such as the Internet, this task is much more involved and requires that the internetwork protocol route the data across the complex topology of the network to the destination computer. The internetwork protocol is not a reliable protocol, so it is possible for data to be lost due to transmission errors or network congestion. If a reliable transport protocol is in use, any loss of data will be detected and the transport layer will request its retransmission.

The lowest level shown in the figure is the network technology, which represents the networking hardware and driver-level software needed to enable communication. TCP/IP operates on a diverse collection of networking hardware such as Ethernet, dialup modems, cable modems, and high-speed optical networks. From the perspective of the application developer, the important attributes of the network technology are the data rate it supports and the reliability of data transfer that it provides.

5.2.1 TCP/IP Transport Protocols

As seen in the previous section, the two transport-level protocols provided by TCP/IP are TCP and UDP. TCP is a reliable, connection-oriented, stream-based protocol. UDP is an unreliable, connectionless, datagram-based protocol. TCP supports only point-to-point communication, while UDP supports both point-to-point and multicast communication. These differences will be addressd in the following sections.

Reliable vs. Unreliable Protocols

A reliable communication protocol provides the following features:

- Error-free delivery
- Assured delivery
- Delivery in the same sequence the data was sent
- No duplication of delivered data

Both TCP and UDP provide (nearly) error-free delivery by computing and placing a checksum in each data packet transferred across the network. The receiving system performs a checksum computation on each received packet. If a checksum error is detected, the receiving system rejects the packet without any error indication. In this approach, only packets that arrive error-free at the destination computer will be delivered to the destination application. This technique does not result in absolute error-free delivery because there is a remote chance that a combination of errors can occur during transmission that will not be detected by testing the checksum computation. This possibility is so unlikely that it is not considered further.

The TCP protocol assures delivery of transmitted data by detecting lost or rejected packets and requesting their retransmission. The UDP protocol does not concern itself with the loss of packets, leading to its "unreliable" designation.

TCP keeps track of the order in which packets were sent. If a group of packets happen to arrive at the destination computer in a different order (due to varying delays across the network), TCP will reorganize them into the correct order prior to delivering them to the destination application. UDP does not keep track of the order of transmitted packets, so it is possible for them to arrive at the destination application out of order.

If a network problem results in the creation of multiple copies of a particular data packet, TCP will only deliver the same packet one time to the destination application. UDP will deliver the multiple copies of the same data to the destination application. When UDP is used, this type of problem should be a rare occurrence.

Connection-oriented vs. Connectionless Protocols

UDP is a connectionless protocol. This means that to send a datagram from one application to another, the sending application simply transmits the data packet addressed to the destination application. This is similar to dropping an addressed, stamped envelope into a mailbox. There is no need to notify the recipient ahead of time of that a message is coming, as long as the recipient's postal address is valid.

TCP is a connection-oriented protocol. This is more like a telephone conversation where one party places a call to another party. The call recipient must answer the telephone and then the caller and recipient both identify themselves in some manner before the actual conversation begins. TCP requires a connection in order to support reliable delivery. The context of the connection enables TCP to detect missing packets, out-of-order packets, and duplicate packets. The necessity to create and maintain the connection has implications for the performance of the communication link, particularly in situations where packet loss occurs.

Stream-based vs. Datagram-based Protocols

TCP is a stream-based protocol, which means that the data transferred across the connection is considered to be a continuous stream of bytes. The protocol will break a large chunk of data into smaller packets for transmission across the network. The transmitted packets can be no larger than the network maximum transmission unit (MTU), which is 1500 bytes on an Ethernet network. At the receiving end, the protocol ensures that the packets are delivered in the correct order. It is possible for a sequence of small transmitted packets to be combined by TCP into one larger packet before delivery to the destination application. This means the number of received packets will not necessarily equal the number of transmitted packets.

UDP is a datagram-oriented protocol, which means that each transmission of data across the network is a separate entity. The UDP transport-layer software does not maintain any relationship such as correct ordering between the datagrams delivered to the receiving application. If a UDP datagram is larger than the network MTU, the protocol will automatically break the datagram into multiple pieces for transmission and then reassemble them into a single datagram at the destination prior to delivery. If no errors occur, the number of received UDP packets should equal the number of transmitted packets.

Point-to-Point vs. Multicast Protocols

A point-to-point communication protocol allows two applications to transmit data between themselves. Bringing a third application into this communication link requires point-to-point communication between one or both of the original applications and the new application. If every application in a set of N applications is able to communicate directly with any other application in the set, we must provide

$$\frac{1}{2}N(N-1)$$

communication paths. If one of the applications wishes to send a data packet to all the other applications, it will have to transmit $N-1$ copies of the data. Note that as N becomes larger, this approach will create an increasing communication burden with decreasing overall performance.

TCP and UDP both support communication in a point-to-point mode, but UDP also provides the ability to communicate in a multicast mode. In UDP multicast, each application joins a multicast group that enables it to receive messages transmitted to a particular multicast network address. Many applications can join the same multicast group, which allows an application to send a datagram to a single multicast address and have it delivered to a large number of recipients. An application can join many multicast groups, so it can receive datagrams sent to a variety of multicast addresses.

The UDP multicast approach minimizes network traffic when data must be passed from one application to several recipients. If the number of communicating applications is large and data must be transferred among them in a one-to-many fashion, UDP multicast can provide substantial performance enhancements compared to the use of point-to-point communication.

5.3 Protocols for Distributed Simulation

As discussed previously, a distributed simulation is a group of simulations that communicate over a network as they execute. The network might be a LAN operating at 100 megabits per second or it may be a larger, slower, less reliable network such as the Internet. A distributed simulation may or may not be a real-time application. In a distributed simulation, a set of rules must be in place that specify

- the method of communication,
- the types of data that are transmitted among the applications, and
- the timing when data is transferred.

This set of rules defines the distributed simulation communication protocol.

For our purposes, a distributed simulation communication protocol is one that uses the basic services provided by TCP/IP to enable distributed simulation for a particular type of application. The two primary types of distributed simulations are real-time and non-real-time. These two categories have quite different requirements for the behavior and performance of a distributed simulation communication protocol.

We expect that a non-real-time distributed simulation will produce identical results for two different runs given the same input data set. This leads to a strict requirement for reliability of the communication protocol used among the simulations. TCP is the natural choice for the transport-layer protocol in non-real-time distributed simulations, given its error-free, assured, in-sequence delivery attributes.

Momentary network problems can occur during distributed simulation execution that result in the loss of data packets. TCP detects the loss of these packets and requests retransmission without any intervention from the application level software. Execution of the distributed simulation is delayed while the retransmission occurs, but because the simulation is not a real-time application, this delay will not introduce errors into the results.

The delays due to packet loss and the timing uncertainties introduced by running a simulation on multiple networked computers lead to a requirement for distributed time management. Distributed time management is the mechanism by which the individual simulations maintain a coherent notion of the current time and advance through time in a coordinated manner.

One approach to distributed time management is to provide a central time advance controller application that sends out a message to all simulations in the distributed system requesting them to advance a small step to a specified simulated time. The simulations provide feedback to the time advance controller to indicate when they have completed advancing. The controller then requests that the simulations advance another time step, and so on. The time advance controller repeats this procedure until it reaches the end of the simulation time interval. During each time step, the individual simulations pass data among themselves as needed.

The use of reliable communication protocols and distributed time management increase the network traffic and reduce overall processing performance, but they make the behavior of distributed simulations precisely repeatable. This is almost always a critical requirement when performing non-real-time simulation.

Real-time distributed simulation, on the other hand, has a rather different set of requirements for communication performance. The timeliness of data delivery is of comparable importance to the need for error-free delivery. To ensure that data arrives as quickly as possible at the destination, we must avoid the use of protocols such as TCP that automatically detect lost data and initiate retransmission. In the case of TCP, the loss of data is not detected until some time after the following data packet arrives, which means that retransmission will delay delivery of subsequent packets even further.

An example of this situation is shown on the upper (TCP) timeline of Figure 5.2, where the upward-pointing arrows represent the arrival of packets. Event A is the expected delivery time of a data packet that happened to be lost. Event B is the arrival at the destination computer of the packet transmitted following the lost packet. With TCP, the receiving computer will buffer this packet and wait for an implementation-dependent period of time in case packet A happens to arrive out of order. Eventually, TCP will recognize the failure of packet A to arrive at the destination and will initiate retransmission. Event C is the delivery of the retransmitted data packet to the destination application. Event D is the delivery of the packet that arrived at Event B, but was buffered while awaiting retransmission of the lost packet.

Figure 5.2   TCP vs. UDP handling of a lost packet.

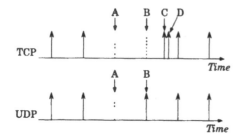

Note that in Figure 5.2, the TCP retransmission delay represented between Events B and C may be highly optimistic. In fact, it may take several hundred milliseconds to detect the loss of the packet and to complete its retransmission [1]. TCP will not deliver any more data to the receiving application until the retransmission process is complete. As soon as retransmission is finished, any undelivered data packets will arrive at the receiving application in a flood. After TCP finishes delivering the backlog of packets, real-time operation of the communication link will resume.

The automatic retransmission of the lost data by TCP causes two problems for us. First, by the time the retransmitted data arrives at the destination, it is too old to be of much use. Second, newer data is already available at the destination computer during retransmission, yet it is not delivered to the destination application until after the retransmitted data arrives.

On the other hand, notice on the lower (UDP) timeline in Figure 5.2 that the loss of packet A is followed by the delivery of packet B as soon as it arrives. The communication continues from that point with no disruption other than the loss of packet A. Although the lost packet is never delivered, the overall performance of the real-time communication link in the presence of occasional packet loss is significantly better than was the case with TCP.

This discussion assumes that the lost data packet does not contain information that is critical to the performance of the distributed simulation. This assumption is reasonable if the lost packet contains updates to the values of variables that will be updated again by the next packet that arrives. However, it is not reasonable if the lost packet contains critical control information such as a command to start or stop simulation execution. For these critical data packets, either use a reliable communication technique or accept a small possibility that they will fail to arrive at the destination application.

5.4 Communication Latency and Jitter

The previous sections discussed the issue of timeliness of data delivery in real-time applications in general terms. This issue will now be examined in more detail, and a way to partially alleviate the problems caused by delays will be considered.

The time it takes a message to travel across the network between two simulations is known as the communication latency. Latency includes the processing time required to move the data between the simulation and the network interface at each end of the communication. If a large number of messages are transmitted from a sending simulation to a receiving simulation and the latency of each message is measured, this set of measurements can be characterized by statistical parameters such as the mean and standard deviation. We will refer to the standard deviation of the latency as the latency jitter.

Ideally, both the latency mean and jitter will be as small as possible. If the distributed simulation communicates over a dedicated, high-speed LAN, this assumption may be satisfied all of the time. If instead the simulation uses a large network (such as the Internet) that involves passing data across a series of routers and competing with other traffic, the average latency and the jitter may both be large values. In the case where the data must make several router "hops," but does not experience significant interference from other network traffic, the average latency may be large while the latency jitter is small. Finally, a high-speed local area network that is congested with traffic may exhibit low average latency along with significant latency jitter, due to occasional interference from the other traffic.

In a situation where data travels in only one direction between two simulations, the average latency may be irrelevant. In this case, the simulation receiving the data can operate delayed in time by the average latency with no ill effects. In fact, the data transferred between the simulations could instead be written to a file and later "played back" into the receiving simulation with identical results. The only problem with real-time operation in this configuration occurs when the jitter is large, causing errors in the timing of the inputs to the received simulation. However, in cases where data travels bidirectionally between two simulations, the average latency becomes critical because it represents a transport delay in the closed loop system.

If there is a way of determining the latency for each data transfer, we can use the technique of extrapolation to estimate the current values of the continuous variables contained in the packet. This minimizes the effects of the average latency and jitter. How can we measure the timing latency for a one-way data transfer? If the system clocks on the two communicating computers are precisely synchronized, this is easily accomplished. The sending computer places a *timestamp* (a reading of the current time) in each data packet it transmits. When the receiving application gets a packet, it subtracts the packet timestamp from the current time to determine the communication latency.

The problem with this approach is that we typically wish to measure the latency to accuracy levels of less than a millisecond and it may be difficult or impossible to synchronize computer system clocks to that degree of accuracy. Given this difficulty, there are two approaches to measure communication latency: a) measure the round-trip latency instead, or b) use a precision distributed time reference.

If the receiving computer sends a response to the initiating computer immediately after it receives a data packet, the initiating computer can use the time between the initial transmission and the arrival of the response to estimate the latency. The estimated one-way latency is the round trip latency (which can be measured precisely) divided by two. This computation assumes that the time required for the computer at the other end to transmit its response is negligible and that data travels at equal speeds in both directions across the network. Unfortunately, this approach does not provide the application that received the initial data transmission with any information about network latency and it increases the amount of traffic on the network.

The alternative approach to latency measurement is to use a precision distributed timing a reference. An example of such a system is GPS (Global Positioning System) receiver, which provides a precise reading of the current time as a byproduct of its position determination. If both computers involved in a communication have interfaces to GPS receivers, the one-way communication latency for every transmitted data packet can be measured with accuracy that is typically in the single-digit microsecond range. The transmitting computer reads the GPS time and places it as a timestamp in each data packet that it sends out. The receiving computer reads the GPS time when it gets a packet and subtracts the packet timestamp from the current time to determine the communication latency. This approach makes the latency information available at the receiving computer where it is needed. The drawbacks to this approach are the expense of GPS receivers and the need to install GPS antennas at each computer location, as well as the need for additional software and processing time to communicate with the receivers.

Latency information must be available at the receiving application so that extrapolation can be used to minimize the effects of the latency. At the receiver, we can extrapolate continuous variable values to the current time if there is a way to estimate their rate of change. As an example, assume that the one-dimensional position p and velocity v of a moving body are contained in a data packet that arrives over the network. The structure of this data packet appears in Figure 5.3. Assume that a distributed time reference is in use that allows the receiving application to compute the communication latency of each packet. The transmitting application places the values for p and v in a data packet along with the timestamp at which the values are valid and transmits the packet across the network to the receiving application.

Figure 5.3   Data packet containing a timestamp.

We can identify the packet timestamp as t_t and the time of arrival at the destination application as t_a. Using the extrapolation formula shown in Equation 5.1, we estimate the position of the body at t_a, where the hat indicates that the computed position is an estimate.

5.1 $$\hat{p}(t_a) = p(t_t) + (t_a - t_t)v(t_t)$$

Use Equation 5.1 when the derivative of the variable is available. If the derivative is not available, as in the case of the velocity v, we can only use the extrapolation formula shown in Equation 5.2 which computes an estimate of the current velocity of the body using the most recent and previous velocity updates. In Equation 5.2, the most recent packet timestamp is t_t and the timestamp of the previous packet is t_p. The time of arrival of the most recent packet at the receiving application is t_a.

5.2 $$\hat{v}(t_a) = v(t_t) + \left(\frac{t_a - t_t}{t_t - t_p}\right)[v(t_t) - v(t_p)]$$

As demonstrated in Section 4.5.2, the extrapolation will have better accuracy if the derivative-based estimate of Equation 5.1 is used rather than Equation 5.2, which relies on previous values of the variable. Alternatively, as was also discussed, higher-order extrapolations will increase the accuracy of the estimate at the expense of some additional computation.

These extrapolation formulas are only useful with continuous variables. If discrete data values are contained in the transmitted data packet, there is no practical way to extrapolate them to the current time. For discrete variables, we must accept the existence of communication latency and monitor it to ensure that it does not become so large as to diminish the overall validity of the distributed simulation. A requirement for discrete variables to travel across the network is an important input to the design of the communication architecture for a distributed simulation.

Having discussed some of the important issues involved in distributed simulation, some communication protocol and software architecture packages will be examined that are intended for use with non-real-time and real-time distributed simulations.

5.5 The HLA Standard

The High Level Architecture (HLA) is a standard for communication among a group of cooperating simulations. The HLA standard was developed with the guidance and support of the U.S. Department of Defense (DoD) to enable the interaction of the enormous number of simulations in use by the DoD, its contractors, and other related organizations. HLA is a mandatory standard that all existing and new DoD simulation applications are required to support.

HLA has been approved by the IEEE (Institute of Electrical and Electronics Engineers) as IEEE Standard 1516.

The HLA standard consists of three major components:

1. A set of ten rules that specify how the communicating simulations must be constructed.
2. The programming interface to the software that performs communication among the simulations. This software is called the Run Time Infrastructure, or RTI.
3. The Object Model Template (OMT), which provides a uniform method for documenting the capabilities and interfaces of individual simulations and entire distributed simulations.

In HLA terminology, a distributed simulation is called a federation. Each individual simulation in the federation is called a federate. The design of the HLA architecture is highly object-oriented: each federate provides an interface to instances of one or more object classes. Each class has a set of attributes associated with it that are shared with other HLA federates during execution. In addition to sharing attribute values among themselves, federates also communicate through interactions, which occur when one object instance has a direct effect on the state of another object instance.

The goal for HLA is to provide the capability to assemble high-fidelity distributed simulations consisting of collections of HLA-enabled simulations using relatively little time and effort. The approach that is intended to make this possible is the documentation and publication of detailed information about the communication interfaces of a large number of HLA-compatible simulations through the OMT. The OMT describes essential information about individual simulations in the form of Simulation Object Models and about entire distributed simulations in the form of Federation Object Models. The information contained in OMTs enables simulation developers to provide the data required by other federates and to make use of data other federates make available.

The HLA specification does not define a particular software implementation or even a communication protocol that must be used by the RTI. Various commercial and free implementations of RTI software are available in programming languages including C++, Ada, and Java. The RTI has a standardized programming interface that is divided into six categories and contains about 130 functions. These categories are shown in Table 5.1.

Table 5.1   RTI API categories.

Federation Management	Create and join federations; perform federation pause, save, and restore operations.
Declaration Management	Declare intent to publish and subscribe to object attributes and interactions.
Object Management	Create object instances; control attribute and interaction publication.
Ownership Management	Transfer ownership of object attributes.

| Time Management | Coordinate the advance of simulation time. |
| Data Distribution Management | Support the efficient routing of data among the federates. |

HLA provides capabilities to enable the creation of very large distributed simulations that make effective use of available network bandwidth. The Data Distribution Management (DDM) component of HLA limits the data passed among object instances to that which is relevant to their needs. For example, a simulation of an air search radar only needs to receive information about object instances that represent aircraft within its maximum search range. Using DDM, network bandwidth is not wasted by passing information about other objects to the radar simulation that would be ignored.

HLA is intended to support both real-time and non-real-time simulation applications. For non-real-time simulation, HLA provides sophisticated algorithms for advancing time that enable good simulation performance while maintaining the required repeatability of results. For real-time simulations, HLA supports data transport using the UDP protocol, which, as seen, is preferable for this application.

HLA is a complete and robust standard for use in the development of small to large distributed simulations that are either non-real time or real time. However, there are a few drawbacks. First, the complexity of the RTI programming interface leads to a fairly steep learning curve. To even create a small distributed simulation, the developer must learn and use a significant subset of the 130 or so functions provided by the RTI. These functions involve concepts that may not be familiar to all developers, such as "updating and reflecting attribute values" and "publishing and subscribing to interactions." Becoming familiar with the terminology and ideas of HLA requires some time and effort for developers who are new to this area.

The second drawback to HLA is that its performance is less than optimal. The RTI is a large, layered piece of software. A considerable amount of processing is required between the time a simulation begins the operation of transmitting an attribute update (or an interaction) and the time the resulting data is placed on the network. Similarly, at the other end of the communication, some processing time is necessary before the information arrives at the destination application. The time required for this communication to occur necessarily depends on the particular RTI software implementation and computer hardware used. We can conclude, however, that the time required to transfer information among simulations using HLA will always be greater than the time required for a direct communication using a lower-level protocol such as TCP or UDP. This will be most problematic in real-time simulation applications.

A third drawback is that each federate in a distributed simulation must use compatible RTI software because HLA does not provide a specification of the communication protocol used by the RTI software. This may necessitate that some federates acquire a different version of the RTI software before a federation can run. While this should not be a serious problem in most cases, it creates potential difficulties when assembling federations.

Another drawback of HLA is that it does not directly handle issues such as the byte ordering of multiple byte values passed between processors. As an example, a 32-bit integer can be laid out in memory so that the least significant byte has the lowest address (called the "little-endian" byte order) or with the most significant byte at the lowest address ("big-endian" byte order). For example, the Pentium processor uses little-endian byte ordering, while many UNIX RISC processors use the big-endian order.

Simulation federates communicating using the HLA RTI must ensure that they use compatible byte ordering to transfer data. One common approach is the use of "Network Byte Order," which is simply a requirement that all multiple byte data values be transferred across the network using big-endian byte order. Systems that are already big-endian do not need to do anything and little-endian systems must reorder all data values as they are sent and received.

Similar problems arise when transferring floating point values across the network. The floating point number format in use must be compatible with all potential recipient computers. A final problem that the simulation developer must deal with occurs when passing multiple-element data structures across the network. An example of such a data structure appears in Listing 5.1.

Listing 5.1 C data structure.

```
struct StateT
{
    unsigned char status_byte;
    float pos[3];
    float vel[3];
};
```

The actual data size of this structure is 25 bytes, but many C and C++ compilers will leave three bytes unused next to the status_byte structure element to align the following floating point values at addresses that are multiples of their size. When passing data structures such as this among different types of computers, it is important to verify that the structure layout matches on all the systems. If the layouts do not match, additional processing must be performed to rearrange the elements each time a structure is sent or received.

More information about HLA is available from the official HLA web site at http://hla.dmso.mil. Several free and commercial HLA-related tools are described on this site, some of which simplify the programming interface for the RTI. Several free RTI implementations are also described there. The web site provides free downloads of the latest version of their RTI software. To download, users must register at http://sdc.dmso.mil/. The web site staff must approve registration before you can download the software. The criteria for approval of user registration requests is not spelled out anywhere on the site. We can assume that anyone associated directly with the DoD or a DoD contractor will be approved to download the software. It is not clear if approval will be granted to students or others who attempt to register on the site.

5.6 Internet Game Protocols

We can think of real-time, multi-player computer games such as the Quake™ series as distributed simulations. These games usually operate in a client–server mode where the actual simulation takes place on a single server. The clients are the remote computers where the game players interact with the simulated world.

Each client computer maintains a copy of the simulated world with which the player interacts. Data transfers from the server to the client provide updates as changes occur in the simulated world. The client computers communicate the actions of each player to the server as they occur. Because the "feel" of these games depends significantly on the round-trip communication latency, it is important for the game developers to minimize latency as much as possible.

Because this is a real-time application with the same kinds of requirements discussed in Section 5.3, UDP is usually the communication protocol of choice. The goal is to minimize communication latency and not to waste any time retransmitting messages that have been rendered obsolete by subsequent updates.

There are some types of messages, however, that must be reliably transferred across the network. An example of this type of message is one that indicates a player has been killed by an explosion. It would be unacceptable for some of the game players to see the player killed while other players see him continue to live.

An approach that provides reliable data transfer is to use a custom protocol within the structure of the unreliable UDP protocol. When sending a UDP message that must arrive at the destination, each client must acknowledge the receipt of the message in some way. If, after a timeout period, a client has not acknowledged the message, the server retransmits it. This process continues until the server receives an acknowledgement or it determines that the connection to the client is lost.

The client–server model used by these games may be useful for some simulation applications such as training simulators. For applications involving distributed HIL simulations, the client–server concept is less appropriate.

One of the most critical factors for distributed multiplayer games is their real-time performance. When developing real-time distributed simulations, it is a good idea to examine the techniques used by developers of similar applications such as these distributed games. In the next section, a communication protocol will be examined that was designed with a similar level of consideration given to the maximization of real-time performance.

5.7 Real-time Simulation Protocol

Although HLA provides a high level of capability for non-real-time simulations, its suitability for real-time applications is more limited. This is a result of its poor real-time performance compared to protocols that make direct use of UDP. The processing requirements of the HLA RTI layers impose a significant burden on each simulation in a federation, which manifests itself as a relatively high average latency with a high level of timing jitter. In an effort to extract as much real-time performance as possible from a given configuration of computing hardware communicating over TCP/IP, I developed a communication protocol called the Real Time Simulation Protocol, or RTSP for short.

RTSP is based on UDP multicast and is intended for use with relatively small groups of simulations (approximately ten federates or less) on an isolated LAN segment. The isolation of the LAN is to minimize the possibility of network congestion; it is not a requirement for operation of RTSP. Using commonly available networking hardware (10 megabit and 100 megabit Ethernet), RTSP provides typical latencies in the 1–2 millisecond range with timing jitter of under a millisecond.

The use of UDP multicast minimizes the amount of traffic traveling across the network. It is possible for any simulation in a federation to receive any of the data packets transmitted by other simulations. Any number of simulations can receive a single data transmission. The result of this is that the total quantity of network traffic increases linearly with the number of simulations in the federation. If, on the other hand, a point-to-point communication protocol were used, the network traffic would increase with the square of the number of simulations in use (assuming full connectivity among the simulations).

The RTSP software was designed with two goals in mind: a) maximize communication performance and b) be as easy to use as possible. Communication performance is maximized because as much work as possible occurs during the program compilation and initialization stages, which makes the runtime operation very efficient. Ease of use is addressed by the Message Definition Format (MDF) file, a text file that defines the simulations in a federation and all messages that pass between them. A software tool provided with the RTSP software translates the MDF file into C++ source code for compilation into the simulations.

RTSP assumes that its interfaces to simulations will be in the C++ language. The RTSP code is implemented entirely in C++ and the source code that the RTSP code generator produces is C++ as well. The RTSP software has been used successfully on Windows NT™, several UNIX systems, and on the VxWorks™ real-time operating system.

RTSP provides some additional benefits that other protocols such as HLA lack. RTSP automatically detects the byte ordering of the processor on which it is running and rearranges the order of incoming and outgoing multi-byte values as needed. The transfer of floating-point data values is addressed by including a requirement that each machine running RTSP must support the IEEE-754 floating point number standard. Most modern computers support this standard by default. Some processors that use other floating point formats, such as an Alpha™ processor running OpenVMS™, can provide IEEE-754 compatibility with the selection of appropriate compiler switches.

The issue of "holes" in multiple-element data structures is addressed by automatically reorganizing the structures so that the largest multi-byte data values come first in the structure, followed by smaller multi-byte values, and so on down to single byte values. Padding variables are automatically inserted as needed to improve the alignment properties of the structures. While this approach is not guaranteed to work under all circumstances, no case has turned up yet where it fails. This strategy has been successful in distributed simulations involving a variety of PC, UNIX, and VME processor types.

In addition to the data values passed among the simulations of a federation, there must be control messages to manage the overall execution of the distributed simulation. In RTSP, one application in the federation must function as the federation controller. The federation controller is responsible for transmitting command messages and receiving responses from each federate. Each command message is a single multicast data packet transmitted by the controller, with a response expected from every simulation in the federation.

Four types of command messages are available in the RTSP: Ping, Initialize, Start, and Halt. The Ping command verifies connectivity among the federates and measures the round trip latency to each federate. The Initialize command instructs each simulation to take any steps needed to prepare for execution. This may involve transmitting state information from some simulations to others. The Start message instructs all the simulations to begin real-time execution. The Halt message stops real-time execution. Each federate returns a success or failure indication in response to each of these messages.

The command messages do not use a reliable protocol, so it is possible for either the command or the response from a particular federate to be lost during transmission. While this seems as though it could cause serious difficulties, in practice, it has not been a real problem. Command messages are a very small percentage of network traffic, which means they are rarely lost on a network with a normal level of reliability. The only time reliability is really needed for command messages is for the Start message. For the other types, the controller can perform repeated transmissions if no response arrives from one or more federates within a reasonable length of time.

If there is no response to the Start message from one or more federates, the controller can send a Halt command and try again by sending an Initialize message followed by a Start message. In applications where I have used RTSP, the transmission of command messages has always been a manually-initiated process. With this arrangement, it is easy to deal with the rare problems that arise from unreliable command message delivery. If reliable command message delivery is critical for a particular application, the RTSP software could be modified to add reliability using techniques similar to the ones discussed in Section 5.6 on game communication protocols.

As discussed previously, the use of the unreliable UDP protocol is the preferred approach for transferring data values in a real-time application. The update rates selected for the transmitted data must be high enough that if an occasional update is lost on the network, it will not significantly affect the behavior of any simulation in the federation. Although occasional lost messages can be tolerated, it is still nice to know which messages get lost during a simulation run. To provide this capability, the RTSP software places a sequence number in each transmitted data packet before it goes out. At each receiving simulation, RTSP keeps track of messages that arrive out of order or that are lost. Following each simulation run, the data on lost and out-of-order message sequences is available for access using functions provided in the RTSP software.

In an application of the RTSP where maximum real-time performance is critical, it is useful to run the message transmission and reception for a federate in separate threads or tasks. RTSP supports this approach by permitting execution of an incoming message processing thread that blocks waiting for messages to arrive over the network. As each message arrives, the blocked thread wakes up and immediately passes the arriving data along to the simulation application. A separate output thread transmits messages onto the network by calling the Send function for each message as needed. In less performance-critical applications, a single thread of execution can handle both message transmission and reception.

The entire RTSP protocol and software package consists of the following items:

- Message Definition File (MDF) syntax and format specifications.
- Translator program to convert an MDF file into C++ source code.
- Runtime software that provides the RTSP real-time communication routines.
- A generic Win32™ controller program that reads any valid MDF file, sends out command messages to the federates in response to button clicks, and displays the response information returned from the federates.

To develop an RTSP federation of simulations, the simulation developer must perform these steps:

1. Develop an MDF file describing the federates and the data that will be transferred among them. This file contains a name for each federate along with the contents of the messages that each federate will send and receive.

2. Run the RTSP translator to convert the MDF file into a set of C++ header files and one C++ source file, which contains static data describing the federation. The translator creates a header file for each federate that sends one or more messages, plus a header file for each federate that receives one or more messages. A federate that both sends and receives messages will have two header files created for it.

3. Integrate the generated C++ code into each simulation in the federation. This consists of the following general steps:

   (a) Create an object of the RTSP class in the simulation.

   (b) Create an object for each different type of incoming and outgoing message in the simulation. These classes are defined in the header files generated by the MDF translator program.

   (c) Call the methods in the RTSP class to initialize it and to identify the callback functions to execute when each type of incoming message arrives.

   (d) Use the RTSP methods to handle simulation initialization, start of real-time execution, and halt of real-time execution. During real-time execution, the PollRcv RTSP member function must be called regularly (perhaps every simulation frame) to process incoming RTSP messages, assuming a single thread of execution is in use.

   (e) Use the outgoing message objects to transmit messages as needed. To do this, simply fill in the values of the appropriate public data members of the class and call the Send member function.

   (f) Implement callback functions for each incoming message to integrate the received data into the operation of the simulation. Each callback function executes during the call to the RTSP PollRcv member function after a message of that type has arrived.

4. Step 3 above assumes that each simulation in the federation is single-threaded. If separate threads are to be used for RTSP data transmission and reception, the program organization is a bit different. In this case, the transmit thread does not call the PollRcv member function and the receive thread calls the RcvMainLoop member function, an infinite loop that blocks waiting for incoming messages. When an incoming message arrives, RcvMainLoop places the data in the object associated with its message type and calls the callback function for that message type.

5.7.1 RTSP Example Federation

A complete example federation using RTSP and the DSSL simulation library will now be developed. The system to be modeled is a continuous plant with a continuous controller and a command generator that drives the controller. This system is shown in Figure 5.4.

Figure 5.4   RTSP example system.

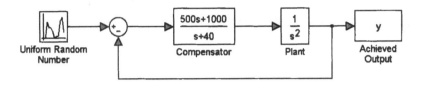

The plant is a "pure inertia" system with the transfer function

$$\frac{1}{s^2}.$$

The compensator is a linear system with the transfer function

$$\frac{500s + 1000}{s + 40}.$$

The command generator outputs a randomly selected command position in the range [0, 10] at ten second intervals. We will divide this simulation into three federates as shown in Figure 5.5.

Figure 5.5   Separation of system into federates.

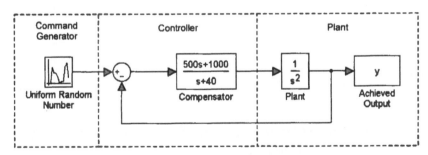

The functions of each federate are described as follows:

1. The CommandGenerator federate creates and outputs the commands to the Controller.
2. The Controller federate computes the difference between the commanded output and the current system output and passes the resulting error signal through the compensator transfer function. The output of the transfer function drives the plant.
3. The Plant federate accepts the Controller output signal as its input and uses it to drive the plant transfer function. The Plant feeds back the current value of its output to the Controller.
4. The generic federation controller application will control the operation of this entire federation.

Given this information, we develop an MDF file that describes the federates and the messages that pass between them as shown in Listing 5.2.

Listing 5.2 Distributed simulation MDF file DistSim.mdf.

```
// Distributed Simulation Message Definition

// Declare names for all federates:
federate CommandGenerator, Controller, Plant;

// Define messages. The federate named with each message is the sender.

message CommandGenerator.Update
{
    double command;
};

message Controller.Update
{
    double drive;
};

message Plant.Update
{
    double output;
};

// Subscription list. Each federate can subscribe to (i.e., receive) any
// message including ones it produces.

// The Controller gets updates from the CommandGenerator and Plant
subscribe Controller : CommandGenerator.Update, Plant.Update;

// The Plant gets updates from the Controller
subscribe Plant : Controller.Update;
```

Then run the MDF translator program with the file in Listing 5.2 as its input. The messages displayed during the translation process are shown in Listing 5.3.

Listing 5.3 Executing the MDF translator.

```
C:\Projects\DistSim>translator DistSim.mdf
Generating CommandGeneratorSend.h
Generating ControllerSend.h
Generating ControllerRcv.h
Generating PlantSend.h
Generating PlantRcv.h
Generating _MsgData.cpp


C:\Projects\DistSim>
```

The C++ header file `CommandGeneratorSend.h` that is created during the translation process appears in Listing 5.4.

Listing 5.4 `CommandGeneratorSend.h` **file.**

```cpp
// CommandGeneratorSend class
// Generated Thu Aug 24 13:33:36 2000 from distsim.mdf
// *** This file was automatically generated. Do not edit it! ***

#include <RTSP.h>
#include <RTSP_Internals.h>

class CommandGeneratorSend
{
public:
    struct Update
    {
        double command;
        uint _TimeTag;
        ushort _SequenceNum;
        uchar _ReceiverIndex;
        uchar _SenderIndex;

        bool Send(RTSP& rtsp, uchar rcv_index = _AllIndexes)
            { return _SendMessage(rtsp, this, 0, rcv_index); }
    };
};
```

In Listing 5.4, the `command` member of the `Update` message appears in the `Update` structure, along with several parameters used internally by RTSP. The RTSP parameter names all start with underscores. The MDF file syntax rules prevent the user from defining variable names that start with underscores, so there is no chance of a name collision.

The contents of ControllerSend.h, ControllerRcv.h, PlantSend.h, and PlantRcv.h are shown in Listings 5.5–5.8.

Listing 5.5 ControllerSend.h **file.**

```
// ControllerSend class
// Generated Thu Aug 24 13:33:36 2000 from distsim.mdf
// *** This file was automatically generated. Do not edit it! ***


#include <RTSP.h>
#include <RTSP_Internals.h>

class ControllerSend
{
public:
    struct Update
    {
        double drive;
        uint _TimeTag;
        ushort _SequenceNum;
        uchar _ReceiverIndex;
        uchar _SenderIndex;

        bool Send(RTSP& rtsp, uchar rcv_index = _AllIndexes)
            { return _SendMessage(rtsp, this, 1, rcv_index); }
    };
};
```

Listing 5.6 ControllerRcv.h **file.**

```
// ControllerRcv class
// Generated Thu Aug 24 13:33:36 2000 from distsim.mdf
// *** This file was automatically generated. Do not edit it! ***


#include <RTSP.h>
#include <RTSP_Internals.h>


class ControllerRcv
```

```
{
public:
    struct CommandGeneratorUpdate
    {
        double command;
        uint _TimeTag;
        ushort _SequenceNum;
        uchar _ReceiverIndex;
        uchar _SenderIndex;

        void SetCallback(RTSP& rtsp, void (*_f)())
            { _AddCallback(rtsp, _f, this, 0); }
    };

    struct PlantUpdate
    {
        double output;
        uint _TimeTag;
        ushort _SequenceNum;
        uchar _ReceiverIndex;
        uchar _SenderIndex;

        void SetCallback(RTSP& rtsp, void (*_f)())
            { _AddCallback(rtsp, _f, this, 2); }
    };
};
```

Listing 5.7 PlantSend.h **file.**

```
// PlantSend class
// Generated Thu Aug 24 13:33:36 2000 from distsim.mdf
// *** This file was automatically generated. Do not edit it! ***

#include <RTSP.h>
#include <RTSP_Internals.h>

class PlantSend
{
public:
    struct Update
```

```
    {
        double output;
        uint _TimeTag;
        ushort _SequenceNum;
        uchar _ReceiverIndex;
        uchar _SenderIndex;

        bool Send(RTSP& rtsp, uchar rcv_index = _AllIndexes)
            { return _SendMessage(rtsp, this, 2, rcv_index); }
    };
};
```

Listing 5.8   PlantRcv.h **file.**

```
// PlantRcv class
// Generated Thu Aug 24 13:33:36 2000 from distsim.mdf
// *** This file was automatically generated. Do not edit it! ***

#include <RTSP.h>
#include <RTSP_Internals.h>

class PlantRcv
{
public:
    struct ControllerUpdate
    {
        double drive;
        uint _TimeTag;
        ushort _SequenceNum;
        uchar _ReceiverIndex;
        uchar _SenderIndex;

        void SetCallback(RTSP& rtsp, void (*_f)())
            { _AddCallback(rtsp, _f, this, 1); }
    };
};
```

The contents of _MsgData.cpp are used internally by the RTSP software and are not generally of interest to simulation developers (except perhaps when troubleshooting), so that file is not discussed here.

The next step is to develop the source code for each federate. This code will make use of the classes contained in the files generated by the MDF translator program as well as the RTSP class and its methods contained in the RTSP.cpp file. We will use the DSSL simulation library to implement the elements of the continuous system simulation.

The CommandGenerator federate is implemented in the file CommandGenerator.cpp, shown in Listing 5.9.

Listing 5.9 CommandGenerator.cpp **file.**

```
#include <RTSP.h>

#include <stdio.h>
#include "CommandGeneratorSend.h"

RTSP* rtsp;

CommandGeneratorSend::Update command_update;

bool ping_callback()
{
    printf("Ping callback\n");
    return true;
}

bool init_callback()
{
    printf("Initialize callback\n");
    return true;
}

bool start_callback()
{
    printf("Start callback\n");
    return true;
}

bool end_run = false;
bool halt_callback()
{
    printf("Halt callback\n");
```

```
        end_run = true;
        return true;
}


int main()
{
    printf("CommandGenerator Federate\n");
    printf("Jim Ledin    August, 2000\n\n");

    // Determine the number of frames per second
    int frames_per_sec = 100;
    printf("\nUpdate rate: %d frames/sec\n\n", frames_per_sec);

    rtsp = new RTSP("CommandGenerator");
    rtsp->SetPingCallback(ping_callback);
    rtsp->SetInitializeCallback(init_callback);
    rtsp->SetStartCallback(start_callback);
    rtsp->SetHaltCallback(halt_callback);

    for (;;)
    {
        end_run = false;
        printf("Waiting for Initialize\n");
        rtsp->WaitForInit();

        printf("Waiting for Start\n");
        rtsp->WaitForStart();
        printf("Running\n");

        double step_time = 1.0 / frames_per_sec;

        rtsp->StartTimer();
        uint frame = 0;
        while (!end_run)
        {
            // Time since start of run
            double Time = frame * step_time;

            // Output a new random command every 10 seconds
```

```
            if (frame % (10*frames_per_sec) == 0)
            {
                double command = 10.0 * double(rand()) / RAND_MAX;
                command_update.command = command;
                command_update.Send(*rtsp);

                printf("Time: %.1lf; New command: %.3lf\n", Time, command);
                fflush(stdout);
            }

            uint end_of_frame = uint(1e6 * ++frame * step_time);
            uint cur_time = rtsp->ReadTimer();
            while (cur_time < end_of_frame)
            {
                rtsp->PollRcv(true, end_of_frame - cur_time);
                cur_time = rtsp->ReadTimer();
            }
        }
        printf("End of run\n");
    }

    return 0;
}
```

The `Controller` federate is implemented in `Controller.cpp`, shown in Listing 5.10. Note that the DSSL library is being used to implement the differential equations of the compensator transfer function.

Listing 5.10 `Controller.cpp` file.

```
#include <dssl.h>
#include <RTSP.h>

#include <stdio.h>

#include "ControllerSend.h"
#include "ControllerRcv.h"

RTSP* rtsp;
```

```
ControllerSend::Update drive_update;
ControllerRcv::CommandGeneratorUpdate command_update;
ControllerRcv::PlantUpdate plant_update;

bool ping_callback()
{
    printf("Ping callback\n");
    return true;
}

bool init_callback()
{
    printf("Initialize callback\n");
    return true;
}

bool start_callback()
{
    printf("Start callback\n");
    return true;
}

bool end_run = false;
bool halt_callback()
{
    printf("Halt callback\n");
    end_run = true;
    return true;
}

void command_callback()
{
    printf("New command from CommandGenerator: %.2f\n",
        command_update.command);
}

void plant_callback()
{
}
```

```c
int main()
{
    printf("Controller Federate\n");
    printf("Jim Ledin    August, 2000\n\n");
    // Determine the number of frames per second
    int frames_per_sec = 100;
    printf("\nUpdate rate: %d frames/sec\n\n", frames_per_sec);

    rtsp = new RTSP("Controller");
    rtsp->SetPingCallback(ping_callback);
    rtsp->SetInitializeCallback(init_callback);
    rtsp->SetStartCallback(start_callback);
    rtsp->SetHaltCallback(halt_callback);

    command_update.SetCallback(*rtsp, command_callback);
    plant_update.SetCallback(*rtsp, plant_callback);

    // Declare a list of state variables and put the state variables in it
    StateList state_list;
    State<> state(&state_list, StateBase::RK4);

    double step_time = 1.0 / frames_per_sec;

    for (;;)
    {
        end_run = false;
        printf("Waiting for Initialize\n");
        rtsp->WaitForInit();

        // State initial value
        state.ic = 0;

        // Set the initial value of the states
        state_list.Initialize(step_time);

        command_update.command = 0;

        printf("Waiting for Start\n");
```

```
        rtsp->WaitForStart();
        printf("Running\n");

        rtsp->StartTimer();
        uint frame = 0;
        while (!end_run)
        {
            // Time since start of run
            double Time = frame * step_time;

            // Compensator transfer function
            double input = command_update.command - plant_update.output;
            state.der = -40*state + input;
            double drive = -19000*state + 500*input;

            drive_update.drive = drive;
            drive_update.Send(*rtsp);

            if (frame % frames_per_sec == 0)
                printf("Time: %.2lf; Controller output: %.3lf\n",
                Time, drive);

            state_list.Integrate();

            uint end_of_frame = uint(1e6 * ++frame * step_time);
            uint cur_time = rtsp->ReadTimer();
            while (cur_time < end_of_frame)
            {
                rtsp->PollRcv(true, end_of_frame - cur_time);
                cur_time = rtsp->ReadTimer();
            }
        }
        printf("End of run\n");
    }

    return 0;
}
```

Finally, we implement the plant model, which uses the DSSL library to implement the differential equations as shown in Listing 5.11.

Listing 5.11 Plant.cpp **file.**

```cpp
#include <dssl.h>
#include <RTSP.h>

#include <stdio.h>

#include "PlantSend.h"
#include "PlantRcv.h"

RTSP* rtsp;

PlantSend::Update plant_update;
PlantRcv::ControllerUpdate drive_update;

bool ping_callback()
{
    printf("Ping callback\n");
    return true;
}

bool init_callback()
{
    printf("Initialize callback\n");
    return true;
}

bool start_callback()
{
    printf("Start callback\n");
    return true;
}

bool end_run = false;
bool halt_callback()
{
    printf("Halt callback\n");
    end_run = true;
    return true;
}
```

```
void drive_callback()
{
}

int main()
{
    printf("Plant Federate\n");
    printf("Jim Ledin    August, 2000\n\n");
    // Determine the number of frames per second
    int frames_per_sec = 100;
    printf("\nUpdate rate: %d frames/sec\n\n", frames_per_sec);

    rtsp = new RTSP("Plant");
    rtsp->SetPingCallback(ping_callback);
    rtsp->SetInitializeCallback(init_callback);
    rtsp->SetStartCallback(start_callback);
    rtsp->SetHaltCallback(halt_callback);

    drive_update.SetCallback(*rtsp, drive_callback);

    // Declare a list of state variables and put the state variables in it
    StateList state_list;
    State<> pos(&state_list);
    State<> vel(&state_list);

    double step_time = 1.0 / frames_per_sec;

    for (;;)
    {
        end_run = false;
        printf("Waiting for Initialize\n");
        rtsp->WaitForInit();

        // State initial values
        pos.ic = 0;
        vel.ic = 0;

        // Set the initial value of the states
```

```
        state_list.Initialize(step_time);

        drive_update.drive = 0;

        printf("Waiting for Start\n");
        rtsp->WaitForStart();
        printf("Running\n");

        rtsp->StartTimer();
        uint frame = 0;
        while (!end_run)
        {
            // Time since start of run
            double Time = frame * step_time;

            // Use the most recent value of the controller drive signal
            vel.der = drive_update.drive;
            pos.der = vel;

            plant_update.output = pos;
            plant_update.Send(*rtsp);

            state_list.Integrate();

            if (frame % frames_per_sec == 0)
                printf("Time: %.2lf; Plant output: %.3lf\n", Time, double(pos));

            uint end_of_frame = uint(1e6 * ++frame * step_time);
            uint cur_time = rtsp->ReadTimer();
            while (cur_time < end_of_frame)
            {
                rtsp->PollRcv(true, end_of_frame - cur_time);
                cur_time = rtsp->ReadTimer();
            }
        }
        printf("End of run\n");
    }

    return 0;
}
```

To build the distributed simulation, compile the three separate programs and link each of them with the compiled code from the _MsgData.cpp source file generated by the MDF translator program as well as the provided RTSP.cpp source file. Because the controller and plant use the DSSL library, these two programs must also link with the compiled code from the StateList.cpp file in the DSSL distribution.

Having built these three applications, we can now execute them as a federation along with the federation controller application. Initially, everything will run on a single computer. On a Windows system, the three program executables can be run plus the generic controller application from a batch file (named run.bat) as shown in Listing 5.12.

Listing 5.12 run.bat file.

```
start controller DistSim.mdf
start CommandGenerator
start Controller
start Plant
```

The run.bat file in Listing 5.12 assumes that all the executable programs and the DistSim.mdf file are located in the current directory or on the directory path. Note that the federation controller accepts the name of an MDF file as a command line parameter and loads it during program startup.

Once all four programs are running, the three federate names will appear in the generic controller window as shown in Figure 5.6. Click the Ping button to verify that all federates respond. If the federates fail to respond, this is an indication that your network may not support multicast, or that there may be a conflict with multicast IP addresses or port numbers. See the *RTSP Programmer's Manual* (included with the RTSP software on the CD-ROM) for more information on how to select alternate multicast IP addresses and port numbers.

Figure 5.6   RTSP controller.

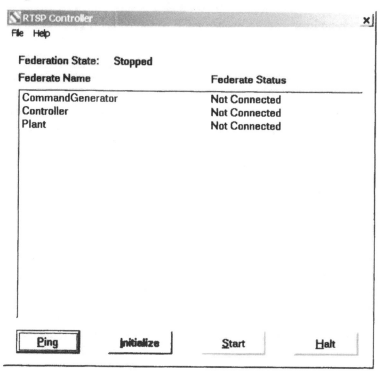

Following a successful Ping command, click the Initialize button and verify that all federates report successful initialization. Then click the Start button to begin real-time execution. The plant and controller transmit Update messages at a 100 Hz rate and display on-screen information at a 1 Hz rate. The CommandGenerator transmits a new command every 10 seconds and displays each new command as it is transmitted.

Observe that the plant output converges to the commanded value within about three seconds after each new command is issued by the CommandGenerator. The Controller output decays to zero within about three seconds of each new command as well.

To distribute the simulation across a network, simply terminate one of the federate applications and run the same executable on a different computer system on the network. As soon as the federate is running on the other computer, click Ping to verify connectivity and then perform a simulation run as discussed previously.

You should be able to compile the source code for these federates with minimal (or no) changes for execution on a UNIX system. No changes are necessary to accommodate byte order differences. Execute one or more of the federates on a UNIX system and repeat the steps above to run the simulation.

This simple federation has not exercised many of the more sophisticated capabilities available with RTSP. Some of the areas you may wish to explore further include:

• Enable logging of message traffic to disk during simulation execution (see RTSP.h). Then, develop an application that reads the log file and analyzes it after a simulation run completes. Some results of this analysis might be the minimum, maximum, and average measured latencies of incoming messages as well as information about lost message sequences.

If no distributed time reference is available, it will be necessary to run the federation on a single computer so that the latency information is valid.

- Synchronize the time on multiple computers using GPS or some other precision timing reference.

- Extrapolate continuous variables to estimate their value at the current time. This requires that all federates execute on a single computer or that a distributed precision time reference be in use because accurate latency measurements are required.

- Display information about sequences of lost messages following each simulation run.

- Develop a real-time viewer application to display the state of the entire federation using the information passed in the messages between the federates. This will require the addition of a new federate to the MDF file that subscribes to all messages from all federates. The viewer federate receives the messages and displays the information they contain in real time, possibly in a graphical manner. Note that the viewer federate does not increase the quantity of network traffic during real-time execution. It merely receives messages that were already traveling across the network.

Exercises

1. Consider the model of a home heating system shown in ExerciseFigure 5.1. The only part of the figure that is not self-explanatory is the output of the thermostat block, which is 1 when the furnace is running and 0 when it is off. The thermostat switches the furnace on when the temperature drops below 20° C and switches it off when the temperature rises above 22° C.

ExerciseFigure 5.1   Home heating system.

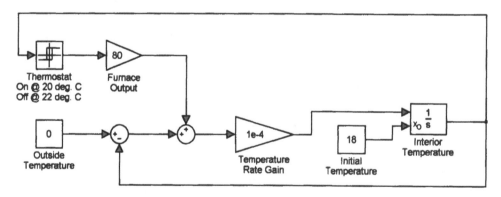

Develop a reference simulation to use later for verification of the distributed simulation results. Develop the reference simulation using a simulation environment of your choice and the forward Euler integration method. Determine the fixed integration step time required for acceptable accuracy. Run the simulation for one hour of simulated time and save appropriate simulation output data for comparison with output from the distributed simulation.

2. Divide the system of ExerciseFigure 5.1 into separate simulations so that one is of the thermostat and the other includes everything else in the system. Develop an MDF file describing the federates in this distributed simulation and the data messages that pass between them. Run the MDF translator program on this file to produce the C++ header and source files for a distributed simulation. Examine the contents of each file produced by the translator program.

3. Develop the individual federates for this distributed simulation using the DSSL library. Determine the update rate required for the output messages from each federate. Include appropriate data display and storage operations to enable verification of correct operation. Integrate the source files created by the translator program along with the RTSP runtime software into the federate source files. Compile and link each federate to create an executable application.

4. Run the distributed simulation (using the generic controller program) for one hour of simulated time on a single computer and save the output data. Compare the results of the distributed simulation with the results you obtained from the reference simulation in Exercise 1. Explain any differences.

5. Run the federates on two separate computers on your network and repeat the comparison with the results of Exercise 1. Is there any significant difference from the results of Exercise 4?

6. Add code to each federate to display information about lost messages onscreen after each federation halts. Run the distributed simulation several times on a single computer and several times on two computers on your network and record the information about lost messages. Do the lost messages (if any) have any significant impact on the overall performance of the distributed simulation?

7. Add a "logger" federate to the federation. The logger receives all messages from all federates and writes them to disk using the facilities available in the RTSP class. Write another program to read the log file for a simulation run and display the type of each message, its transmission time tag, and communication latency. Note that for the communication latency to be meaningful, the federates must all be running on a single computer or you must be using a precision distributed time reference.

8. Modify each of the federates to execute at a "speedup" from real time. This involves increasing the time covered by each integration step by a multiplying factor. Make the speedup a command-line parameter that defaults to 1 if it is not supplied. Find the largest speedup possible for simulating one hour of execution of the distributed simulation that does not cause significant errors in the results.

References

[1] Lynch, Daniel C., and Marshall T. Rose, *Internet System Handbook*. Reading, MA: Addison Wesley, 1993.

Chapter 6

Data Visualization and Analysis

6.1 Introduction

The previous chapters discussed techniques for building simulations of dynamic systems, and covered topics such as the development of mathematical models of system components and the selection and use of numerical integration algorithms. This chapter assumes that development is complete and that an executable simulation is available for use. You can now define test scenarios and execute them. Each scenario simulates the behavior of the system under a specific set of conditions. The specification for a scenario consists of the initial conditions of the system and environment as well as any input signals that vary over time.

When setting up a simulation scenario, we must identify which variables to save during execution for later analysis. This output data must contain information sufficient to make judgments about the behavior of the simulation and of the system being simulated, and enough information must be collected to answer as many reasonable questions as possible about the performance of the simulated system, but not so much to overload the capabilities of the data storage devices and analysis tools. This requires some care in the selection of what information to collect and how frequently to save samples of time-varying values.

The data saved during simulation execution falls into three general categories:

Initial conditions These values define the starting conditions. Initial conditions are required for states in differential and difference equations. In addition, a number of parameter values are usually necessary to determine the initial condition of the system and its environment. Ideally, we should store enough initial condition information to exactly duplicate the simulation run in the future.

Time histories This type of data is collected as the run progresses. Typically, these variables are sampled at a fixed rate and saved to disk during the run or after it completes. This information can also be displayed in text format or graphically as the simulation executes. The number of variables saved and their sampling rate affect the amount of disk space consumed on each run. Often, data saved as time histories will use much more disk space than the initial and terminal condition data.

Terminal conditions These variables represent critical parameter values that occur at or near the end of a run. An example of a terminal condition is the miss distance in an air-to-air missile simulation, which indicates how close the missile came to its target. Not all simulations have meaningful sets of terminal conditions. For instance, a pilot training session in a simulator may end without any particular concern for the exact conditions by simply turning off the system.

At the completion of each run, a data set is available that contains variables in the three categories above. The next task is to examine this data and attempt to determine the answers to general and specific questions about the simulation and the simulated system, such as:

1. Is the simulation an accurate representation of the simulated system?
2. Are the models of the environment that influence performance of the system sufficiently accurate?
3. Is the performance of the system in the simulated scenario satisfactory?
4. Do each of the inputs and outputs of the component models of the system behave as expected?

This chapter discusses approaches for analyzing the output data from simulation runs to help find answers to these questions and identifies ways to make information available to users as quickly as possible. A benefit of quickly presenting results to the user is to minimize the time spent running a simulation in a scenario that was not set up properly. We can use immediate displays to observe important system parameters as the simulation runs.

6.2 Immediate Displays

An immediate display presents data as the simulation runs. This ability is useful in both real-time and non-real-time applications. Immediate displays give the user instant feedback that indicates whether the simulation is operating as expected. If an input parameter has been set incorrectly, the error is often obvious from viewing immediate displays. Upon observing erroneous behavior the operator can abort the run, change the parameter value, and restart the run. This avoids waiting for a potentially lengthy run to complete before the error is detected.

Many different kinds of immediate display are possible.

Text displays   A text display can be as simple as placing print statements in the code that display a group of variables at regular intervals. A more complex text display has a set of fixed display fields located onscreen. The simulation updates the displayed values of the variables at regular intervals as it runs. Text displays can provide a large amount of detailed information, but the observer must focus on each individual field for some time to get a feel for how that parameter behaves as the simulation runs. This can make it difficult to gain an understanding of overall system performance. A simulation with text displays appears in Figure 6.1.

Figure 6.1   Simulation with text displays.

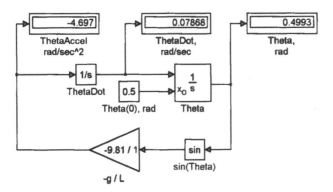

Time plots   A time plot is a two-dimensional graph of a function versus time. When running a simulation, time plots can be displayed on the computer screen or another medium, such as a paper strip chart. When displayed on the computer, there is the issue of what happens when simulation time reaches the end of the graph time axis. For some simulations, it will be enough to make the time axis long enough that the plot never reaches the end during any reasonable run. Alternatively, the plotting routines could scroll the plot window sideways or restart the plot at the left edge of the window. Time plots can make it instantly clear to even an uninitiated viewer when the simulated system undergoes an unexpected period of behavior. Figure 6.2 shows time plots of some variables.

Figure 6.2 Time plots of simulation variables.

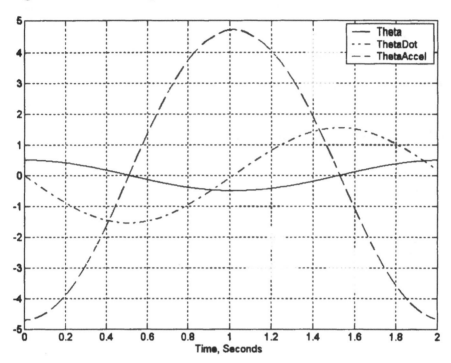

Two-dimensional graphics This category includes more complex graphical displays than the text displays and time plots discussed above. Two-dimensional graphical displays can contain such things as graphical representations of analog meters or storage tank fill levels and can present a realistic arrangement of instruments for an automobile or aircraft simulation. This type of display can also present a complete and authentic arrangement of controls to a user familiar with the actual system. Figure 6.3 shows some examples of aircraft instruments displayed by the DataViews® product [1].

Figure 6.3 Two-dimensional graphical displays.

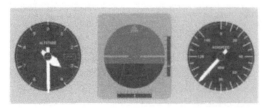

Three-dimensional graphics The ultimate in graphical displays, particularly for a complex dynamic system with many moving components, is a three-dimensional view of the system in simulated operation. A 3-D display can contain information about a large number of system components and present this data in a way that makes it immediately apparent whether the overall system is performing as expected. The three-dimensional graphical display does not present information in a format that provides numerical information, so the benefit of this type of display is that it provides a qualitative view of system performance. Quantitative comparisons must be made using other types of data displays, such as time plots. Figure 6.4 is a three-dimensional rendering of an electromechanical system that can display the behavior of the system during simulated operation.

Figure 6.4   Three-dimensional graphical display.

Immediate data displays are useful during simulation development and during production simulation runs to monitor system behavior as execution proceeds. These displays provide instant feedback to users about the behavior of the simulated system. If immediate data displays are unavailable, the alternative is to store output data as the simulation executes and analyze it later. Even when immediate displays are available, post-run analyses of data saved during execution need to be performed.

Post-run data analysis is necessary because immediate displays only provide general information about the operation of the simulated system. Many of the specific questions about the performance of the system can only be answered by examining the simulation output data in detail. The next section discusses some of the tools and approaches we can use for performing post-run data analysis.

6.3 Plotting Tools

A basic tool for analyzing time history data from simulation runs is the two-dimensional time plot. A useful 2-D plotting tool allows the analyst to produce multiple plots simultaneously and to have multiple variables displayed on a single plot. Additional features that are valuable in a two-dimensional plotting tool include the ability to

- add annotations, both in the form of text strings and as labels, that display the numerical value of the variable at user-selected points on the plot;
- add labels to the plot x- and y-axes and provide a title that describes the entire plot;

- zoom in on time periods of interest;
- plot data from different sources as overlays on a single plot; for instance, overlay data from a simulation run on top of telemetry data that was recorded during a real-world test of the simulated system;
- perform mathematical operations on signals prior to plotting them; for example, subtracting an actuator command from its current position to derive the position error, which is then plotted. It is valuable for a plotting tool to support the usual trigonometric, logarithmic, and other functions normally available within a programming language. Additional examples of useful capabilities are numerical estimates of signal integrals and derivatives and operations to filter signals over time in various ways;
- print plots and copy them into word processing documents.

Simulation software products such as VisSim or Simulink provide the ability to plot variables as the simulation runs. The plotting features may not include all of the capabilities mentioned above, particularly the ability to mathematically manipulate data prior to plotting. In this situation, the desired mathematical operations must be performed as part of the simulation itself. The result of the calculation can then be plotted.

When developing a simulation using a high-level programming language, or if the development environment does not provide sufficient plotting capability, it will be necessary to provide another method for plotting simulation data. This need can be satisfied by developing a plotting tool from scratch or by purchasing a plotting software package that provides the needed capabilities.

One important choice that must be made in implementing a plotting capability is deciding whether immediate plots will be displayed as the simulation runs. The alternative is to store the output data during the run and create plots at a later time. It is usually easier to plot the data after the end of the run because it is then a simple matter of reading data from a disk file into the plotting software. If it is necessary to plot data as the simulation runs, additional work is required to implement an interface that passes data from the simulation to the plotting software during execution.

The two-dimensional plot is the workhorse of simulation data analysis. These plots make it easy to understand the behaviors of specific system elements at a glance and to perform comparisons between data from a variety of sources. As we perform tasks such as verification, validation, and testing of the simulated embedded system, we will present many of the results of our simulation runs as two-dimensional plots.

6.4 Animation

Sometimes the most useful and powerful way to display simulation results is to generate a 3-D animation driven by simulation output data. An example of this is an automotive suspension system. Although it is valuable to generate 2-D time plots indicating the position, angle, and other parameters for each suspension component, nothing gives an immediate, overall impression of system performance like a 3-D view of the system in operation. This type of a display is very useful for presenting the results of a simulation to people who are not experts on the simulated system. Another benefit that should not be ignored is that the animation tends to be a natural focus when VIPs are brought on tours through the simulation facility.

Over recent years, high-performance 3-D graphics accelerator video cards have become ubiquitous and inexpensive. Today, it is difficult to buy a new personal computer that does not contain a fast 3-D graphics card. We can use this capability to produce high-quality 3-D displays of a simulated system as the simulation executes or when playing back recorded data from previous simulation runs.

To create a display that is smooth and pleasing to the eye, a 3-D animation must update its display in the range of 20 to 60 frames per second. Each update of the display requires passing data that describes the system state from the simulation or the file of stored data to the 3-D rendering application. Upon receiving each data update, the 3-D application creates an image of the system components and environment and displays it onscreen. 3-D graphics hardware generally uses a double buffering technique, where the "front" buffer is displayed on the screen and the "back" buffer is used to draw the next update of the display. After rendering the new scene is completed, the buffers are swapped so that the newly drawn scene becomes the front buffer and the previous front buffer becomes the back buffer. This approach displays smooth changes in the scene without the flickering that would occur when only one buffer is used to erase and redraw the screen.

Several different approaches are available for developing the 3-D application software. In all cases, we must either develop or obtain a set of 3-D models of the dynamic system components and important elements of the surrounding environment. If CAD (computer aided design) diagrams of the simulated system are available, they can be used as the basis for a 3-D model. It may be necessary to convert the CAD system model to a file format suitable for use by the 3-D rendering software. If an existing 3-D model of the simulated system is not available, it may be necessary to develop one with the help of suitable 3-D modeling software either by working from scratch or by modifying an existing model of a similar system.

The 3-D models of the system components contain information about the geometrical shape and location of each system part as well as the part's appearance, such as its color, shininess, and transparency. These models must be accurate enough, but not overly complex. Models that are more complex will take longer to render. A real-time display is severely limited by the time between frame updates. Updating the display at 60 frames per second allows only 16.67 milliseconds to process the incoming data from the simulation and render each scene. Even if the simulation does not run at real-time speed, rendering efficiency is still an issue. If the display updates too slowly, observers will lose interest and not put it to effective use.

Several tools are available for 3-D display development. In the Win32 environment, Direct3D and OpenGL are the primary low-level 3-D APIs in current use. Using one of these APIs provides maximum flexibility and real-time performance, but the learning curve is steep. Alternatively, several higher level software products, such as the open-source Genesis3D project [2], provide 3-D scene rendering capabilities. Many of these tools tend to be oriented toward 3-D game development, but their capabilities are applicable to real-time simulation animation as well.

6.5 Automated Analysis and Reporting

Dynamic system simulations have the potential to generate far more data than would be reasonable for a human to analyze in detail. Instead of ignoring much of this potentially large quantity of output data, it may be worthwhile to develop a capability for analyzing the data automatically. A relatively simple initial approach to automated data analysis might be to check simulation data for things that should always be true. This analysis tool could scan the data from each run and alert the user to any problems it found.

Developing a tool with this capability makes sense when the variables saved during each run are well defined and unlikely to change from run to run. It does not make so much sense if, on different runs, completely different sets of data are saved. It also would not be very useful if some variables that are crucial to the analysis process are left out on some runs. For these reasons, it is best to include a core set of variables in the collected data for each simulation run that serves as input to the automated analysis tool.

As an example of an application of this approach, it might be useful to verify that data on simulated system parameters, such as electrical power supply voltages and currents, fall within specified tolerances at all times. As another example, an automated analysis tool can check that an expected series of events occurs on each run.

This type of automated analysis tool can check for indications of problems in the simulation, as well as within the simulated system itself. Given a simple initial automated analysis capability, it is easy to see how to add more complex analysis checks. Some examples of potential automated analysis tasks appear in Table 6.1.

Table 6.1   Automated analysis techniques.

Analysis task	Description
Parameter limits	Verify that parameters stay within prescribed limits at all times.
Parameter relationships	Verify that proper relationships are maintained among parameters. Example: Actuator error (actual position minus commanded position) remains within prescribed limits.
Input–output relationship	Verify that subsystem output signals are consistent with the input signals within tolerances. Example: execute a simplified version of the model during analysis using the simulation inputs to determine expected model output and compare with the simulated subsystem output.
Comparison with other results	Verify that differences between the current simulation run and data from some other source (perhaps a previous run) are within limits. This technique is useful for regression testing. There must be a way to identify which existing data set to use for comparison.

In addition to performing the types of analyses shown in Table 6.1, the automatically generated reports should present sufficient raw data and analysis results to clearly indicate system behavior. As an example, a parameter limit check might include plots of the limits superimposed on a time plot of the signal. The report may contain conditional plots that appear only if the analysis discovers a related problem.

Automated analysis and reporting can present the results of regression testing that is performed as changes are made to the simulation and to the system hardware (in the case of an

HIL simulation). When performing regression tests, the system must have some way to identify a particular existing data set to use for comparison with the results of the current test. One relatively simple way to do this is to assign each run a sequential integer run number. The latest run number must be stored in a disk file and incremented following each run. The run number then identifies the data files that are output from the associated simulation run. One way of doing this is to use the run number as part of the output data filename; for example, `1234.dat` is the output data from run number 1234.

The automatic comparison of new results against stored data requires the number of the previous simulation run to use in the comparison. After the simulation completes, the automated analysis executes and performs the comparisons between the new and old runs. The analysis results provide input for a report on the results of the regression testing. This report may be created manually from the plots and other data produced from the automated analysis, or the automated tool can assemble the report document itself.

Some simulation software tools provide built-in capabilities for automated data analysis and report generation as discussed in this section. One example is Simulink, combined with the optional MATLAB Report Generator and Simulink Report Generator components. These report generator tools allow the user to specify the contents of a report using a setup file. After the setup file has been defined, the report can be generated and viewed immediately. These tools support a variety of output document formats, including RTF, XML, SGML, and HTML. The generated report can be imported into a word processor for further additions and modifications to produce a final document.

6.6 Data Analysis Techniques

This section covers some techniques for the analysis of simulation output data. The goals of these analysis techniques are to gain a better understanding of the behavior of the simulated system, to determine if the simulation is an accurate model of the simulated system, and to identify if the behavior of the system is correct under the conditions of each run.

These techniques can be broken into two broad categories: graphical techniques and numerical techniques. Graphical data analysis techniques present information in a manner that enables the extraction of useful information visually. Numerical data analysis techniques provide numbers to compare to thresholds or results from other sources to determine information about the behavior of the simulation. Before discussing these techniques, I will describe an example simulation of a continuous dynamic system with a digital controller that we will use to generate data for analysis.

6.6.1 Example Simulation

The system simulated here is a rotating turntable driven by a DC motor, as shown in Figure 6.5. The digital controller inputs are the commanded position for the turntable and its measured position. The controller generates an output signal to drive the DC motor via a power amplifier, which moves the turntable to the commanded position. This is a combined discrete–continuous system which we be simulated using multiframing in Simulink.

Figure 6.5 Turntable system and controller.

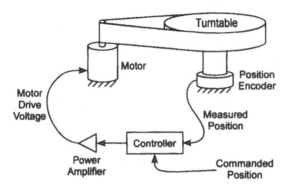

The controller is modeled as a digital system that operates at an update interval of 5 milliseconds. The input to the controller is the turntable position, as measured by a quadrature position encoder. This device outputs a digital position reading with a resolution of 4,096 steps per turntable revolution. The controller output signal is converted to a voltage via an 8-bit DAC, which drives the DC motor through a power amplifier. To avoid the cost of a high-performance processor, controller processing will be modeled as taking 4 milliseconds to complete during each update cycle.

When modeling a dynamic system, we must decide how much detail to include in the representation of each component. The amount of detail required depends on the intended uses for the simulation. In this case, the primary goal is to design and implement a digital controller for the turntable system. Consequently, the motor and turntable dynamics will be modeled with good accuracy, the dynamic behavior of the power amplifier will be ignored, and the behavior of the digital control algorithm will be modeled as accurately as possible.

Figure 6.6 shows a Simulink block diagram of this system. The motor and turntable dynamics are modeled as a second-order linear transfer function. The input to this transfer function is the motor drive voltage, and the output is the turntable velocity. Several parameters appear in the turntable velocity transfer function. These parameters and their nominal values for this system are

- J, the effective moment of inertia of the motor plus turntable, = 0.012 kg-m^2;
- b, the damping ratio of the motor–turntable system, = 0.2 N-m-second;
- K, the motor electromotive force constant, = 0.013 N-m/amp;
- R, the motor electrical resistance, = 1.1 Ohms;
- L, the motor electrical inductance, = 0.6 Henries.

The turntable velocity is integrated to determine its position. The position encoder measures the turntable position and outputs a quantized reading to the digital controller. The measured turntable position and its commanded position are inputs to the digital controller. The controller output is an analog voltage that drives the power amplifier, which in turn drives the motor. The boxes labeled "DAC Output" and "Position (radians)" represent signals that are saved during simulation execution for later analysis.

Figure 6.6   Simulink diagram of turntable system with controller.

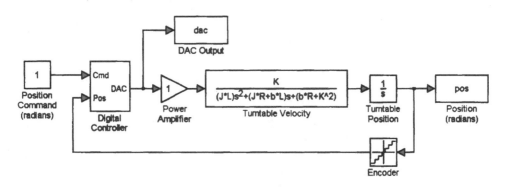

Inside the box labeled "Digital Controller" is the implementation of the control algorithm, which appears in Figure 6.7. Because this algorithm is to be executed at intervals of 5 milliseconds, Simulink requires the addition of blocks labeled "Zero-Order Hold1," "Zero-Order Hold2," and "Unit Delay." Each of these blocks has a parameter associated with it that has been set to indicate 5-millisecond updates. The remainder of the algorithm consists of a proportional-derivative controller that uses the discrete-time transfer function labeled "Derivative Estimate" to produce an estimate of the turntable angular rate. The output of the control algorithm is fed to an 8-bit DAC model that limits and quantizes the signal. The "4 mS Transport Delay" block delays the output of the algorithm by 4 milliseconds, which simulates the computational delay.

Figure 6.7   Digital controller model.

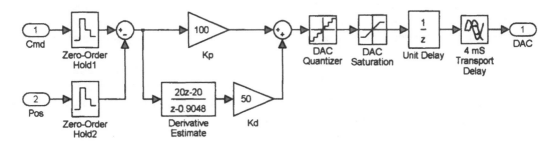

In addition to implementing the models for the simulation, we must also specify the integration algorithm to use and, if the algorithm is of the fixed-step type, the integration time step. A 1.0-millisecond time step size combined with Simulink's fourth-order Runge-Kutta integration algorithm provide satisfactory results for this simulation. It is easy to confirm this by performing a run with a step time of 0.1 millisecond and verifying that the results do not change significantly.

This simulation is used in the following sections as a source for data in performing graphical and numerical data analysis. To produce data for comparing the "actual" and "simulated" systems, we can modify the model parameters to approximate the differences between simulation and reality that occur normally in the development process. These parameter variations will cause both obvious and subtle differences in the output. Much of the difficulty of the data analysis task is identifying the cause of an unexpected result in the output data by tracing it back to its source.

6.6.2 Graphical Techniques

As discussed previously, the most basic form of graphical representation of data is the two-dimensional time plot of individual simulation variables. To develop additional information about the behavior of the system, we can perform mathematical manipulations on the data before producing a plot. One common computation is to subtract two signals to determine their difference, which is called a difference plot. The difference plot is useful in cases where, for example, we want to subtract an actuator's commanded position from its achieved position to determine the error signal. Another case where difference plots are useful is when comparing data from two different sources, such as data from an actual system test and from a simulation run under identical conditions.

We will assume that we have two signals in the form of data sequences x and y each consisting of N samples. For the moment, we assume that the values in both sequences occur at the same sample times. We compute the difference signal $z = x - y$ using Equation 6.1 for $i = 1, ..., N$.

6.1 $z_i = x_i - y_i$

If the sequences were not sampled at corresponding sample times, we can use the function interpolation techniques discussed in Chapter 2 to extract data suitable for use in Equation 6.1. Usually the most efficient alternative will be to convert just one of the data series to an interpolation funciton and then perform interpolation on that function at times corresponding to the sample times in the other series. Occasionally, there will be advantages to creating interpolation functions for both series so that both functions can be sampled at any point in time.

Either of these approaches provides two time series for comparison with equal lengths and with samples that occur at identical times. Of course, the results will be usable only if the samples are taken frequently enough that interpolation between the samples produces valid results.

Depending on the nature of the simulation, in addition to the simple subtraction of signals discussed above, it may be helpful to:

- Convert variables to more appropriate units; for example, convert radians to degrees.
- Perform a Fast Fourier Transform (FFT) on segments of the signal to determine the frequency spectrum. We can plot the magnitude squared of the FFT coefficients (or more commonly their decibel values) as a two-dimensional plot of frequency versus magnitude squared. Alternatively, we can compute the FFT on sequential segments of the signal data and produce a three-dimensional plot of the magnitude squared of the coefficients over

time. The three axes on this plot (which is called a spectrogram) are time, frequency, and magnitude squared.

- Extract meaningful information from difficult-to-comprehend data. For example, given the elements of a 3 x 3 direction cosine matrix, compute the body Euler angles (yaw, pitch, and roll).

- Perform function interpolation to convert raw data to meaningful values. For example, given a raw temperature sensor reading from a thermistor with a nonlinear output characteristic, perform a function interpolation using its transfer curve to determine the calibrated temperature.

So far, I have discussed the manipulation of simulation output data to produce new signals that can be plotted as functions of time. Implicit in this was the idea of plotting a single signal on a graph. Alternatively, multiple signals can be plotted on the same set of axes to provide additional information about system performance. This technique is called overplotting.

A way to clearly display how closely two signals match is to provide two separate plots: The first is an overplot of the two signals and the second is a plot of the difference between the signals. The overplot gives a view of the overall behavior of the signals from both sources, whereas the difference plot displays the variation between the two signals.

Returning to the example turntable system, Figure 6.8 shows the system step response. The initial state of the system is with the turntable stopped at the zero position. At time zero, a command is applied to move the turntable to the 1-radian position. After about 5 seconds, the turntable has essentially reached the desired location. From this plot, there is little indication that the modeled nonlinearities have any effect on the system. This plot provides a broad overview of the system performance but does not provide the type of information that is important for detailed analysis. Developing a series of graphs to present the overall performance of a system normally starts with this kind of plot to give a high-level indication that the system is performing correctly. Additional plots provide the details of system component operation.

Figure 6.8 Simulation of system step response.

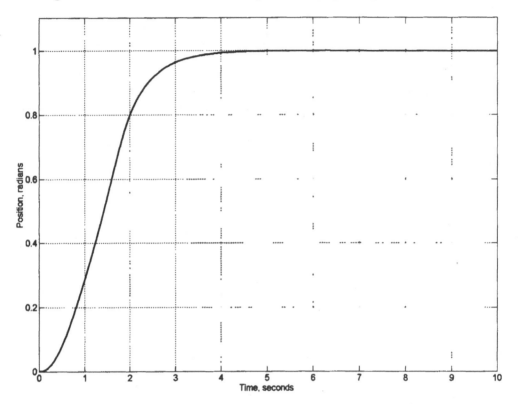

To determine the effects that the system nonlinearities have on system performance, we examine the DAC output signal as shown in Figure 6.9. Here, the effects of the quantization of the position encoder signal are clearly evident in the spiky behavior of the DAC output signal. This plot also shows that the DAC output signal is saturated at its maximum value for about the first 1.7 seconds of the simulation. A close examination will also reveal artifacts due to the quantization of the DAC output signal voltage.

Figure 6.9   Simulated controller DAC output voltage.

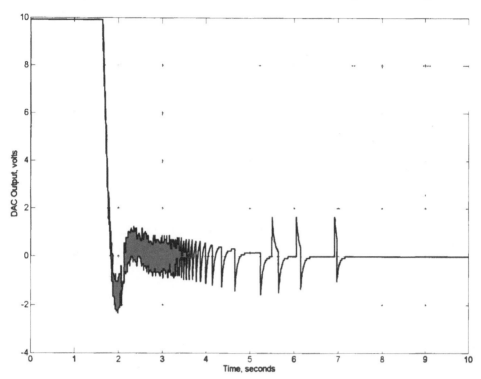

The simulation of the turntable and controller provides a great deal of information about the dynamic behavior of the overall system. The details of nonlinear system behavior are crucial when developing designs that must work in the real world. The use of simulation allows you to determine the system performance under a wide variety of conditions by changing model parameters and by including additional effects and complexity in the component models. Simulation-based trade studies can determine the behavior of the system in response to design modifications such as a different controller update rate, different number of DAC bits, or different encoder resolution.

The graphical techniques discussed above (overplotting and difference plots) can be applied to the results of this simulation by performing a series of runs with model parameter variations. These variations approximate the differences that naturally occur between a real-world system and a simulation of that system, which necessarily includes assumptions and simplifications. To determine how closely the two different versions of the model agree with each other, we can compare the output data from runs of each model version.

As an example of a system variation, we will double the parameter J, the effective moment of inertia of the motor plus turntable to 0.024 kg-m^2 and then run the simulation over the original time interval using the same integration time step. Overplots of the turntable position and DAC output voltage for the two runs appear in Figures 6.10 and 6.11. In these two figures, the solid line is the data from the original run and the dashed line is from the run with the increased value of J.

Figure 6.10 Overplots of turntable position.

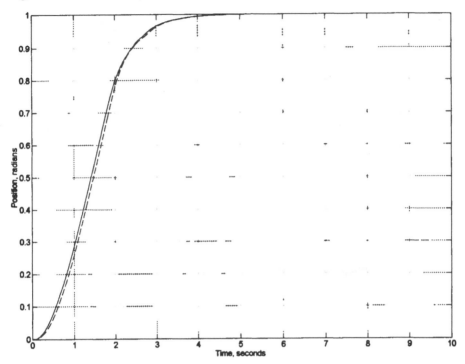

Figures 6.10 and 6.11 imply that the two data sets represent similar behavior, though some differences are clearly visible. Small differences in the turntable position in Figure 6.10 occur during the first 5 seconds of the run, and there is a significant difference in the DAC output voltage from about 1.7 to 2.5 seconds. Difference plots of these parameters will make these differences more visible.

To create the difference plots, we subtract the turntable position and DAC output voltage of the second run from those values computed during the original run. The difference in turntable position is plotted in Figure 6.12, and the difference in DAC output voltage is plotted in Figure 6.13. These plots allow direct determination of how closely the two different versions of the simulation agree with each other. The difference plot is particularly useful because there is a clear figure of merit for determining if two simulations agree. If the difference plot is zero everywhere, the parameter matches exactly between the two data sets. Small deviations from zero represent small differences, and large deviations represent large differences.

Figure 6.11 Overplots of DAC output voltage.

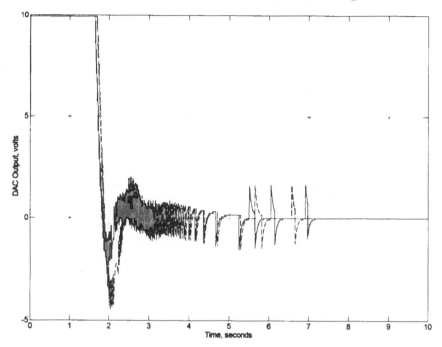

Figure 6.12 Difference plot of turntable position.

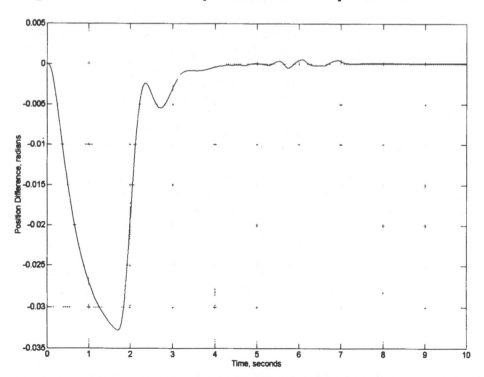

Figure 6.13 Difference plot of DAC output voltage.

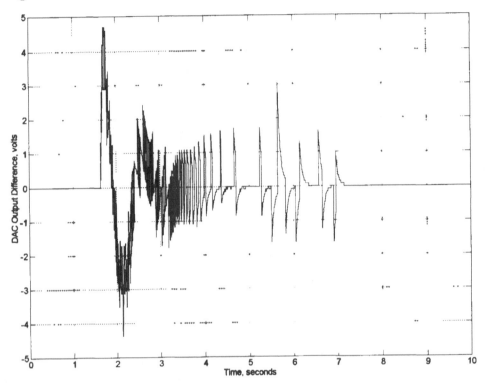

However, it is not always a straightforward task to go from observing large amplitudes on a difference plot to the determination that there are significant differences between the two systems used to generate the data. An example of this is visible in Figure 6.13, the DAC output voltage difference plot. During the period from about 5 to 7 seconds, there are large spikes on the plot, where Figure 6.12 shows that the turntable position is in close agreement during this time.

These differences in motor voltage are a consequence of small differences in the timing of steps in the position encoder output. This type of behavior, where minor differences in system behavior produce relatively large excursions on difference plots, is common in the simulation of real-world systems. It is one reason we must rely heavily on human interpretation of output data rather than the use of purely automated data analysis techniques.

Having said that, we must also understand that numerical data analysis techniques such as the Theil Inequality Coefficient, discussed in the next section, have their uses and can provide a quick overview of how well two sets of data agree. In particular, numerical analysis techniques are valuable for determining if two sets of data match closely. If the numerical results do not indicate good agreement, on the other hand, human analysis is usually required to determine the causes of the disagreements between them.

6.6.3 Theil Inequality Coefficient

The previous section examined ways to compare sets of data graphically so that the eye of the analyst is the ultimate tool in discriminating good result matches from bad. This section considers ways to automate this task, assuming that the quantity of data available for comparison is limited, which constrains the possible types of analysis techniques. There are many statistical techniques that rely on large sample sizes that are less useful for smaller data sets. One example is comparing the spectrum estimates resulting from the spectral analysis of two data sets [3]. Techniques such as this provide less valid results when the quantity of data available is relatively small.

Comparison data is often limited when it is expensive and time consuming to perform system testing in its operational environment, such as aircraft flight testing. The primary tools we will use for automated analysis will be techniques for performing comparisons between two sets of time series data that indicate the degree to which the data sets match.

Many different techniques have been proposed for this task. One approach that is fairly simple to implement and has been shown to produce reasonable results in practical applications is the technique called the *Theil Inequality Coefficient* [4], or TIC. The formula shown in Equation 6.2 will produce the TIC for the data sequences x and y. As discussed previously, the two data sequences must be of the same length, N, and must have sample times that coincide.

$$6.2 \quad U = \frac{\sqrt{\dfrac{1}{N}\sum_{i=1}^{N}(x_i - y_i)^2}}{\sqrt{\dfrac{1}{N}\sum_{i=1}^{N}x_i^2} + \sqrt{\dfrac{1}{N}\sum_{i=1}^{N}y_i^2}}$$

Equation 6.2 shows that for any two data series the TIC always lies in the range $0 \le U \le 1$. The two extremes for this value occur as follows:

- $U = 0$ when the two data sequences agree exactly. Each term in the numerator sum is equal to zero in this case.
- $U = 1$ when the disagreement between the series is maximum. This happens when the corresponding elements in each series are the negative of each other or when each element of one of the series is zero.

A special case occurs when all elements in both data series are zero. This leads to the undefined result

$$U = \frac{0}{0}.$$

Because the data series match exactly, we would expect the value $U = 0$ to be the result in this situation. A robust computation of the TIC computation should return zero in this special case.

It may seem odd to worry about comparing two data sets that are entirely zero, but there are times when it does occur in practical situations. The TIC formula is applicable to discrete signals as well as continuous signals; for example, we may want to compare the values of a flag variable that can take the values 0 and 1. Suppose this flag is an error indication that did not occur during either simulation run in the comparison. In this case, both data series are entirely zero, so the TIC computation should produce a zero result, just as it would if the flag had the value 1 throughout both runs.

Continuing this example, if both data series contain a single transition from 0 to 1 (or vice versa), the TIC will be 0 if the transitions occur at the same times. If the transitions do not occur at the same times, the TIC increases linearly with the difference between the transition times and has a maximum value of 1 when the transitions occur at the opposite ends of the simulation execution interval. Thus, increasing differences between two sets of data result in increasing values of the TIC.

The $U = 0$ and $U = 1$ extremes of behavior will rarely occur in the comparison of continuous variables from dynamic system simulations and real-world system tests. For the purposes here, it is necessary to determine threshold values for the TIC that indicate "good" agreement between two sets of data. Several factors make the selection of this threshold a difficult task.

The first difficulty in applying the TIC to simulation output data is that it computes only a single value for a pair of data series that may be quite lengthy. There may be portions of the data series with excellent agreement and other parts that do not match well at all. An example of this is shown in Figure 6.12, where there is a large error in the turntable position from about 0 to 3 seconds then good agreement after that point. How do we interpret this behavior in terms of a single number generated by comparing the data sets? The answer to this question appears to be that we must select a small value of U as the threshold for a "good" match.

Another problem is that there may be differences in the data sets due to minor variations in parameters or in behavior stemming from noise. Often these differences are considered to be insignificant in comparing the data sets, yet they may produce relatively large values in the numerator term of Equation 6.2. An example of this is illustrated in Figure 6.13 during the 5- to 7-second time period, where differences in the timing of position encoder pulses caused spikes in the difference plot of the motor voltage. In this situation, it appears that a relatively large value of U needs to be selected as the threshold to avoid falsely indicating poor agreement due to these effects.

The application of some engineering judgement can resolve these difficulties by limiting expectations for the robustness of this technique. Perhaps the best hope is to use the TIC to test whether two data series have "very good" agreement. If the series do not pass this test, human review is required to determine if the source of differences is significant. This means that the threshold value of U must be a small value that can be expected to trigger where the agreement is still "good" in some cases.

In addition, because different system variables will have different characteristics related to noise and sensitivity to minor parameter variations, we will most likely need to tune the threshold value of U for each variable individually. As an alternative to this approach, we could set up threshold values of U for different categories of variables so that the problem then becomes a matter of identifying the category in which to place each variable.

The tuning of the threshold value of U for each variable can be performed by producing overplots and difference plots of various data sets and using expert opinion to determine if each pair matches. Each pair of data series will have a value of U associated with it and (hopefully) a threshold value of U will become apparent from this examination.

6.6.4 Example Application of the Theil Inequality Coefficient

This section uses the turntable simulation discussed in Section 6.6.1 in an attempt to determine the robustness of the controller performance in the presence of system parameter variations, we will use both graphical and numerical techniques to present the results of the analysis.

To determine the system behavior for expected variations of the parameters related to the motor and the load on the turntable — the sources of which are factors such as manufacturing tolerances, differences between components provided by different suppliers, components aging over the system life cycle, and varying system operating conditions — assume that the variations of each parameter are described by a normal distribution about the nominal parameter value. This assumption allows the complete characterization of the variation of each parameter by its nominal value and the standard deviation about the nominal value. The nominal values and standard deviations for the example problem are shown in Table 6.2.

Table 6.2   Nominal parameter values and standard deviations.

Parameter	J	b	K	R	L
Nominal value	0.012	0.2	0.013	1.1	0.6
Standard deviation	0.004	0.025	0.0016	0.14	0.12

Initially, we would like to develop a feeling for the consistency of the system performance in the presence of worst-case parameter variations. In the normal probability distribution, there is a 99.73% chance that any sample will fall within three standard deviations of the mean, so we will assume this to be the worst-case parameter deviation. A run with each parameter in Table 6.2 at its nominal value and one run each at the nominal value plus and minus three standard deviations will cover the full range of that parameter. To do this in all combinations of the five parameters results in 3^5, or 243, total simulation runs.

We will assume that the system response plots shown in Figures 6.8 and 6.9 are the desired system behavior and that you would like to be alerted to parameter combinations that result in significant variations from these targets. This set of requirements is enough information to set up and perform the simulation runs. The MATLAB script shown in Listing 6.1 will run the existing Simulink model once for each of these parameter varifications.

After running the simulation for each combination of parameter values, the script in Listing 6.1 computes the TIC by comparing the nominal run turntable position against the turntable position for the current run using Equation 6.2. It also computes the TIC that results from comparing the nominal and current run DAC output voltage signals. These TIC values are each saved in arrays for later examination and plotting.

Listing 6.1 Run script for parameter variation scenarios.

```
clear all
close all

J0 = 0.012;
b0 = 0.2;
K0 = 0.013;
R0 = 1.1;
L0 = 0.6;

J_sig = J0 / 3;
b_sig = b0 / 8;
K_sig = K0 / 8;
R_sig = R0 / 8;
L_sig = L0 / 5;

J = J0;
b = b0;
K = K0;
R = R0;
L = L0;

sim('Turntable')
Pos_nom = pos;
Dac_nom = dac;

i = 1
for iJ = -1:1
    J = J0 + 3*iJ*J_sig;
    for ib = -1:1
        b = b0 + 3*ib*b_sig;
        for iK = -1:1
            K = K0 + 3*iK*K_sig;
            for iR = -1:1
                R = R0 + 3*iR*R_sig;
                for iL = -1:1
                    L = L0 + 3*iL*L_sig;
                    sim('Turntable')
                    pos_TIC(i) = theil(Pos_nom.signals.values, pos.signals.values);
                    dac_TIC(i) = theil(Dac_nom.signals.values, dac.signals.values);
```

```
              param(i,1:7) = [i pos_TIC(i) iJ ib iK iR iL];
              i = i + 1
         end
    end
  end
 end
end
```

After executing the script in Listing 6.1, the vector variables pos_TIC and dac_TIC contain the angular position and DAC output voltage TIC values for all combinations of the five parameter values. Figure 6.14 shows the TIC values for the turntable position plotted against the run number.

Figure 6.14 TIC values for turntable angular position.

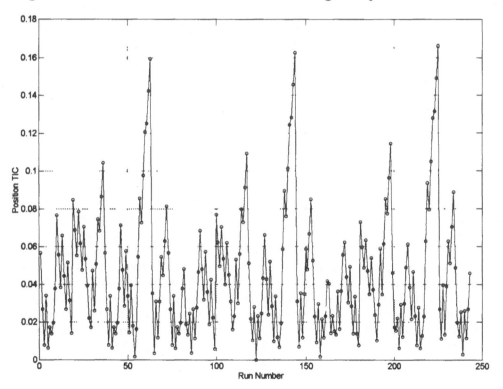

Figure 6.15 shows the TIC values for the DAC output voltage plotted against the run number.

Figure 6.15 TIC values for DAC output voltage.

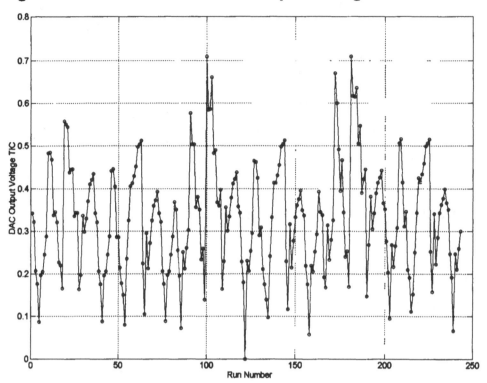

Comparing Figures 6.14 and 6.15, we see the TIC values for the turntable position tend to be much smaller than those of the DAC output voltage and there does not appear to be much correlation between the worst-case (largest) values in the two plots. Of primary interest is the motion of the turntable; we know the DAC output voltage tends to have large noise-like variations due to relatively insignificant differences in system behavior, as seen in the very large magnitude of TIC values in Figure 6.15. As a result of these factors, we will restrict the analysis to the turntable position and do not use the DAC output voltage TIC values further.

To gain some confidence that signal pairs with relatively high values of TIC produce overplots that show large variations, observe Figure 6.16, which is a plot of the turntable position for the 10 simulation runs that have the largest TIC values for the turntable angular position. The nominal turntable position trace is shown as a dotted line. The difference between the nominal position and each of the 10 runs is shown in the bottom plot.

Figure 6.16 Ten runs with highest position TICs.

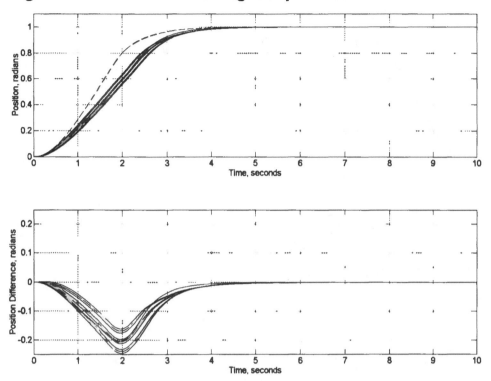

Figure 6.17 shows the turntable position for the middle, or median, 10 TIC value runs of the set, along with the nominal position and the differences of the runs from the nominal run.

Figure 6.17 Ten runs with median position TICs.

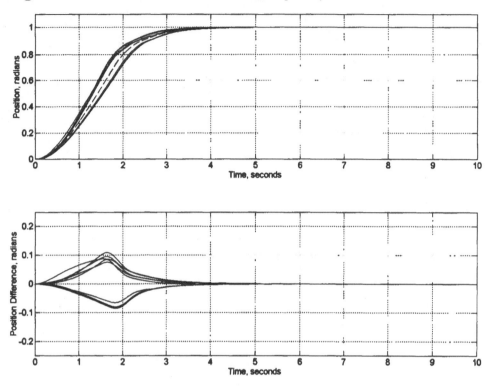

Figure 6.18 shows the turntable position and difference for the 10 runs with the lowest TIC values of the set. Note that one of these runs is the run where all parameters were at their nominal values, which results in a TIC of zero and a difference trace that is zero everywhere.

Figure 6.18 Ten runs with smallest position TICs.

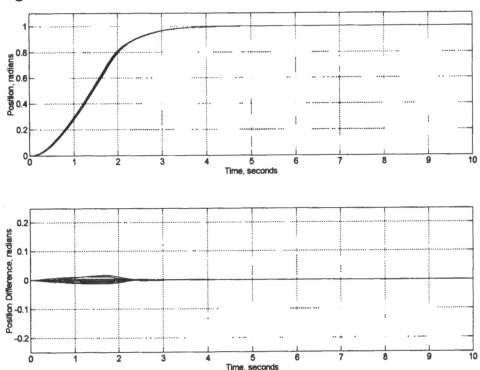

Figures 6.16–6.18, show that, at least in this example, the TIC provides a good way of determining if two signals match closely (as determined by examining an overplot or difference plot visually). The result agrees with an intuitive sense of when two signals "match" or "do not match." Therefore, it can be used as a tool in the execution of automated data analysis under certain conditions. In this example, the turntable position, but not the DAC output voltage, is suitable for TIC analysis. A computation of the TIC can rapidly determine if something, such as system instability, has gone drastically wrong during a particular run.

The goal for this example analysis was to determine the difference in the system behavior due to changes in parameter values. Figure 6.16 shows the system position response in the 10 worst cases, in terms of TIC values. Table 6.3 shows the parameter variations for these 10 worst runs. In this table, a plus symbol (+) indicates that the parameter value was incremented by three standard deviations, a minus symbol (–) indicates the parameter was decremented by the same amount, and a blank indicates that the nominal parameter value was used. It is clear that for these runs the combination of incremented b and R along with decremented K results in the worst-case deviations.

Table 6.3 Parameter changes for the 10 highest TIC runs.

Run	TIC	Change in J	Change in b	Change in K	Change in R	Change in L
225	0.1661	+	+	−	+	+
144	0.1627		+	−	+	+
63	0.1594	−	+	−	+	+
224	0.1490	+	+	−	+	
143	0.1457		+	−	+	
62	0.1424	−	+	−	+	
223	0.1315	+	+	−	+	−
142	0.1283		+	−	+	−
222	0.1280	+	+	−		+
61	0.1252	−	+	−	+	−

As this example has shown, there are some things to bear in mind when considering the use of Theil Inequality Coefficients.

- It is probably better to use the relative values of the TIC across a set of runs instead of attempting to determine a specific threshold value to indicate "good" matches between signals. Each signal has its own characteristics that would affect the choice of a threshold TIC value.

- TIC values provide the most useful results when the signals being compared are relatively smooth. In mechanical systems, this means that positions are preferable for TIC analysis in comparison to velocities and accelerations. In some cases, it may be possible to increase the signal smoothness with the use of low-pass filtering prior to TIC analysis.

In this section, an automated analysis identified worst-case combinations of parameter variations for a particular system design. A linear analysis of this system could have reached a very similar conclusion about which parameter deviations would combine to produce worst-case results as well. What have we gained by going to the effort of developing a system simulation and performing a large number of runs along with analysis of the output data? The answer is that a number of nonlinearities in the simulation — the effects of quantization, limiting, and transport delay — could not be modeled by linear analysis techniques.

The linear analysis tells us much about the system behavior, but it cannot provide the same level of confirmation that the control algorithm will perform acceptably in an actual implementation when compared to the nonlinear system simulation. The linear model contains more assumptions and simplifications than the nonlinear simulation.

In addition, the techniques used in generating results from linear analysis and from nonlinear system simulation are nicely orthogonal, in the sense that errors that occur in one analysis approach are relatively unlikely to occur in the other. If the results of the linear analysis agree with the result of the nonlinear analysis, the confidence in the correctness of both analyses is increased. This confirmation of design correctness is desirable before building expensive system prototypes.

On the other hand, the results of the linear analysis may vary significantly from the results of the system simulation. If this occurs, and if we determine that there are no errors in either analysis, we must conclude that the nonlinearities in the system render the linear analysis results invalid, or at least questionable. Thus, the simulation can help determine the degree of validity of the linear system model.

Even in cases where the linear model is shown to have a high level of validity and is used as the primary design tool, a nonlinear system simulation is useful to verify its validity over the system performance envelope. The validity of the linear model may be called into question at extremes of system behavior, or specific tests may be required, such as determining system performance in the event of a component failure. In these cases, the nonlinear system simulation may be the only way to generate the desired results other than by performing tests on actual system hardware.

Exercises[1]

1. Implement a simulation of the turntable system shown in Figures 6.6 and 6.7 using your choice of development environment. Design it so you can perform Monte Carlo simulation by selecting values for the five parameters listed in Table 6.2 using pseudorandom numbers. The approach for this is: Prior to starting each run, for each parameter, generate a pseudorandom number from a normal distribution having the mean and standard deviation shown in Table 6.2. Set up the simulation so it can perform a selectable number of runs in this manner, generating new parameter values before starting each run. Also, make sure that you can change the random number seed before starting a set of runs so that you do not always generate the same sequence of parameter values.

*2. Implement the TIC computation shown in Equation 6.2 in a way that is suitable for use in comparing output time histories from the simulation you developed in Exercise 1. Test it by generating sequences of pseudorandom data. What is the expected value of the TIC for sequences of uncorrelated random numbers from a normal distribution having zero mean and unit variance? Test your implementation to confirm that it agrees with this result. Also, test it in cases where both sequences are identical, where one sequence is the negative of the other, where just one sequence is all zero, and where both sequences are all zero.

3. Perform a simulation run with all five parameters in Table 6.2 at their nominal values and save reference time histories from this run for the turntable position and the motor DAC voltage. Compare these plots to Figures 6.8 and 6.9.

4. Perform a set of 250 simulation runs using Monte Carlo variations of the five parameters, as shown in Table 6.2. Compute the TIC comparing the turntable position and motor DAC voltage from each run with their nominal time histories that you saved in Exercise

---

1. Answers are provided for those exercises with an asterisk in Appendix A, page 294.

3. For each run, save the run number, both of the TIC values, and the variations in each of the five parameter values from the nominal in terms of number of standard deviations.

5. Examine the data you saved in Exercise 4 to determine the 10 highest TIC values for the turntable position. Look at the parameter variations on these runs and compare the results to those shown in Table 6.3. Do your results agree? Comment on the relative strengths and weakness of the Monte Carlo approach you used and the approach of using only nominal parameter values and nominal values plus or minus three standard deviations, as in the example in Section 6.6.4.

6. Make an overplot of the turntable position time history for the runs with the 10 highest TIC values on top of the nominal turntable position. Make another overplot of the differences between the turntable positions on these runs and the turntable position of the nominal run. Compare these plots to Figure 6.16.

7. Examine the data you saved in Exercise 4 to determine the 10 highest TIC values for the motor DAC voltage. How do the simulation parameter values for these runs compare to those for the TIC runs for the 10 highest turntable positions you analyzed in Exercise 5?

8. Make an overplot of the motor DAC voltage time history for the runs with the 10 highest TIC values on top of the nominal motor DAC voltage. Make another overplot of the differences between the turntable positions on these runs and the turntable position of the nominal run. Compare these plots to those you generated in Exercise 6.

9. Compute the statistical correlation between the turntable position TIC and the motor DAC voltage TIC over the 250-run set. What does this tell you about the relative usefulness of the turntable position TIC versus the motor DAC voltage TIC?

References

[1]   For more information, visit `http://www.dvcorp.com`.

[2]   For more information, visit `http://www.genesis3d.com`.

[3]   Fishman, G.S., and Kiviat, P.J., *The Analysis of Simulation-Generated Time Series*, Management Science 13, No. 7, 1967, pp. 525–557.

[4]   Kheir, N.A., and Holmes, W.M., *Modeling and Credibility of Random Ensembles*, Simulation, March 1982, pp. 93–128.

Chapter 7

Verification, Validation, and Accreditation

7.1 Introduction

A simulation of a dynamic system only has value if it represents the simulated system with sufficient accuracy for its intended purposes. Any simulation development effort must take steps to demonstrate that the resulting simulation provides a satisfactory level of accuracy. These steps are an integral part of the simulation effort and should be planned from the start of the project.

The accuracy of a simulation is demonstrated using a process called verification, validation, and accreditation, or VV&A for short. I will provide a brief definition of each of these terms and then discuss the entire process in detail in the remainder of this chapter.

Verification   demonstrates that a simulation has been implemented correctly according to its design specifications.

Validation   demonstrates that a simulation accurately represents the behavior of the simulated system and related external effects for the simulation's intended purposes.

Accreditation   is an authoritative statement that a simulation is acceptable for its intended uses, usually provided by the ultimate users of the simulation results.

VV&A is a process involving three major steps that generally proceed in the order listed above. The verification step is relevant for any software development process and simply indicates that the software performs as its designers intended. In simulation work, verification can occur in the early stages of a product development project. It is not necessary to have data derived from system prototype testing to perform verification. As a result, we can perform verification for a simulation of a system that does not yet exist. This allows a simulation to be built and used early in the concept definition phase of product development. If the simulation is available early, it can be used to perform early design trade studies. Of course, because there is no actual system to compare the simulation against, we must use extreme care in the verification of an early-phase system simulation.

Once hardware prototype versions of subsystems and the entire system become available, we can perform simulation validation. Many approaches are used for validation, all of which have the overall goal of demonstrating that the performance of the simulation agrees with that of the actual system to an acceptable degree. For reasons discussed in Chapters 2 and 3, simulations of real-world systems will never match the behavior of the actual systems exactly. When comparing results from a simulation against the results from tests of the real-world system, we must determine if the differences that arise are significant. Significant differences are those that impair the ability of the simulation to accurately predict system behavior.

Another aspect of validation is that it is defined only in the context of the intended uses for the simulation. In practice, simulations model only a subset of all the possible modes of behavior for a system. In selecting the behavior modes to include in a simulation, we attempt to choose those that are of the most relevance to the system design process and for which there is sufficient information to develop models with acceptable accuracy. As a result, there may be significant areas of system performance that are not included in a simulation, either because they are not relevant or because not enough is known about them.

If a particular mode of system behavior is not simulated, that does not make it a bad simulation; rather, it means that during the simulation, operation of the system in the unmodeled mode does not occur. The intended uses of the simulation must be restricted to preclude operation in unmodeled modes of behavior. When validating the simulation, ensure that the validation scenarios do not involve a precluded mode of operation. This is what is meant by saying that validation is only defined in the context of the intended uses of the simulation.

As an example, suppose an aircraft simulation models the aerodynamic behavior of an aircraft under normal flight conditions, but does not model the behavior when the aircraft has stalled. In this situation, the post-stall behavior is a precluded mode of simulation operation. Although it may make sense to perform aircraft testing and flight crew training in stall recovery, the simulation is not an appropriate tool for this task because this is not modeled the relevant behavior. The validation of this simulation must avoid the use of flight test data that includes post-stall behavior because the intended use does not include simulating the aircraft operation in a stall.

The final step in the VV&A process is accreditation, which is a combination of political and technical processes. Accreditation consists of presenting the results of the verification and validation (V&V) steps to the ultimate users of the simulation results and asking for their approval that the simulation will meet their needs. The "ultimate users" of the results may be the people who will operate the simulation to test system behavior, or they may be people further down the line who will receive reports on the results of simulation runs.

It is important to clearly identify who the users of the simulation results will be before attempting to perform accreditation. People in various areas of the design and development process may be able to use the results. Some of those people might have the option of using simulation data or using information from other sources. Individual or group attitudes may exist that discourage the use of simulation results in making key product development decisions.

One goal of accreditation is to reach these people who might otherwise avoid the use of simulation and to address their concerns about the validity of the output data. Before beginning the accreditation process, visit the simulation skeptics and ask, "What would it take to demonstrate the validity of this simulation to you?" Answers to this question can then feed into the design of the VV&A process.

A complete accreditation includes a thorough demonstration of simulation validity over its intended range of operation. It also contains background information about the design, development, and operation of the simulation and its constituent models. The entire accreditation package should include enough information to give the reader a complete understanding of how the simulation was developed and how it was tested. The test results must be included along with an analysis that describes the test conditions and the comparison of the simulation results with results from testing the actual system.

The final step in accreditation is to gain agreement from the users that the simulation validity is acceptable for its intended purposes. This step typically consists of signatures from representative users on a statement of accreditation. The value of this final step is that it provides an endorsement of the simulation by the users. This provides an incentive for the users to be diligent in their assessment of simulation validity. The completion of accreditation, in turn, may sway users who have the option of using other data than simulation results to give more credence to the simulation output. It also may convince the skeptics to consider making use of simulation results in situations where they previously would not have done so.

The proposed steps of VV&A for a particular project must be documented in a VV&A plan, and the results of the process must be documented in a VV&A report. The VV&A plan identifies the products to be examined, along with the specific tests and analysis techniques to be performed. Expected results and acceptable margins for error must also be included in the plan. The VV&A report documents the results of the tests and analyses in a manner that provides a level of confidence in the ability of the simulation to accurately represent the behavior of the simulated system. Deviations from expected results and untestable system behavior modes must be clearly identified. As a result of these deviations and untested behaviors, it may be necessary to limit the acceptable purposes for which the simulation may be accredited.

The entire VV&A process is designed to demonstrate for the users of simulation results that the simulation is properly constructed and produces results that reliably represent the behavior of the simulated system. In addition to performing these steps, the VV&A process must also proceed in a timely manner and have a reasonable cost. The remainder of this chapter will discuss techniques for performing the steps required by VV&A in ways that attempt to minimize the amount of effort and expense required.

7.2 Verification and Validation

As discussed in the previous section, verification is the process of demonstrating that a simulation is an accurate implementation of the mathematical models of an embedded system and its environment. The first step in simulation verification is to identify the approaches to use in determining the degree of simulation correctness and then to apply these verification approaches to the simulation and its output data. Finally, the results are evaluated to determine whether or not the simulation satisfies the verification requirements.

If the simulation fails to pass verification testing, it may be necessary to perform additional simulation design, development, and testing to improve its fidelity. It is also possible that errors in the simulation implementation will be discovered during the verification testing process. If simulation enhancements or bug fixes are required as the result of verification testing, it will be necessary to repeat some or all of the verification testing on the modified simulation version.

The version of the simulation software that passes verification testing should become a baseline in the configuration management system. Subsequent simulation changes must be carefully tracked to maintain the integrity of the verification process. As the models and other elements of the simulation change, it will be necessary to repeat verification tests that are relevant to the affected area. By carefully following this process of ongoing simulation verification, we can ensure that the simulation will satisfy the verification requirements over its entire life cycle.

Validation demonstrates that the simulation models the embedded system and the real world operational environment with acceptable accuracy. A standard approach for validation is to use the results of system operational tests for comparison against simulation results. This type of validation test involves running the simulation through a test scenario that is identical to one that was performed by the actual system in an operational environment. The results of the two tests are compared and any differences are analyzed to determine if they represent a significant deviation between the simulation and the real world.

Depending on the size of the simulation project, the amount of planning effort and other resources required for VV&A may be substantial. For a small project with only one developer, it may be possible to have that individual perform the VV&A assessments as well as the development work. In larger projects, it may be necessary to have a person (or even a group) dedicated to the VV&A process separate from the simulation developers.

The following sections discuss a variety of VV&A techniques suitable for use in simulation development projects of various sizes. In planning the VV&A process for a particular project, we must identify the techniques to be used and the point in the development cycle at which each technique will be applied. Not all of these techniques are appropriate for every project. It is important to carefully select which ones will provide the most effective VV&A while minimizing the cost and time required for the effort.

7.2.1 Informal Verification Techniques

This section lists verification techniques that are informal in the sense that their implementation depends heavily on human interpretation and the results tend to be somewhat subjective. However, these methods are some of the most commonly used and best accepted techniques for software verification. These approaches are not limited to simulation development projects. They are useful for software development projects of any type.

Desk Checking

A desk check is an intense examination of work products to verify their correctness, completeness, and clarity [1]. A person other than the developer should perform desk checking because it is frequently difficult to detect one's own errors. Desk checking should occur early in the development process, preferably after the design has been coded but before systematic testing begins.

A thorough desk check should include a careful examination of design documents and software products to verify that the design is correct and understandable and that the software is a correct implementation of the design. The desk check should also verify that simulation coding, commenting, and documentation procedures are being followed.

Desk checking is considered to be the first step in the VV&A process; hence, it should occur early in the development cycle. These sessions are usually planned and carried out in a very informal manner. A developer typically arranges with a peer to perform the desk check and then provides the relevant information to the checker in the form of printouts or disk files for examination. The checker examines the provided information and responds with feedback in the form of comments, questions, and suggestions to the developer. Management is not involved in this process other than to receive notification that the desk check took place along with a brief summary of the findings.

Walkthroughs

For simulation development purposes, a walkthrough is a group peer review of some elements of the design and implementation of a simulation [2]. In a walkthrough, a developer provides an explanation of the design and implementation of simulation components for which he or she is responsible to a group of peer simulation developers. The walkthrough should be a two-way exchange of information, with the audience providing comments, suggestions, and constructive criticism to the developer about the subject matter during the presentation. It is important that these comments be recorded in some form during the review and provided to the presenter, or some of the information may be lost before it can be used.

The goal of a walkthrough is to provide high-quality feedback into the simulation development process in a timely, efficient manner. To meet these requirements, it is often best that the walkthrough be a relatively informal process that does not require a large amount of preparation or lead time before the review can be held. A formal review might involve having the developer prepare a stack of transparencies and send out invitations for everybody to show up for the review in two weeks. An informal, and often more effective, approach is to have the developer print copies of the relevant source code and design documentation and ask the group to get together later the same day.

Of course, there should be some structure to the review in order to produce the best results. Any but the most informal walkthrough should have an agenda and a time limit. There should also be some rules for the walkthrough that are understood by all participants. These rules include such things as the responsibilities of the walkthrough coordinator and an understanding that all participants will study any documentation or code listings provided by the developer prior to the review.

There is a question of when it is best to hold walkthroughs during a development project. Should they occur during the design phase, after implementation but before testing, or after testing is complete and the developer believes there are no remaining defects? The correct answer may be that multiple walkthroughs are sometimes appropriate. An initial walkthrough can take place after the design is completed, prior to the start of implementation. This early review allows feedback to the developer about unjustified assumptions or errors that occurred during the design process. It can also point out areas of confusion or unnecessary complexity in the design that will make the implementation process easier and less prone to error. However, the design walkthrough is usually only necessary in cases where the design is quite complex or it relies heavily on data or models that may be questionable for some reason. If the design is relatively simple and is based on well-understood physical principles, a design walkthrough may be unnecessary.

After implementation is complete and before testing begins is usually the best time for a walkthrough. The developer has likely found and eliminated many of the defects in the design and implementation, but some tricky ones may remain. A walkthrough at this point in the cycle can be effective at locating those problem areas that the developer would not have discovered, while avoiding the additional expense that is typically required to detect and isolate the problems during testing.

Each individual developer in a simulation project is usually involved in the design and implementation of models of several system components or effects related to the external environment. It is important to break these different models into components of reasonable size. Each component of the system should undergo its own walkthrough process during development.

Reviews

A review is similar in concept to a walkthrough, but it is more formal and involves management as an integral part. The purpose of reviews is to provide evidence to managers, customers, and others that the goals of the development process are being satisfied in an appropriate manner. In a review, the developers present information to demonstrate that the development effort is producing the desired results within budget and schedule constraints.

Reviews are more formal than the other techniques discussed in this section. They function at an oversight level rather than at the level of technical details. Reviews focus more on determining the quality of the product than on verifying its correctness. The review team is generally concerned that development policies and procedures are being followed and that the design is based on a reasonable set of assumptions. The review should also demonstrate that satisfactory modeling methodologies are being used and that the resulting models are appropriately documented.

Because the customers and end users of a simulation are often present at reviews, these are often the best times to communicate the status and progress of the simulation development project to them. The review should satisfy the customers and users that development efforts are being focused appropriately. If the customers or users identify areas where they feel more attention is required in the development process, this is the time to make the development team aware of those concerns. For example, the users may identify a particular effect that they feel is being modeled too simply and may suggest that a model design of higher fidelity is more appropriate for their needs.

7.2.2 Static Verification Techniques

Static verification techniques are popular and widely used approaches for software verification. The techniques discussed in this section are less subjective than those of the previous section. These techniques do not require execution of the source code, though mentally executing parts of the software is sometimes useful. Automated tools are available to perform many of these analyses.

Control Analysis

Control analysis includes techniques such as calling structure analysis, concurrent process analysis, control flow analysis, and state transition analysis.

Calling structure analysis for a particular routine identifies which routines call or are called by that routine. The result of this analysis is a summary that identifies dependencies among the different routines that make up a complete program. This summary can be examined to verify that it makes sense for the intended design, and it is also useful in debugging problems with the software.

Concurrent process analysis is useful in multitask and distributed simulations. This analysis identifies which processing threads are active simultaneously on a single processor or on multiple processors. The processing time requirements and synchronization requirements for communication among these threads are analyzed to determine if the simulation will operate properly. Potential problems such as deadlocks should become apparent from this analysis.

Control flow analysis involves creating a graph that contains nodes where conditional branches occur and where the flow merges again. The nodes are connected by edges, which represent blocks of sequential code statements. Control flow analysis is useful in verifying the correctness of a design and for identifying inefficiencies in a design.

State transition analysis is used when a control algorithm in a model can be represented by a finite state machine. In this situation, the conditions under which the model transitions between states is shown in a state transition diagram, which is analyzed to determine its correctness and to verify that the implementation matches the design.

Data Analysis

Data analysis includes the techniques of data flow analysis and data dependency analysis. These approaches ensure that data objects used in a simulation are properly defined and that appropriate operations are applied to them.

Data flow analysis involves the construction of a data flowgraph to visualize the use of data objects within the simulation. This type of flowgraph is similar to a standard control flowgraph, with enhancements to indicate the operations applied to data. The data flowgraph contains nodes that represent statements and the corresponding data items. The nodes are annotated to indicate when variables are declared, defined, and used. The graph edges represent the flow of control.

Data flow analysis is useful in detecting undefined and unused data elements and is also helpful in identifying inconsistencies in data structures and improper linkages among data items.

Data dependency analysis is the determination of which data items depend on other data. This analysis is particularly important in the case of multithread and multiprocessor simulations. The analysis must determine that the operations applied to data elements retain consistency and correctness before, during, and after each access by a thread or process.

Interface Analysis

Interface analysis applied to simulation involves the techniques of model interface analysis and user interface analysis.

Model interface analysis is a detailed examination of the interfaces between the models that compose a simulation. This analysis must determine if the interface to each model is correct, complete, and unambiguous. As one element of this analysis, the units of each input and output variable must be clearly defined. Because the interfaces to models are defined early in the development process, this analysis should ideally occur before full model development begins.

User interface analysis is an examination of the interaction between the simulation user and a particular model in the simulation. This analysis examines the parameters and any other settings the user interacts with to affect the model behavior. The goal of this analysis is to determine the potential for the introduction of errors during user interactions with the model. An example of a problem that this analysis should detect is a Boolean variable name that does not clearly identify what *true* represents. For instance, a Boolean variable called `valve_state` does not indicate whether the valve is open or closed when it is true. A better variable name might be `valve_open`. This name is less likely to confuse users when attempting to interpret its value.

Traceability Analysis

A traceability analysis attempts to match the elements of different forms of a model to each other in a one-to-one manner. An example of this is a comparison of the requirements specification of a model to the implementation of that model in source code. The traceability analysis identifies requirements that have not been implemented, and it identifies elements in the code that do not correspond to requirements. The resolution of issues raised by this analysis may lead to changes in the requirements, the code, or both.

Syntax and Semantic Analysis

Syntax analysis occurs during the compilation of source code into object code. This analysis ensures that the source code obeys the rules of the programming language in which it is implemented. Semantic analysis also occurs during compilation and determines the intent of the software developer as expressed in the source code.

The compiler produces a variety of types of information during syntax and semantic analysis that is useful to the simulation developer. During syntax analysis, the compiler produces error and warning messages to indicate incorrect and suspicious constructs in the source code. Semantic analysis produces a variety of forms of information, many of which can be displayed by selecting appropriate compiler switches. Some examples of this information include

- symbol tables, which describe the attributes of data objects and functions defined by the developer,

- cross-reference tables, which identify where in the source code the symbols are used, and

- link maps, which provide information such as the size and memory location of data objects and functions in the compiled code.

In addition to the facilities provided by the compiler, other tools are available that provide more depth and capability for performing some of these functions. For example, lint tools for C and C++ perform a large number of checks for consistency, questionable syntax, and potential errors in source code. These tools can detect a much wider variety of problems than a typical compiler, so performing lint testing as a regular part of software development can be a very cost effective way to improve software quality.

Other automated source code analysis tools are available that perform such tasks as complexity analysis and documentation of interfaces to functions. These tools are often low in cost (or sometimes free) and should be used during simulation development as appropriate to help prevent errors and improve understanding of the software implementation.

7.2.3 Dynamic Verification and Validation Techniques

Dynamic V&V techniques involve the execution of the model to determine its behavior. These techniques require the collection of data as the model executes. This may occur as a normal part of simulation operation or it may be necessary to add instrumentation code to the model at selected points to collect and store information about model behavior. This code may be inserted temporarily to perform these tests only when needed.

There are two drawbacks associated with adding code temporarily for testing purposes and later removing it for the "final" model version. First, merely removing the test code may introduce errors that cause incorrect model behavior that will not be detected since the model has already passed the tests. Second, during later maintenance, we may decide to rerun the same tests. This requires placing the instrumentation code into the model for the tests and then removing it again. A better approach, when available, is to use conditional compilation for this code. C and C++ permit the use of preprocessor variables to determine whether to compile a section of source code into object code. Using this facility, can add and remove instrumentation code without any changes to the source files of the simulation. It is only necessary to recompile the simulation with appropriate preprocessor variable definitions, which can be supplied in the compiler command line.

An even better approach is to avoid the need for recompilation by using parameters in the simulation to enable or disable the collection of instrumentation data. In this approach, the instrumentation code is always compiled into the simulation and only executes when the user sets the parameters to turn it on. This allows the dynamic V&V tests to be rerun at any time. The drawback to this approach is that the code size for the simulation is larger than it would be if the instrumentation code were not present. This is rarely a serious problem because simulations are normally run on computers with abundant memory and disk space resources.

The execution of dynamic V&V tests is typically a three-step process. The first step is the instrumentation of the source code. The second step is the setup and execution of the test run.

The third step is the analysis of the data collected during the test. This analysis seeks to determine if there are errors in the model or problems with insufficient model fidelity. The following sections discuss various types of dynamic V&V tests that are carried out using this procedure.

Graphical Comparison

One of the most popular tools for comparing the results of V&V testing from different data sources is the graphical comparison of time history data. This comparison technique is necessarily subjective, but when carried out by people familiar with the simulated system, it is quite effective. In Chapter 6, I discussed techniques for comparing signals from different sources, such as a test of an actual system and a simulation of the same test.

The most basic techniques for graphical comparison of data from two different sources are the overlay plot and the difference plot. The overlay plot is a time plot of a signal containing a separate trace for each source of data. Differences between the behavior of the signal in the actual system and the simulation are apparent from the deviations between the two traces.

Subtracting one of the signals from the other in a point-by-point manner and plotting the result produces a difference plot. If the two signals are not sampled at identical points in time, additional processing is necessary to resample one of the signals at the same time points as the other before the subtraction can be performed. The difference plot is useful in highlighting segments where deviations are relatively larger between the data from the two sources. This is useful in situations where the overlay plot of the signals does not indicate clearly visible differences.

Execution Testing

Execution testing involves the use of software tools that perform functions such as profiling and tracing program behavior. Profiling gathers high-level information about program behavior during execution, such as which source code statements were executed and how many times each function was called during a run. A profiler may also collect information that indicates how much time is spent in each function during the run.

Information collected during profile runs is useful in determining if sections of code that were expected to be executed during a test actually did execute. Profile results are also helpful in designing V&V test cases to ensure that all source code statements are executed during testing.

Tracing is a line-by-line execution of the simulation under manual control. During tracing, the developer examines the results of each statement after it executes to verify agreement with expectations. Tracing generally occurs in a debugger environment. To perform effective tracing, the debugger must provide the abilities to single-step through the source code and to examine and modify the values of program variables. Most high-level programming language development environments provide debugging tools with these capabilities. Some block diagram simulation development tools provide these capabilities as well.

Tracing provides an excellent early test of the correctness of a software implementation. A single module at a time should trace tested. This test should exercise all paths through the source code. Using the capabilities of the debugger, it is usually possible to set up conditions that enable testing of all code paths. For example, a call to a system service may produce a return value that is almost always successful. If you execute this system call in the debugger and then modify the variable containing the returned result to indicate an error, you can test the error-handling code.

It is a good practice to require that all models undergo a trace test prior to incorporation into the controlled configuration of the simulation. This approach can dramatically reduce the number of errors that make it into the simulation [3].

Comparison Testing

Comparison testing is applicable when more than one version of a model or system simulation is available for use in testing. Comparison testing involves setting up the different models or simulations with identical inputs, running them, comparing the outputs with each other, and analyzing any differences between the results to determine if there are significant differences between the models or simulations.

If significant differences are found, we must identify the sources of the differences and determine if there are errors or improper assumptions in either implementation. As part of this analysis, we consider the degree to which each model has already undergone V&V testing. A simulation that has passed a full suite of V&V testing is more likely to be the correct version, although this result is not guaranteed.

Comparison testing is particularly valuable when developing an HIL simulation based on an existing non-real-time simulation. The HIL simulation often requires simplifications and optimizations to meet the requirement to run at real-time speeds. Careful comparison testing between the two simulation versions will determine if these changes have had a significant effect on the accuracy of the resulting real-time simulation.

Regression Testing

Regression testing ensures that changes made to a simulation do not introduce errors or cause unintended side effects. Regression testing normally involves repeating a test performed with an earlier version of the simulation on the new simulation version. The inputs that specify the test must have been saved from the earlier test for use in setting up the regression test. The output data from the earlier test must have been saved as well, because it will be used as the comparison basis to determine if the results of the current test are correct.

Regression testing should be a part of any V&V testing process, particularly after a baseline simulation version is in place that has been verified and validated. The natural evolution of a simulation project involves continuous change and enhancement of the simulation models, so it is vital to maintain the integrity of the V&V work that has taken place. Regression testing is the primary tool for maintaining this integrity as changes take place in the simulation.

For a medium to large simulation development project, it may make sense to automate regression testing when possible. Much of the time, simulation enhancements can be expected to have little or no effect on the behavior of existing models in the simulation. An automated analysis using the Theil Inequality Coefficient (TIC) (see Section 6.6.3) can compare the test output results from the current and previous simulation versions and identify which variables have changed by more than a small threshold amount.

As discussed in Section 6.6.3, care must be used when applying the TIC to variables that exhibit noise-like behavior. If, for example, we change the seed value of a pseudorandom number generator used to simulate noise on a system parameter, the result may be a large TIC result indicating a significant difference between the two simulation versions. In this case, the TIC reading is likely to be a false indication of differences between the two versions. As this example indicates, it is wise to ensure that identical pseudorandom number sequences are used for initial tests and for later regression testing. This is true even in cases where visual comparison, rather than the TIC, is used to determine if the test results agree.

Beta Testing

Beta testing involves the operation of early versions of a simulation by the simulation users rather than by the developers. This type of testing is typically the first direct experience the users have with the simulation. As the users work with the simulation, they will encounter problems and have questions that they pass along to the developers. The developers incorporate this feedback into subsequent updates of the simulation and its documentation.

Beta testing follows the alpha testing phase, which is testing performed by the developers. Alpha testing results in a simulation in which all problems that the developers have been able to find are fixed (or at least documented). Beta testing often uncovers additional simulation bugs as the users work with the simulation. In addition, because the users have a different set of assumptions about how the simulation should work, they may make requests to change the simulation user interface to match their expectations.

Functional (Black Box) Testing

Functional, or black box, testing is an assessment of the correctness of the processing performed by a model. In a functional test, a given set of inputs is applied to a model, and the resulting output is examined to determine the correctness of the model. The actual processing performed by the model is not directly analyzed during this test, which results in treatment of the model as a "black box."

Using this approach, it is not realistic to expect to test all possible combinations of input and output for even a simple model. For instance, a model that merely multiplies two 32-bit integers together to produce a 64-bit output would require 2^{64} or 1.8×10^{19} test cases to cover all possible input–output combinations. Functional testing requires the intelligent selection of test cases that provide good coverage over the range of operation while avoiding an excessively large number of cases.

A variety of methods is available to help select test cases. A primary source of information is the requirements documentation for the model or simulation to be tested. It should be possible to identify one or more test cases to assist in determining the correct implementation of each documented requirement. Other test cases can be devised by considering extreme situations and the possibility of invalid input to the model or simulation. A thorough functional test should consider all possible modes of system operation and all of the expected failure or error modes of behavior.

For each function test case generated, we also need to specify the expected test results. The combination of input data and expected results for each test goes into the test plan. During test execution, we record the actual behavior of the system and identify any variations from the expected behavior. Analysis of the variations between expected and actual behavior determines if the test passed or failed.

Statistical Tests

Many statistical tests are available for use in simulation V&V applications. The predominant application for these tests is in the validation comparison of actual system operation data against data from a simulation executed under identical conditions. Statistical validation techniques require the collection of separate complete sets of validation data from the system and its simulation. A multivariate statistical analysis can then determine the correlation between output variables from the two data sources.

The TIC (see Section 6.6.3) is one example of such a statistical analysis technique. The computation of the TIC results in a zero value when there is perfect agreement between the two data sources. Larger TIC values indicate poorer agreement, with 1 indicating maximum disagreement between the two data sequences.

Many other statistical techniques are available that are applicable to simulation validation. Some of these are listed below.

Spectral Analysis

Spectral analysis involves performing a discrete Fourier transform (DFT) [4] on each of the data sequences and comparing the resulting spectra. This comparison can determine the degree of agreement between the data sequences in the frequency domain.

The DFT formula is shown in Equation 7.1. In this equation, the data sequence x (which may be real or complex) is N elements long starting at index zero, $e = 2.71828182...$, and $j = \sqrt{-1}$. The resulting (complex) sequence X is of length N with the index k representing the frequency.

7.1
$$X[k] = \sum_{n=0}^{N-1} x[n] e^{-j(2\pi n k/N)}$$

Equation 7.1 is the underlying computation of the DFT, but much more efficient algorithms exist in the form of the fast Fourier transform (FFT) to compute this result. The FFT is the preferred method for computing the DFT, particularly when the length of the sequence N is large.

The power spectrum of the signal can be estimated from the result of Equation 7.1 using the periodogram as shown in Equation 7.2.

7.2
$$I(\omega_k) = \frac{1}{N}[X[k]]^2$$

Equation 7.2 provides an estimate of the power spectrum at frequency $\omega_k = 2\pi k/N$ radians/second. Evaluating this expression for all values of k from 0 to $N-1$ provides the complete power spectrum estimate. Other techniques, such as spectrum overplots and the TIC, can be used to compare the resulting spectrum to another signal's spectrum.

Correlation Analysis

Correlation analysis uses statistical techniques such as auto- and cross-correlation functions and their Fourier transforms, which are called spectral density functions [5]. These techniques are similar in many ways to the spectral analysis approach discussed above.

Correlation analysis is useful in developing linear models from noisy measurements of system response. Models developed in this fashion from simulation results can be compared to models developed from tests of the actual system. This comparison is useful in determining the degree of validity of the simulation.

Analysis of Variance

Analysis of variance (ANOVA) is a statistical technique for comparing two or more groups of observations to determine the probability that the means of the groups are identical. This analysis assumes that the observations contain noise with a normal probability distribution and that the different groups have equal variances.

ANOVA is a useful technique when a simulation produces results with noise-like properties. An ANOVA comparison of simulation results with the results from system tests can provide confidence that the average behavior of the simulation matches that of the actual system.

Confidence Intervals

This technique uses the sample mean and variance to determine that the probability of the true mean of a variable lies within a specified interval surrounding the sample mean. This technique relies on the assumption that the variable is normally distributed. In this approach, it is common to select a probability (such as 95% or 99%) and then determine the confidence interval that satisfies that probability level.

A potential problem with this approach is that if the true variance is unknown, it may be necessary to estimate the variance from the measured data. This measurement often requires a large number of samples to estimate with acceptable accuracy. In many simulation situations, the sample size for data derived from system tests may be severely limited because of the expense and time required to perform system tests. For this reason, statistical techniques such as confidence intervals often have limited usefulness when applied to simulation validation testing.

The Kolmogorov-Smirnov Test

The Kolmogorov-Smirnov (or K-S) test measures the difference between two cumulative distribution functions. It is applicable in situations where each point in the data set is associated with a single number. The N data points are converted into an estimator, $S_N(x)$, of the cumulative distribution function [6]. $S_N(x)$ gives the fraction of the data points that are less than the function input x. Given a cumulative distribution function $P(x)$ to compare with $S_N(x)$, we can compute the K-S statistic using Equation 7.3.

7.3 $$D = \max_{-\infty < x < \infty} \left| S_N(x) - P(x) \right|$$

The K-S statistic D measures the maximum absolute difference between the two cumulative distribution functions. A zero value of D indicates perfect agreement of the distributions, and larger values of D indicate a greater amount of disagreement. For nonzero D, you can compute the probability of a value of D greater than the observed value in the case of matching distributions. This gives the likelihood that the distributions are in fact the same.

A primary benefit of the K-S test is that it works well with small data sets, which are common in simulation validation.

The Chi-Square Test

The chi-square test [7] tests the validity of the assumption that the results of experimental observations match a particular expected statistical distribution. The test procedure involves determining the number of degrees of freedom in the experiment and computing the chi-square value from the experimental data. Using this information, it is possible to determine the probability that the computed chi-square value could occur by chance. This test is useful in situations where simulation results are expected to fit a specified statistical distribution.

Predictive Validation

Predictive validation uses input and output data from a test of the actual system to test the simulation. The same input data that was used in the system test is used to drive the simulation. The simulation outputs are then compared to the outputs of the system test. This type of test determines the ability of the simulation to predict system behavior.

Predictive validation is a primary tool for providing evidence that a simulation is an accurate representation of an actual system. Demonstrations of predictive validity provide confidence in the overall accuracy and usefulness of the simulation. After performing predictive validation for a carefully selected set of test scenarios, we have a high degree of confidence in the accuracy of simulation scenarios that are interpolations between the validation conditions. We can also extrapolate beyond the conditions for which predictive validation has been performed, but with diminishing confidence in the results as the amount of extrapolation increases.

Assertion Checking

An assertion is a logical statement that is expected to be true each time it is evaluated. Assertion checks are statements placed into source code that perform this type of check. If the check is successful (that is, the logical statement turns out to be true), the assertion check takes no action and program execution continues normally. If the check fails (the logical statement is false), the assertion check reports the error and may take another action, such as aborting the execution of the simulation.

The following are some uses for assertion checks in simulations:

- Verify that assumptions about the inputs to a model are correct. For example, test that inputs are within the allowable range or that the magnitude of a unit vector is one to within floating point precision.
- Verify that relationships among data values are valid. For example, use matrix operations to verify the orthogonality of the direction cosine matrix for a three-axis rotation.
- Verify that control flow is executing correctly. For example, if a state of a finite state machine can only be reached from one other state, verify on entry that the previous state is the expected one.

C and C++ provide an `assert` macro that makes performing assertion checks easy. It is also possible to disable the checks in these languages by defining the preprocessor symbol `NDEBUG` and recompiling the source code. When the checks are disabled, we lose the ability to catch errors using this facility, but the code size is reduced and execution performance is increased.

However, you normally these assertions should be left in the code even in the final production versions of a simulation because of the additional support they provide in detecting errors and ensuring correctness. Assertion checking should be disabled only when all available performance is needed for real-time execution or when a sudden simulation halt due to an assertion failure would create a hazard. In these situations, it is necessary to develop a more sophisticated way to detect errors and notify the user when they occur.

7.3 Accreditation

Accreditation is the go-ahead decision to use a simulation for a particular purpose. In the case of a small, single-developer simulation project, the accreditation decision may occur implicitly when the developer becomes satisfied with the results of verification and validation testing. In larger projects, the accreditation process is more formal and may involve a number of people with varying interests in the simulation development and V&V processes. In this section, I will assume a simulation project that is sufficiently large that some degree of formality is essential to the accreditation decision. This will be the case when the results of simulation runs will be used as inputs to critical program decisions that have significant financial or safety consequences.

One of the first steps in planning for accreditation is the identification of the proper accrediting authority. This is normally a person or organization different from the simulation developers. The accrediting authority should be capable of analyzing the details of V&V reports and of determining if the simulation satisfies its requirements. Also, the accrediting authority should be a user of simulation results throughout the project life cycle. In many cases, the best selection of accrediting authority is an individual or organization with responsibility for the success of the overall project.

After examining the results of V&V testing, the accrediting authority must make a decision on acceptability of the simulation for its planned purpose. The result of this decision is usually one of the following:

- The simulation is acceptable for its intended purpose.
- The simulation is acceptable for its intended purpose, except there are some limitations on its use.
- Additional V&V must be performed before the simulation can be accredited.
- The simulation must be modified and additional V&V must be performed before it can be accredited.
- The simulation is unacceptable for its intended purpose and must not be used.

The last three decision results listed above will cause additional costs and delays to the project, or may result in drastic changes to the project plan. A well-planned VV&A process should include feedback from the accreditation authority as it progresses so that the authority remains aware of the results of ongoing testing. If the authority has a good understanding of the results of V&V testing and feels that all necessary information has been provided, the actual accreditation decision becomes a formality.

On the other hand, if the accrediting authority is not aware of ongoing V&V work and the information to support an accreditation decision is delivered at the end of the process, an unsatisfactory accreditation decision is much more likely. The authority may have particular data requirements or other information needs that have not been met, so there is likely to be a request for additional testing or other information that delays the accreditation decision. This can result in unacceptable project delays while the additional testing and information gathering occurs.

A thorough accreditation decision process should take into account more than just the results of simulation runs and comparisons with other data sources. It should also consider factors in the development process, such as coding standards, configuration management, and release criteria. These additional factors determine the degree to which the simulation can be maintained and upgraded over its life cycle.

As changes and enhancements are made to the simulation, it may be necessary to revisit the accreditation process from time to time. With the use of regression testing, it should be possible to ensure that previously accredited capabilities are maintained as changes are implemented in the simulation. New simulation capabilities may require accreditation when they represent significant differences from the point of view of the user. The accreditation of these simulation enhancements can take the form of an addendum to the original accreditation document.

7.4 VV&A Plans and Reports

Careful planning and reporting of results are essential to the VV&A process. Planning for VV&A begins with the planning for the design of the simulation. The accreditation authority should be made aware of simulation development plans by receiving copies of planning documents and through invitations to design reviews. This enables the accreditation authority to understand the design approaches used and to provide feedback into the design process when appropriate.

Planning for verification can proceed in parallel with simulation planning and development. When a baseline simulation configuration is available that includes satisfactory versions of all models and all significant problems have been fixed, verification testing can begin. The verification tests are specified by the verification plan, and the results of those tests provide the basis for the verification report. The accreditation authority should receive a copy of the verification report as well as an invitation to any reviews of the results of verification testing.

Planning for validation can also occur as part of planning for simulation development. Validation testing normally follows the completion of verification testing and requires test data from an actual system operating under specified test conditions. The real-world test specifications and inputs provide the information needed to set up and execute simulation validation tests. Comparison of the results from these simulation tests with those of system tests provides confidence in the validity of the simulation. This comparison is documented in the validation report, which is provided to the accreditation authority along with an invitation to the review of the validation test results.

The accreditation authority uses the planning documents for the simulation and V&V along with the V&V reports, to reach an accreditation decision. By including the accrediting authority in the process of simulation development and V&V from the beginning, there is likely to be a quick and positive accreditation decision when the results show satisfactory simulation performance. On the other hand, even if the V&V results show excellent simulation performance, if nothing is provided to the accrediting authority until the end of the V&V process, there may be difficulty getting a quick decision on accreditation. If the authority is unfamiliar with the simulation development project and the decisions that went into its design and V&V processes, it may be difficult to reach an accreditation decision. There may be many questions and changes required by the authority before accreditation can be granted. When a formal accreditation process is used in a project, it is critical to keep the accrediting authority in the loop on the simulation development and V&V efforts.

Figure 7.1 summarizes the complete VV&A process. Planning for simulation development, verification, and validation can proceed in parallel during the initial phases of a project. Verification testing, analysis, and report creation occur after the simulation has reached a sufficient level of maturity. Validation requires data from tests on actual system hardware, so this is likely to occur much later in the product development cycle, at least in cases where new hardware is being developed. Finally, inputs from verification and validation planning and tests along with information about the simulation design and development are used to reach an accreditation decision.

Figure 7.1   VV&A process.

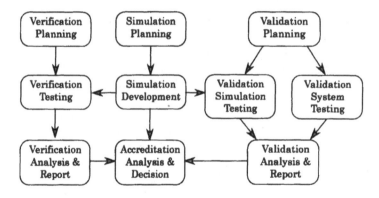

The VV&A process described here is flexible and applicable to both small and large simulation projects. Each part of the process can be as simple or formal as required. A small simulation project may have only one person to perform the entire simulation development and VV&A processes. Although this approach has some obvious drawbacks, the limitations of budgets, personnel, and other resources may necessitate this type of operation. Even in this situation, it is still possible to perform all the tasks shown in Figure 7.1 and to provide a high-quality, validated simulation for use in product development and testing.

In a larger project, where simulation development is a full-time job for one or more people, it is appropriate to have a different person or group responsible for coordinating V&V activities. The V&V group performs tasks such as developing V&V plans, testing, and reporting on the test results. Usually the accrediting authority will not perform the V&V work, in which case, the group prepares the reports and presents the results to the accrediting authority along with a recommended decision on accreditation.

The VV&A process is a critical element of simulation development. Unfortunately, in many simulation projects, the VV&A process occurs informally and results are not captured and made available to people outside the simulation project. This can lead to the rejection of simulation results by those people. This is a reasonable thing for them to do, since they have seen no evidence that the simulation is credible and accurate. To gain maximum credibility and usefulness for simulations, it is important to plan for VV&A and to make the results of the process available to all parties in the product development process. Allowing input from those outside the simulation development project into VV&A planning can provide valuable feedback that improves the overall simulation effort and increases the usefulness of the simulation to the organization.

Exercises

1. Choose a simulation that you have worked with or one that is described in this book. Write the outline of a verification plan for this simulation.

2. In the verification plan outline you developed in the previous exercise, define a series of static and dynamic verification tests for the simulation. Identify sources of data for determining the correctness of these tests. Do not assume that an actual system is available for testing. Ensure that the tests cover all modes of system operation and extremes of system behavior.

3. Write the outline of a validation plan for this simulation.

4. In the validation plan outline you developed in the previous exercise, define a series of dynamic validation tests for the simulation. Identify the system tests that are required to generate data for comparison with the simulation. Try to ensure that the tests cover all modes of system operation and extremes of system behavior. Are there system behaviors that cannot be tested due to safety concerns or other unacceptable risks?

5. Assume that you are an accrediting authority who is not a simulation developer. Perhaps you are a customer for the product under development. Define the criteria you would apply to make an accreditation decision for the simulation. Do the verification and validation plans you developed in previous problems address these criteria adequately?

6. Identify a set of regression tests to be applied following significant changes to the simulation. How do these tests differ from the tests in the validation and verification plans? To what degree can the execution and analysis of results from the regression tests be automated?

References

[1] Defense Modeling and Simulation Office, *Verification, Validation & Accreditation (VV&A) Recommended Practices Guide*. U.S. Department of Defense, 1996.

[2] Yourdon, Edward, *Structured Walkthroughs*. Englewood Cliffs, NJ: Prentice-Hall, 1989.

[3] Maguire, Steve, *Writing Solid Code*. Microsoft Press, 1993.

[4] Oppenheim, Alan V., and Ronald W. Schafer, *Discrete-Time Signal Processing*. Englewood Cliffs, NJ: Prentice-Hall, 1989.

[5] Bendat, Julius S., and Allan G. Piersol, *Engineering Applications of Correlation and Spectral Analysis*. New York, NY: John Wiley, 1980.

[6] Press, William H., Saul A. Teukolsky, William T. Vetterling, and Brian P. Flannery, *Numerical Recipes in C: The Art of Scientific Computing*. Cambridge, England: Cambridge University Press, 1992, §14.3.

[7] Mood, A. M., and F. A. Graybill, *Introduction to the Theory of Statistics*, 2nd ed. New York, NY: McGraw-Hill, 1963.

Chapter 8

Simulation Throughout the Development Cycle

8.1 Introduction

Simulation provides valuable benefits to a product development project, starting with the initial requirements definition phase and continuing through support for a mature fielded product. By making use of simulation techniques at every stage of the process where they are appropriate, overall product quality can be enhanced while development cycle time and risks are reduced. In the remainder of this chapter, I will discuss the ways simulation can be used in each of the development phases shown in Figure 8.1 to enhance product quality, shorten the development cycle, and reduce project risk.

8.2 Requirements Definition

The requirements definition phase of the product development cycle is where the basic functionality of the product is determined. In a typical approach to requirements definition, the product requirements are determined by asking potential system users to identify the things they want and need the product to do. The product designers examine the resulting desired capabilities and identify those that they can realistically provide and those that they believe they cannot satisfy given the available development time and resources. There may be several iterations of this process between the customers and designers before a final agreed-upon list of requirements for the product is reached. The result of this phase of the project is a list of requirements along with the expected time and cost for the development effort.

Figure 8.1   Steps in the product development process.

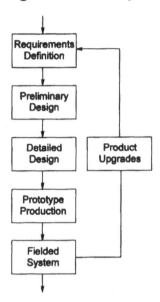

This approach to requirements definition frequently leads to difficulties because it requires the customers to identify the ways they will use the product before it exists. It is up to the imagination of the users to identify the potential ways of using the product. As fallible humans, the users frequently fail to include all the aspects of the desired design in their imaginary explorations of the product. This leads to missing or conflicting requirements.

The process of requirements validation is intended to identify and fix these problems. Requirements validation involves examination of a set of product requirements to determine if they are complete, consistent, and feasible for the planned development project. This process attempts to locate and repair any problems in the initial set of system requirements. Again, however, the people performing the requirements validation must use their imaginations to determine if the requirements are correct and appropriate. The validation process can help find some of the problems in the initial set of requirements, but it may not find all of them.

Simulation can be used to explore and validate requirements during this phase of the development cycle. As an example, suppose that we are planning to build a passenger airliner. Early in the requirements definition phase of the project, we could build a flexible high-level simulation of the aircraft performance. Rather than containing a full set of detailed models, this simulation would more likely include simplified models of gross effects and would perhaps include some rules of thumb for describing system performance. Simple linearized models may be used rather than detailed nonlinear models of system elements. We can use this simulation to examine the relationship among major system parameters such as passenger capacity, cargo capacity, and fuel economy.

By manipulating the parameters of this simulation, we can try out different aircraft configurations and identify which of the initial set of requirements can be met and which may be unrealistic. The use of simulation in this phase of the product development cycle does not replace the requirements definition and validation processes that would normally be used. Rather, it is an enhancement to those processes that enables more accurate specification of the system requirements and that has the potential to identify problems such as conflicts among the requirements. Locating these problems early in the product development cycle provides a powerful benefit that has the potential to avoid disastrous difficulties much later.

The use of simulation to support the requirements definition and validation phases means that simulation run results will be used to support decisions with great financial impact. It is critical that any simulation used for these purposes must have undergone a thorough verification, validation, and accreditation process (see Chapter 7) prior to its use for this purpose. Because this simulation is for a system that does not yet exist, it may be difficult to perform the simulation validation step. In some cases, it may be possible to perform validation using comparison data from a system that is similar to the product that is to be developed. In the case of the airliner example, perhaps another aircraft type exists with some similarities to the planned aircraft, and results from its flight tests are available. In this case, it may be possible to adjust the parameters of the simulation to match the existing aircraft and perform a validation against that set of data. After completing this procedure, the only difference in using this simulation for the new aircraft design will be the variations of the system parameters between the existing and new aircraft designs. In most situations, however, more changes to the models will be required than merely adjusting the parameters. However, the technique of validating a simulation for a new product using data from a similar existing product often provides great value.

It is important that the system parameter variations explored during simulation testing for requirements definition and validation realistically represent the potential system design variations under consideration. This places a responsibility on the simulation developers and users to ensure that the results they generate are valid. There should be an appropriate review process in place to analyze the inputs and outputs of simulation runs to ensure that they accurately reflect the intent of the planned tests.

For many kinds of products, simulations developed during this phase can give the users of the final product a chance to "try out" the product. Continuing with the airliner development project example, if a sufficiently sophisticated simulation of the aircraft is built during the requirements definition phase, it can be converted into an air crew trainer cockpit. This will give pilots a chance to "fly" the new aircraft. Feedback from this group can provide important input to the design of the external configuration, control system, and other features of the aircraft. The alternative approach of building a prototype aircraft and performing test flights to gather this type of information is obviously a vastly more expensive and time-consuming approach to achieve similar results.

The benefits realized by using simulation in the requirements definition and validation phases of product development can be summarized as reductions of project risk. Risk is reduced because the requirements have been tested and because users have seen how a system that implements the requirements will perform. This reduction of risk means that there is a lessened chance of unpleasant surprises later in the development cycle when the cost in time and money to deal with those surprises will be much higher.

8.3 Preliminary Design

During the preliminary design phase of the product development cycle, simulations can provide essential information concerning high-level design trade-offs. Simulations used in the preliminary design phase may be enhanced versions of those used during requirements definition. The early simulations used in requirements definition tend to be relatively simple and are focused on the gross behavior of the system. Those simplified models must be enhanced or replaced with higher fidelity versions for use in preliminary design.

If the simulation used in the requirements definition phase employed an architecture suitable for expansion and model upgrades, it should be a minor task to incorporate new versions of models as they become available. As the design process proceeds, new versions of system component models and of the external environment will be developed in the normal course of engineering work. Models that include nonlinear effects such as backlash, friction, and limiting will replace simple linear models. As these more complex models are integrated into the system simulation, it will be necessary to perform regression testing to verify correct system behavior and to identify the sources of any system performance difficulties that arise from the use of the new models. The verification process that was used during initial development must continue as new models are integrated into the simulation. Each time a model is replaced with a newer version, there must be a verification phase that ensures the correctness of the model implementation and of its integration with the rest of the simulation.

Often, the integration of higher fidelity models will indicate problem areas in the system design that simplified engineering analysis techniques fail to uncover. This is because there are often interactions between the nonlinear behaviors of different elements of the system that those techniques overlook. A simulation that grows in detail as the system design becomes more clearly defined allows the designers to analyze interactions among the system components and overall system behavior at an early phase of the development process.

The system simulation can also find use as an experimental tool, where the system designers try out a variety of potential design variations in a search for an optimal solution. The relative simplicity of implementing and modifying models is preferable to the alternative approach of building a variety of prototype system components to gather similar information. As always, the techniques of configuration management and careful verification must be employed to ensure that the results of simulation tests are meaningful. This is particularly important when a variety of model implementations are to be tested. The goal of configuration management must always be kept in mind: It must be possible to identify all model versions that went into a simulation run, as well as the complete set of input data for each run. This information is crucial when questions arise about the results at a later time.

Often, high-fidelity models in the simulation have high-frequency effects or for other reasons take a very long time to execute. For example, it is conceivable that the inclusion of a high-fidelity model of one subsystem may increase the execution time of the overall simulation by a factor of 10. When this happens, it is often useful to maintain two or more different versions of that model in the simulation simultaneously. A user input parameter then selects which version of the model to execute on a particular run. This organization permits the use of the detailed, slow-running version of the model when the precise behavior of that subsystem is to be analyzed. When more approximate modeling of the subsystem is acceptable, it is often appropriate to use the simplified model, which may result in a significant speedup of the simulation execution. This may be particularly important when tests are performed that require a large number of runs, such as Monte Carlo testing. The inclusion of multiple versions of subsystem models in a simulation allows the user to make a trade-off between fidelity and execution time.

Effective use of simulation during the preliminary design phase results in a significant project risk reduction compared to an otherwise equivalent design process that does not use simulation. The simulation development effort requires additional work on the part of the product designers, but this additional investment pays off in many ways. The benefits of the simulation effort flow back to the designers as a verification of design correctness and the availability of a tool for performing "what-if" tests on potential design alternatives. The overall project benefits from the ability to integrate subsystem designs using a tool that can identify incompatibilities and performance limitations at the system level. By identifying problems early in the development process and verifying that subsystem designs work together properly, simulation will lead to a better preliminary product design with reduced project risk.

8.4 Detailed Design

The preliminary design phase discussed in the previous section involves high-level trade-offs in the product configuration. As an example, for a passenger aircraft design, these decisions would determine such things as the number of engines, the number of passengers and amount of cargo that could be carried, the wingspan, and so on. At the completion of the preliminary design phase, a broad outline exists of the design of the product, but a vast number of details must be clarified before production of a prototype can begin. This information is developed during the detailed design phase.

The inputs to the detailed design phase are the system requirements and the results of the preliminary design phase. Detailed design fills in the information needed to begin production of a product that meets the system requirements and is consistent with the preliminary design. A larger group of people is involved in the detailed design than in the preliminary design, and many of these people are experts in specialized areas. In the aircraft example, aerodynamicists will be concerned with the precise exterior shape of the aircraft, and structural specialists will analyze the strength and shape of the internal components of the aircraft.

As their work proceeds, many of these specialists will develop engineering models of the system components that concern them. The aerodynamicists will perform wind tunnel testing of subscale models and develop a model of the aerodynamic forces and moments exerted on the aircraft under a variety of flight conditions. The control system designers use this model as an input to the design of the control system sensors, actuators, and algorithms. The control system design will also require mathematical models of the sensors and actuators it employs. The point of this discussion is that many of the models needed to develop a high-fidelity simulation of the entire system are available for "free" as part of the normal engineering design process. The development of the complete system simulation becomes an effort to coordinate the transfer of models from design specialists to simulation developers and then integrate those models into a simulation.

The system simulation developed during the requirements definition phase and refined during the preliminary design phase naturally serves as the basis for the simulation of the detailed system design. Using the same approach as in the preliminary design, specific models can be replaced with new models of higher fidelity as they become available. As the models grow in sophistication and complexity with each simulation revision, the execution speed will typically degrade. As discussed in the previous section, Preliminary Design, it is often a good idea to maintain multiple levels of fidelity for some simulation models. Judicious use of lower fidelity, faster executing models can make the use of Monte Carlo techniques more feasible during the detailed design phase.

It is possible to begin performing some degree of validation on the models as the detailed design proceeds. Even though prototype system hardware has not yet been developed, as design decisions are made about specific system components, validation data will frequently become available. For example, once specific vendors and part numbers are selected for the sensors and actuators to be used in the control system, manufacturer test data can be used to integrate models of those components into the simulation. Specific test sequences may have been performed on the hardware components that can be duplicated with the simulation model. Comparison of these data sets provides a degree of validation for the component model.

Manufacturers often provide information about component tolerances in a statistical format. For example, a minimum and maximum value for a parameter may be provided. The manufacturer guarantees only that the parameter will lie within the allowed range. To determine the effects of these parameter variations across a large number of components, the technique of Monte Carlo simulation is useful. First, we must identify all the parameter variations of concern and associate a probability distribution with each one. We then perform a large number of runs that randomly select values from these probability distributions for each parameter. After running a sufficient number of simulations in this manner, we will develop a good understanding of the system performance in response to expected parameter variations.

The Monte Carlo technique uses pseudorandom sampling techniques to identify system behavior variations in response to a large number of parameter changes. It is possible to use a deterministic approach to develop similar information. For example, one approach would be to perform a set of runs where all combinations of the minimum and maximum values for the parameters are tried. If there are N parameters to vary, this approach will result in 2^N simulation runs. Regardless of the method used, effective testing of a variety of parameter combinations will require a large number of simulation runs. Depending on the availability of computational resources and the speed of execution, it may be necessary to use simplified versions of some component models to complete these tests in a reasonable amount of time. The decision to use simplified models should be appreciated carefully and in consultation with the design experts in the area of the specific models that are to be simplified. It is also a good idea to perform some runs for comparison using the higher fidelity model that will not be used for the Monte Carlo runs. The results of this comparison between the simpler and more complex models should provide confidence that the use of the simplified model will not result in erroneous conclusions about system behavior in response to parameter variations.

During the detailed design phase, the experts in each discipline are available for model development and consultation activities. When these experts do not perform model development themselves, they can provide oversight and verification and validation support to others who develop and test the models. It is common in design and development organizations for experts in specific areas to move from project to project as work becomes available. When the detailed design phase of a project has been completed, these experts are likely to move on to other projects and become less available to provide support for model development and verification and validation work. Consequently, it is important to make effective use of their expertise during the time that it is available.

The simulation developed during the detailed design phase will be a detailed, high-fidelity representation of the intended performance of the system. Using this simulation, it is possible to perform a wide variety of studies to determine system behavior under nominal and extreme conditions. The amount of validation that is possible during this phase of the project will be limited, so this fact must be kept in mind when analyzing the results of simulation tests. Although there will be caveats associated with the results of tests performed with this simulation, it is still an extremely valuable tool for the entire development project. Analysis techniques other than simulation are used during the design process, and it is important that the results support those from the other analyses. Agreement between these disparate sources of information will provide assurance of the correctness of the design. Disagreement between the simulation and the other sources of information will indicate the possibility of errors or oversimplification in at least one of the approaches.

8.5 Prototype Development and Testing

When the detailed design of the system has been substantially completed, the development of prototype system hardware will begin. Initially, this may involve a limited number of subsystems, but in many cases, a complete system prototype is eventually built. For some types of products, the prototype may actually be the final delivered system. For example, a one-off space vehicle development project may go directly from design to production with minimal need for prototype development.

During the prototype development phase, it is common practice to develop an HIL simulation. In development environments where this has not been done in the past, it is worthwhile to consider performing HIL simulation for new projects because of the substantial benefits it provides. In one program that experienced a catastrophic failure, an HIL simulation of the system would have readily identified the problem.

On June 4th, 1996, the maiden flight of the Ariane 5 launcher experienced a problem that caused the rocket to veer off course, break up, and explode [1]. The source of the problem was traced to the inertial navigation system (INS), which is used to determine the position and orientation of the launcher during its flight. The sensors of an INS consisted of three accelerometers and three gyroscopes, oriented so that an accelerometer measures linear motion along each orthogonal body axis and a gyroscope measures the rotational motion about that axis. The INS computer used techniques similar to those discussed in Section 2.5.2 to determine the position, velocity, angular orientation, and rotation rates of the launcher for use in guidance computations.

In this case, the specific problem occurred when the INS computer attempted to convert a 64-bit floating point number to a 16-bit signed integer. This conversion failed because the floating point number had a value greater than could be represented in a 16-bit integer. This resulted in the generation of an exception, which was not handled in a meaningful way. The exception caused the INS computer to report that it had failed and it began transmitting diagnostic information to the primary guidance computer. The guidance computer attempted to interpret this data as valid INS information, which resulted in the loss of control of the launcher. The design of the Ariane 5 launcher included dual redundant INS systems that would automatically switch to the backup unit if the active unit failed. In this case, the redundancy provided no relief because both units experienced the same failure at almost the same time.

It turned out that the source of the problem was in embedded code that performed alignment computations that were only required prior to launch for the Ariane 5. Portions of the source code for the Ariane 5 INS computers were reused from the Ariane 4 system, where this function was intentionally enabled after launch. The specific variable that caused the overflow and exception was the launcher horizontal velocity, representing its velocity across the ground. The Ariane 5 system had a much higher horizontal velocity during the early phase of flight than the Ariane 4, which is why the overflow never occurred with the Ariane 4 system.

The failure review board that analyzed this accident made a number of recommendations. The first was the obvious suggestion that software functions should not run during flight when they are not needed. The second recommendation was as follows:

Prepare a test facility including as much real equipment as technically feasible, inject realistic input data, and perform complete, closed-loop, system testing. Complete simulations must take place before any mission. A high test coverage has to be obtained [1].

This is a concise description of an HIL simulation. Clearly, this type of testing was not done with the Ariane 5 INS computer system prior to its first flight. It is just as clear that if an HIL simulation had been developed using the actual INS computers and software, this problem would have been apparent the first time a launch simulation was run.

The developers of the Ariane 5 INS hardware and software were not careless people. Even when using the best available software development practices, it is not possible to eliminate all bugs from delivered code. That is why the hardware and the code must be tested using a variety of approaches. HIL simulation is a particularly effective method for testing embedded software because it operates on the actual hardware of the embedded system in a realistic environment.

It is not necessary to wait for the delivery of a complete system prototype before beginning HIL simulation testing when we can test subsystems in isolation. For example, a particular sensor or actuator can be connected to a real-time simulation to enable testing of its performance under realistic conditions.

Development of an HIL simulation proceeds naturally from the high-fidelity system simulation that comes out of the detailed design phase. The critical requirement for the HIL simulation that is not present in the previous simulation versions is that it must be a real-time application. Depending on the particular models and the dynamics of the simulated system, this may entail optimizations and simplifications to the models that represent the system. If the simulation cannot run in real time on the available computing resources, a suggested approach for implementing modifications is listed below. This assumes that the desired fidelity of each model has been identified for use in HIL simulation applications. Overly complex models should be avoided if they do not significantly enhance the quality of the results from the HIL simulation.

1. Perform optimizations to the models that do not alter the model results. For example, use a more efficient algorithm for table interpolations or move code from the real-time portion of a model that is only needed once during initialization.

2. Look into the possibility of procuring a faster processor for the real-time simulation, or split the simulation across multiple processors running in parallel. Take care that delays are not inadvertently introduced between components of the system that are modeled on different processors.

3. Identify simpler, faster executing versions of particular models that will permit the system to execute in real time. This option should be avoided whenever possible if it results in the use of models that are excessively simplified. On the other hand, the use of simplified models may be the only way to perform a real-time HIL simulation. The trade-offs necessary to enable real-time operation should be considered carefully when designing the HIL simulation and when analyzing its results.

In addition to the requirement that the simulation execute fast enough for real-time operation, it must satisfy additional requirements in order to serve as an acceptable HIL simulation. One of the most important requirements for an HIL simulation is that the I/O operations must occur reliably at the appropriate times. As a result of this requirement, HIL simulations are usually implemented within real-time operating systems or with the use of dedicated real-time kernels. The software environments provided by general-purpose operating systems do not give the degree of determinism required by high-performance simulations.

At this point, we will assume that the system simulation produced during detailed design has been modified for real-time operation and implemented on a computer with suitable I/O devices and a real-time software environment. This is the full system simulation, so we can compare its results to the results of the non-real-time simulation. This approach allows verification of the HIL simulation implementation before integrating any of the system hardware with it. You should perform verification of the real-time simulation across a variety of test scenarios that exercise all modes of system behavior. In particular, we should examine the effects of any simplifications and optimizations that were performed on the models to enable real-time operation. Any variances from the behavior of the non-real-time simulation using its highest fidelity models should be noted and incorporated into the analysis of future results from the HIL simulation.

Once verification of the real-time simulation has been completed, we can integrate the prototype system hardware as prototypes become available. Often the prototypes will be valuable, one-of-a-kind items that must not be damaged during simulation operations. To protect these prototypes, it may be wise to install hardware protection, such as limit switches and overcurrent protection. Additionally, it is often necessary to provide a variety of protection methods in the simulation software. When triggered, each of these protection mechanisms typically causes the simulation to shut down in an orderly manner and report the specific problem to the operator.

Following the implementation of the hardware and software interfaces for a specific system hardware component, an orderly integration test phase should be performed. This may begin with a set of ridealong tests (see Section 4.9) to confirm that the I/O interfaces to the system hardware are working correctly and the hardware is behaving as expected. This step is followed by closed-loop tests, with the prototype hardware operating in conjunction with the simulation. Each time a new element of system hardware is integrated with the simulation, a verification test series should be performed to confirm that the subsystem is behaving as expected under all modes of operation. This testing provides a degree of validation for the models of the prototype hardware because the results of runs with the actual hardware can be compared to identical test scenarios that were run with a software model of the hardware.

Various elements of the embedded system hardware are candidates for incorporation into an HIL simulation. Often, the most critical element to include in an HIL simulation is the embedded processor and its associated software. For many types of embedded systems, a large fraction of the overall system complexity lies in the software for the embedded processor. As a result, HIL testing of the processor provides the highest payoff in terms of its ability to thoroughly test system functionality and reduce project risk. In addition, many types of embedded systems include complex hardware elements, such as radar systems, hydraulic systems, and mechanical transmissions. It is often cost effective to develop an HIL simulation that incorporates these system components as well. The cost of an HIL testing facility that exercises these complex systems may be high, but it often costs much less than alternative test approaches that do not provide the ongoing value of an HIL simulation.

The cost of an HIL simulation that only incorporates the embedded processor and its software may be quite low relative to the test capability it provides. The hardware for this simulation facility consists of a computer with a set of real-time I/O devices plus the embedded processor and its embedded I/O devices. It is necessary to interface the two computers with each other through their I/O signals and to operate the simulation computer in real time so that it behaves in a realistic manner as seen by the embedded computer.

It should be a goal for the HIL simulation implementation that the embedded software does not require any modifications or the selection of special modes for use in the simulation environment. It may be tempting to use a test mode of operation for the embedded processor that allows signals to be more easily injected or monitored for HIL simulation testing. However, this approach will always leave doubts about the validity of results because it does not run the embedded software in the same manner as in actual operation. Similarly, it may seem like a minor thing to modify the embedded software to bypass a check of some kind that is difficult to perform in an HIL environment. In this case, the embedded software in the HIL simulation does not match the software in the actual system, which creates another set of doubts about the value of HIL simulation results. Ideally, it should be possible to run the embedded software in the HIL simulation in exactly the same manner that it runs in an equivalent test of the actual system.

The integration of the prototype hardware into the HIL simulation environment, followed by verification and partial validation of the resulting system simulation provides a powerful tool that is useful in many ways to the entire development project. The most obvious use for the HIL simulation is to provide a proving ground for the embedded software as it matures. The detection of a serious software problem, such as the Ariane 5 problem discussed previously, often will more than pay for the entire simulation effort.

Because an HIL simulation operates in a laboratory environment with a significant degree of protection for prototype hardware systems, it is possible to use the simulation as an experimental tool in developing the embedded software. This approach allows the embedded software developers to try out a variety of algorithms in attempting to optimally solve a particular development problem. The thorough testing possible in the HIL simulation provides a high degree of confidence that the strong points and weak points of each alternative algorithm have been identified.

HIL simulation also is useful under conditions that cannot be attempted during system tests for safety or cost reasons. An example of such a situation would be a test of an aircraft in a stall condition at a very low altitude. Such a test might be unacceptably risky to perform in a flight test, but in an HIL simulation, there would be no risk to the hardware or to the pilots. When performing tests such as these that are outside the envelope of actual system testing, we must take care to justify that the verification and validation of the simulation support its use in the desired operational regime. In the example of the low-altitude aircraft stall, we would have to demonstrate the ability of the simulation to accurately model the behavior of the aircraft in a stall and to model any effects related to the low altitude.

Another potential use for the HIL simulation is the testing of sensors and actuators used in the embedded system. These items can be tested by directly interfacing them to the HIL simulation computer, or they may be tested in conjunction with other system hardware components such as the embedded processor. If these components are sufficiently complex, it may make sense to use an HIL simulation as part of an acceptance test for each item as it comes off the production line. Assuming that the HIL simulation consists of a computer system and a set of I/O devices running the simulation software, it should be fairly inexpensive to build multiple copies of the simulation computer hardware. If this is the case, the engineering group might use one copy of the HIL simulation while other copies are used in the factory.

Similarly, an HIL simulation could serve as the basis for a complete embedded system test set. A system test set normally performs a large number of low-level component tests to detect and diagnose problems. These test sets usually have some capability to perform more complex test sequences that exercise the components of the system as an interacting group. As these tests execute, the test set monitors system behavior and verifies that it remains within acceptable limits. This monitoring typically takes the form of checking parameters for limit violations and other simple tests for proper behavior.

By integrating an HIL simulation with the standard capabilities of a system test set, we can test the system much more thoroughly as it operates under realistic conditions. HIL simulation does not replace the lower level testing capabilities of the test set; rather, it augments those capabilities so that, overall, the set provides a much more thorough and complete test. With this configuration, the test sequence typically begins with low-level component tests followed by intermediate-complexity system tests and finishes with a set of HIL simulation test scenarios.

Problems identified during the low-level test phase should be easy to diagnose because those tests are usually performed on a single component at a time. Failures of the intermediate-complexity tests may be more difficult to diagnose because they may be the result of subtle interactions between components. Problems detected during HIL simulation tests may be even more difficult to diagnose for similar reasons. The difficulty of diagnosing these system-level problems should not be a deterrent to thorough testing, however. It is generally easier to solve these problems in the laboratory environment of the HIL simulation where the problem is more likely to be repeatable and the effects of system modifications can be readily determined. In comparison, attempts to fix system problems identified during full system tests (such as aircraft flight tests) normally require a great deal more work to analyze and repair. This is because it is more difficult to diagnose the problem from the limited amount of system test data available, and additional system tests must be performed to verify the correctness of the solution following its implementation.

Effective application of HIL simulation techniques can provide many benefits during the prototype development phase of a complex embedded product. For example, system components can be tested in an HIL simulation before they are integrated into the system prototype. The primary beneficiary of the HIL simulation effort, however, is often the embedded software development process. The ability to test the embedded software in a realistically simulated operational environment is a tremendous benefit that leads to early identification of problems and to higher overall software quality. The HIL simulation is also useful for testing the behavior of the system in extreme situations that would not be attempted during system tests because of the risks to equipment or people. Finally, the HIL simulation can find use as part of a factory test set that enables thorough testing of products as they come off the assembly line or as a readiness check after maintenance or repairs.

8.6 Product Upgrades

System simulations, in particular HIL simulations, provide excellent facilities for testing proposed upgrades to embedded systems. Probably the most common change made to complex embedded systems is a change to the software. Anan HIL HIL simulation provides an environment for testing software changes easily and thoroughly.

If the system software change does not affect any of the interfaces between the HIL simulation computer and the embedded hardware that operates in the HIL environment, preparation for testing easy. All that is required is to load the software upgrade into the embedded processor before testing begins. However, in cases like this, it is also a good idea to perform some regression testing in addition to testing the new capabilities provided by the software change. The regression tests should be carefully selected to verify that any functionality affected by the software change is still correct. It is also a good idea to perform a suite of regression tests under various operating conditions to verify that basic system performance remains acceptable. As always, when regression testing, it is preferable to automate the test execution and results analysis as much as possible. This minimizes the amount of work required and tends to increase the amount testing performed, which is always helpful for ensuring product quality.

As upgrades are implemented in the embedded software, tests to verify the new functionality should be incorporated into the regression test suite. This enables regression testing to identify whether future changes to the software degrade the new capabilities. In addition, these added tests will indicate if the new capability is inadvertently removed from a future software build.

Changes to the system hardware require additional effort to include in the HIL simulation. These changes may be corrections to flaws in the original design or they may provide additional product capabilities. Either way, it is usually necessary to modify the simulation software, hardware, or both to reflect the changes in the product design.

If a change is limited to portions of the system that are modeled in the HIL simulation software, it may be necessary to modify only the models for those system elements to implement the change. If the change affects the hardware interfaces between the simulation computer and the system hardware, it will be necessary to change the HIL simulation hardware configuration. Often, this task requires the integration of a new I/O interface. In addition to any computer hardware changes, it will be necessary to implement any new models or changes to existing models required by the altered hardware configuration. In addition, software must be implemented to perform I/O using the new interface.

System changes can create significant complications for the HIL simulation effort if it is necessary to maintain a capability for performing tests on multiple system hardware configurations. For instance, this situation can occur when the HIL simulation provides support for testing fielded versions of a system and for testing new system versions with design upgrades. When operating in this type of environment, it is necessary to make decisions about how to maintain the various simulation software and hardware configurations that must be supported simultaneously.

A basic decision is whether to use a single HIL simulation facility to support the different system hardware configurations or to dedicate a test facility to each configuration. If the hardware differences are minor, it often makes the most sense to use a single facility, whereas extensive hardware differences tend to make separate HIL simulations a more reasonable approach. Another factor involved in the single- or multiple-HIL simulation question is the planned workload for tests of the different system configurations. If there is sufficient testing planned for each configuration, it may make sense to develop multiple HIL simulations, even in cases where the hardware differences between the configurations would not indicate that choice.

In cases where the same HIL simulation is used for multiple hardware configurations, any changes to the computer and its associated devices that must be made when switching from one system configuration to another must be clearly documented. Ideally, the software should perform checks to ensure that the computer hardware configuration matches that of the system hardware under test. Each time the hardware configuration is changed, a set of low-level tests should be performed to make sure that all the components of the newly selected configuration are operational. If possible, this testing should take place before the first simulation attempt with the system hardware following the configuration change. This will reduce the risk of damaging the hardware as a result of improper cable connections or other problems.

Another decision that must be made when developing the ability to test multiple system configurations is whether to maintain a single simulation application or to maintain a separate one for each system configuration. It is usually best to maintain a single version for the multiple system configurations whenever possible. This is because it is easier to make improvements to the models if these things only need to be done in one place. If enhancements and error fixes must be repeated across multiple simulations, the chance of error will be increased and the testing requirements will multiply. It is also likely that the implementation of the changes in all affected simulations will not occur because of time constraints. For these reasons, it is best to use a single simulation for multiple product configurations whenever possible.

In the software, the selection of the system configuration can be performed using variables that identify the configuration in use. To guard against errors, checks should be carried out where possible to confirm that the actual system hardware in use matches the settings of the configuration variables. Based on the values of the variables, the simulation can execute the proper versions of the models for the chosen configuration.

Changes to the models that are independent of the system configuration only need to be made one time. Verification and validation of these model changes can be performed using one or more of the system configurations as appropriate. Sometimes it is possible to verify and validate a model adequately using just one of the possible system configurations. This is feasible when the interaction of the model with the system hardware does not vary significantly among the different system configurations. In some cases, however, it is necessary to test model changes in all of the various supported configurations. The amount of testing required depends on the specifics of the model changes and their interactions with the various system configurations.

Sometimes the best approach is to implement a complete new HIL simulation when a significant product upgrade is planned. One potential reason for developing a new simulation is to make use of improved hardware and software technology for the simulation computer system. If the HIL simulation currently in use is several years old, the improved computing and

I/O capability of newer processors and bus technologies may justify the implementation of a completely new simulation. Similarly, if the current HIL simulation software is implemented in a dated language (FORTRAN, perhaps), it may make sense to start a new simulation development effort from scratch using a modern block diagram-oriented tool. The potential improvements in modeling fidelity and I/O speed that newer computer systems provide, as well as the improvements in developer productivity possible from using more sophisticated software tools, may produce a significant return on the investment in developing a new simulation.

The support of complex embedded products during the upgrade process is a major application for HIL simulation. Although the need for testing may be less intense than during the development cycle, there are still many benefits to be gained from the use of simulation. HIL simulation provides a tool for performing regression testing to ensure that modifications do not degrade previously existing system capabilities. In addition, the simulation can be an experimental tool that allows system developers to try out a variety of methods to fix a particular problem or to provide a product enhancement. With adequate planning, one or more HIL simulations can provide support for a variety of product hardware configurations throughout their life cycles.

8.7 Fielded System Problem Analysis

Occasionally, problems arise with systems after they have been delivered to users. When a serious difficulty manifests itself in a fielded system, it is imperative to quickly diagnose the problem and develop a solution. There may be severe financial consequences if, for example, an airline is unable to fly a particular aircraft model because it has been grounded due to a problem in its design. In this situation, there will be intense pressure on the engineering staff to rapidly develop an acceptable solution. In addition to devising a solution to the problem, sufficient testing must be performed to confirm that the solution is effective under all conditions and that the solution does not degrade the existing capabilities of the product.

Simulation can provide critical support in this situation. The first step, if the cause of the problem is not immediately obvious, is to replicate the problem using the simulation. Depending on the specifics of the problem, it may be possible to perform this step using the non-real-time system simulation. If the problem involves the software of the embedded system, however, the best place to attempt replication of the problem is usually the HIL simulation. If data is available from an incident where the problem occurred, this information can be used to set up a scenario to duplicate the problem situation. If the problem depends on factors that are not implemented in the simulation, it may be necessary to add new models or to enhance existing models to include these factors. As always, when adding new models or modifying existing models, it is necessary to perform adequate verification and validation to ensure the accuracy of the resulting simulation. Even (especially!) under the pressure of the need for a quick problem resolution, it is important to avoid skipping the necessary steps of verification and validation. It may be acceptable to perform limited verification and validation of new models and of enhancements to old models as long as this testing includes the regions involving the problem situation. In this case, the limitations of the model testing should be prominently documented and care should be taken that the models are not used outside the region where verification and validation have been successfully completed.

On some occasions, after the simulated scenario has been matched to the problem situation as well as possible, the problem still cannot be readily duplicated in the simulation. This may be caused by differences between the simulated system and the actual system that experienced the problem. Improved models may be required in this case. An inability to reproduce a problem in the simulation could also be due to variations between the simulated scenario and the actual scenario. If error in the simulated scenario is a possibility, it may be a good idea to perform Monte Carlo variations about the expected problem scenario. This approach attempts to identify a particular combination of parameter values that cause the problem to appear. Even in the case where the problem can be duplicated in the simulation, it may be valuable to perform some Monte Carlo variations of parameters to identify the range of values over which the problem appears.

Given the conditions under which the problem appears have been identified in a simulation environment, it should be possible to replicate the problem behavior at will. If the appearance of the problem is intermittent when tested in a simulation environment, this indicates that the system itself is behaving in an intermittent manner or that the simulation has intermittent behavior. In the laboratory environment of an HIL simulation, it should be possible to connect test equipment to the system hardware and simulation computer hardware to detect and isolate the source of such intermittent behavior.

With the ability to reliably replicate the problem in a simulation environment, it is often a straightforward matter to isolate the source of the problem and test proposed fixes. When testing a potential problem fix, the test results must verify that the fix works properly under all conditions where the problem is expected to occur. In addition, there must be sufficient regression testing to ensure that the fix does not degrade previously existing system capabilities. The regression testing must include all areas of system behavior that the fix has the potential of affecting. As a check for unanticipated interactions, regression testing should also include a variety of tests under scenarios where the fix is not expected to have an effect.

Using simulation as a tool for supporting the resolution of problems in fielded systems implies that the simulation project must continue in operation over the life cycle of the product. This results in a significant financial investment that will be cost effective if the simulation is valuable in solving system problems after delivery to customers. The benefits that accrue from use of simulation in resolving these problems begin with the obvious financial benefits of quickly providing robust solutions to problems customers experience with delivered products. Other, less quantitative, benefits result from quickly and effectively solving system problems. These benefits include higher perceived quality on the part of the customers and the increased likelihood of future business. In a competitive marketplace, one of the factors that customers will surely examine when contemplating future purchases is the record of a vendor on resolving problems with previously purchased products.

Exercises

1. Imagine that you are a program manager for a new rocket launch system that will deliver satellite payloads to low earth orbit. Develop the outline of a plan for how you will use simulation from the very beginning of the project through post-flight data analysis. Identify the specific types of simulations to be used in each phase and the applications for each simulation.

2. You are working on a project to develop an embedded product that uses a complex ASIC (application-specific integrated circuit). The ASIC designers have a simulation of the circuit in a hardware design language that precisely models all aspects of its behavior, but this model runs 1,000 times slower than real-time speed. You also have a model of the external behavior of the ASIC in C that can run at real-time speeds. Naturally, the C version of the ASIC model is highly simplified in comparison to the hardware design language version. Identify situations in the product development phases shown in Figure 8.1 where each of these models would be appropriate for use in a complete system simulation.

3. Identify a set of cost–benefit trade-offs that can be applied to the selection of appropriate applications for simulation in a product development project. Be sure to include a means for balancing the costs of simulation against the potential benefits of avoiding low-probability/high-cost events such as the crash of a prototype aircraft during testing.

4. Using a product development process with which you are familiar, perform a brainstorming session to identify as many applications as possible of simulation to that development process. Include even silly and clearly inappropriate ideas in the list of simulation applications that you generate.

5. Go through the list of simulation applications that you developed in the previous exercise and see if any of them represent new approaches that you had not previously considered. Select the most promising untried approach and perform a cost–benefit analysis to determine if it would provide a meaningful benefit to the product development process.

6. Working with an embedded product with which you are familiar, develop a top-level troubleshooting tool selection flowchart. The chart should begin with the identification of an arbitrary problem with the product and end with the selection of an appropriate tool for problem diagnosis. The possible tool choices are the non-real-time system simulation, the HIL system simulation, or a prototype test system (such as a flight test aircraft). The decision points in the flowchart should ask questions that lead to the identification of the tool that is most likely to provide significant findings in the shortest time. Consider the strengths and weaknesses of each category of tool in terms of its ability to duplicate the problem and the speed of test development and execution.

References

[1] Lions, Jacques-Louis, *Ariane 5, Flight 501 Failure, Report of the Inquiry Board.* http://www.esrin.esa.it/htdocs/tidc/Press/Press96/ariane5rep.html, Paris, 1996.

Chapter 9

Simulation Tools

This chapter provides an overview of several software tools for simulation model development, non-real-time simulation, and HIL simulation. Like other software products, these tools undergo constant development and improvement, while introducing the occasional bug along the way. However, most of these products have been on the market for several years, which means that the basics of the user interface and the approach to simulation development used by each one can be expected to remain relatively unchanged for some time to come.

I will demonstrate each of the simulation tools by implementing and executing a model of the same example dynamic system. The modeling of the same simulated system with each tool will help to clarify differences between the tools and will also permit a comparison of results.

The system chosen for implementation on each of these tools is the turntable driven by a DC motor described in Section 6.6.1. In this system, a digital control system receives a position command input signal and drives the turntable to the desired position using the turntable's measured position as a feedback signal. This system includes a number of nonlinear effects that require accurate modeling. Although this is a relatively small simulation, it exercises a number of features that are important in simulating complex dynamic systems.

Accurate simulation of this system requires support for combined discrete-time and continuous-time simulations, as well as nonlinear elements such as the DAC and the position encoder. It is also helpful to have supoort for elements represented in the form of transfer functions in the s and z domains. In addition, there is a transport delay in the digital controller that must be modeled properly. By implementing this system model, we can get a feeling for the basic capabilities provided by the library of components provided with each tool. Of course, the list of elements in this example system is limited in comparison to those needed to model a truly complex system. Depending on the particular application areas involved with a simulation (hydraulics or gear trains, for example), a potential purchaser should carefully examine the completeness of the component library included with a particular tool.

For each simulation tool examined in this chapter, the example system model was implemented and a simulation run was performed to collect data for plotting and comparison with the other tools. The discrete-time controller was always run with a 0.005-second frame time, and the continuous system simulation was always run with a 0.001-second frame time. The Runge-Kutta fourth-order integration method was used in all cases. One would hope that, by implementing the same models and using the same integration algorithm and update rates, the answers would agree between the various simulation tools. As you shall see, this did not always turn out to be the case.

The simulation tools discussed below include only those that provide capabilities for modeling the system elements needed to model the turntable and its controller. Other tools on the market that do not support capabilities needed for this simulation (such as combined discrete and continuous system simulation) were not considered for inclusion in this comparison.

In addition to the collection of system simulation tools, this chapter also includes information about other products that perform simulation functions, such as specialized model development tools and real-time HIL simulation computers. Although it is necessary to limit the number of different tools that can be discussed, this chapter provides a general idea of the capabilities of modern simulation development products.

9.1 Desired Simulation Tool Characteristics

This section provides a brief list of the capabilities that a robust simulation development and execution tool should provide, in the author's opinion. Each user will undoubtedly have various preferences in these areas. This listing might be a starting point that a developer can use to help select an appropriate set of simulation tools for a given project.

Graphical model development   This capability usually takes the form of block diagram modeling, although other types of graphical models (such as bond graphs) are available.

Equation modeling   As nice as the graphical modeling capability is for many types of model development, there are still many cases where the most concise way to specify the behavior of a simulation model is through a set of equations.

Real-time HIL simulation   There should be a reasonable path to enable the use of models developed in a non-real-time environment to be compiled and executed in a real-time HIL simulation environment.

An extensive library of low-level simulation models   The more models that are provided with the simulation tool, the less time the developer will need to spend on simulation development. This assumes that the models provided in the library are relevant and useful for the simulation developer.

Support for vector/matrix operations Many simulation computations rely on, or can make effective use of, vector and matrix operations. A robust simulation development environment should make it easy to implement models in terms of vectors and matrices.

The ability to create data displays while the simulation is running The quickest way to gain an understanding of the behavior of a simulated system is to examine plots or animations of its behavior as it is executing. In cases where there are obvious problems, the user can stop the simulation run, fix the problem, and start a new run.

The ability to store simulation data and create plots and tabulations offline In situations where multiple simulation runs are performed as a group, it is necessary to be able to save simulation output data from each run for later analysis and display.

9.2 Dynamic System Simulation Products

This section contains descriptions of a variety of dynamic system simulation development and execution tools. The tools are mainly of the block diagram form, but C++ is included as an alternative and as a base-level case for comparison against the other tools. Among the block diagram tools, there exists a wide range of prices and capabilities. Many of the tools have add-on products available at additional cost for performing tasks such as HIL simulation or generating embedded C code for execution on an arbitrary target computer system. This discussion will deal primarily with the basic simulation development, execution, and data analysis tools. Where additional capabilities are available, they will be noted.

9.2.1 C++/DSSL

This simulation development environment represents the low end of the spectrum of dynamic system simulation tools. This toolset consists of a C++ compiler and the Dynamic System Simulation Library (DSSL) source code. A variety of C++ compilers is available, with prices as low as free. This represents a minimum-cost route to a modest simulation capability.

There are two primary reasons why one might use these tools to implement a system simulation: There is no money available to purchase a more expensive and complete simulation development tool, or the developer requires the ability to control every aspect of the implementation of the simulation.

The first reason for using C++ (or another general-purpose programming language) for simulation development, cost, is rarely valid. It will probably take a significant amount of additional effort to implement and verify a simulation in C++ than it would with a block diagram-based tool. In most cases, the cost of this additional work will rapidly overtake the savings from avoiding the purchase of a more appropriate tool. The cost argument for using a general-purpose language is only meaningful if the project is very small and the simulation development work is a correspondingly minor task.

The second reason, a requirement for complete implementation control, may be valid under some conditions. If the system contains components that are not included in libraries provided with simulation tools, the developer will have to develop some models from scratch anyway. Another possible justification for requiring this level of control is the existence of a large quantity of existing code that models some or all of the system to be simulated. Although this argument may be valid in some cases, most simulation development tools discussed below provide a capability for interfacing with models written in arbitrary programming languages. The possibility of integrating legacy models into a modern simulation tool using this approach should be investigated before starting a new project using out-of-date simulation products and methods.

Listing 9.1 is a simulation of the turntable and its digital controller. The digital controller is implemented as a C++ function that is called at the 5-millisecond update interval. The main simulation loop uses fourth-order Runge-Kutta integration for the continuous states and has a 1-millisecond update interval. The program writes an output file named Turntable.csv as it executes. This file is in the comma-separated variable format, which Microsoft® Excel can read directly. Figures 9.1 and 9.2 are plots of the simulation output variables displayed within Excel.

DSSL and C++ provide a simple capability for implementing continuous and combined discrete and continuous system simulations. Comparison of Listing 9.1 with the block diagrams in the following sections demonstrates the magnitude of additional work required to implement a system simulation using this approach. In most cases, the prudent simulation developer will select one of the tools discussed below rather than C++ or another general-purpose programming language.

Listing 9.1 C++/DSSL turntable simulation.

```
// Turntable simulation
// Simulate a turntable driven by a DC motor with a digital controller.
// Jim Ledin                                        December, 2000


#include <dssl.h>


#include <cstdio>
#include <cmath>

double digital_controller(double pos_cmd, double pos_measurement)
{
    static StateList state_list;
    static State<> controller_num(&state_list, State<>::DISCRETE),
        controller_deriv(&state_list, State<>::DISCRETE);

    // Compute the output error
    double error = pos_cmd - pos_measurement;

    // Derivative estimate transfer function. Note that I set the ".der" member
    // of the State variables here even though these are really the "next frame"
    // values for the DISCRETE update method.
```

```
    controller_num.der = error;
    controller_deriv.der = 20*(error - controller_num) + 0.9048*controller_deriv;

    // The control law
    double dac_input = 100*error + 50*controller_deriv;

    // Simulate the DAC output
    double dac_output = limit(quantize(dac_input, 20.0/256),
        -10.0, 10.0-20.0/256);

    // Update difference equations
    state_list.Integrate();

    return dac_output;
}

int main()
{
    static StateList state_list;
    static State<> motor_accel(&state_list, State<>::RK4),
        motor_vel(&state_list, State<>::RK4),
        motor_pos(&state_list, State<>::RK4);

    // Constants for frame times and multiframe ratio
    const double step_time = 0.001, controller_step_time = 0.005,
        end_time = 10.0;
    const int frame_ratio = nint(controller_step_time / step_time);

    // Constants related to model parameters
    const double J = 0.012;        // kg-m^2
    const double b = 0.2;          // N-m-sec
    const double K = 0.013;        // N-m/amp
    const double R = 1.1;          // ohms
    const double L = 0.6;          // Henries

    // Compute the transfer function coefficients
    const double a2 = J*L;
    const double a1 = J*R + b*L;
    const double a0 = b*R + K*K;
```

```
// Other constants
const double pi = 4*atan(1);
const double pos_cmd = 1;          // radians

state_list.Initialize(step_time);

// Open the output file
FILE* iov = fopen("Turntable.csv", "w");
if (!iov)
{
    printf("Unable to open output file 'Turntable.csv'");
    return 1;
}

fprintf(iov, "time, dac_output, motor_pos\n");
int frame_count = 0;
for(;;)
{
    // Measure the position of the turntable using the position encoder
    double pos_measurement = quantize(double(motor_pos), 2*pi/4096);

    // Execute the digital controller at the proper time interval
    static double dac_output = 0;
    if (frame_count % frame_ratio == 0)
        dac_output = digital_controller(pos_cmd, pos_measurement);

    // Simulate the 4 millisecond computational delay of the controller
    double delayed_dac_output = transport_delay<double, 4>(dac_output);

    // Write output to file
    fprintf(iov, "%6.3lf, %9.6lf, %9.6lf\n", state_list.Time(),
        delayed_dac_output,  double(motor_pos));

    // Model the motor transfer function
    motor_accel.der = (K*delayed_dac_output - a1*motor_accel -
        a0*motor_vel) / a2;
    motor_vel.der = motor_accel;
    motor_pos.der = motor_vel;
```

```
    // Perform end-of-frame activities
    if (state_list.Time() >= end_time)
        break;

    state_list.Integrate();
    frame_count++;
}

    fclose(iov);
    return 0;
}
```

Figure 9.1 Plot of DAC output signal in Excel.

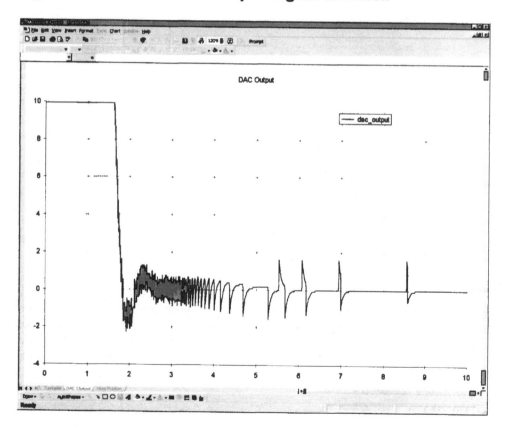

Figure 9.2   Plot of motor position in Excel.

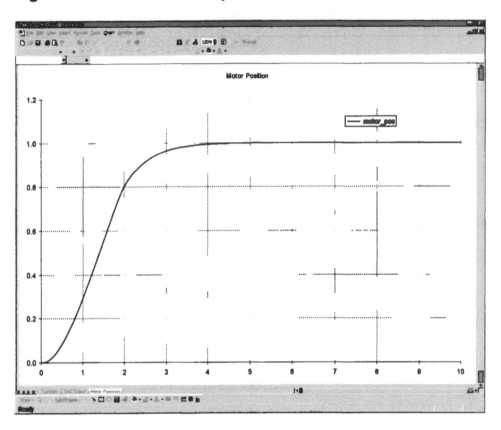

Product Name and Version

The DSSL library v1.0 and Microsoft Visual C++ compiler v6.0 were used in this example. Microsoft Excel 97 SR-1 produced the plots.

Pricing

The DSSL library is included with this book. C++ compilers are available from a variety of sources; some are free. The GNU compiler is one example of a free compiler. It has been ported to a wide variety of architectures, and extensive support is available through newsgroups. For more information, see http://www.gnu.org/gnulist/production/gcc.html.

Supported Platforms

The DSSL library runs on any system for which a standard C++ compiler is available.

Capabilities of Core Product

The DSSL library provides facilities for state variable integration using a variety of integration algorithms, vector and matrix operations, random number generation, multidimensional function interpolation, and a limited number of library functions, such as quantization and transport delay.

Add-On Products

The Real-Time Simulation Protocol (RTSP) discussed in Chapter 5 can be used with DSSL to create distributed simulations.

Product Availability

DSSL v1.0 is included on the CD-ROM that comes with this book. C++ compilers are available from a variety of sources.

Installation and Licensing

See the CD-ROM contents for licensing information. Installation consists of copying the files from the included CD-ROM to a disk drive.

Development of an HIL Simulation

Because DSSL is provided in source form and uses only standard C++ capabilities, it can be ported to any system that provides a standard C++ compiler. Integration of real-time I/O devices involves calling the driver routines from C++ as needed to initialize and access the particular devices.

Development of a Distributed Simulation

The RTSP software is described in Chapter 5 and is included on the enclosed CD-ROM. This protocol is implemented in standard C++ and can be used in any operating environment that provides networking with support for the `select` C/C++ library function.

Technical Support

Send questions about DSSL and RTSP to `jim@ledin.com`. Questions about a C++ compiler should be directed to the compiler vendor.

Available Integration Methods

All the DSSL integration algorithms are of the fixed-step type as follows.

Euler   The forward Euler integration algorithm. Because of its low accuracy, its use should normally be avoided except when performing experimental comparisons of different algorithms.

Adams-Bashforth 2nd order   This is an explicit algorithm with second-order accuracy. It is a good choice for real-time simulations of systems with relatively smooth derivative functions.

Adams-Bashforth 3rd order   This is an explicit algorithm with third-order accuracy.

Adams-Bashforth 4th order This is an explicit algorithm with fourth-order accuracy.

Runge-Kutta 2nd order This algorithm provides second-order accuracy and good performance in the presence of discontinuities in the derivative function.

Runge-Kutta 4th order This algorithm provides fourth-order accuracy and good performance in the presence of discontinuities in the derivative function.

Supported I/O Devices

No I/O devices are directly supported. The available I/O devices depend on the capabilities provided by the compiler, operating system, and target system computer hardware.

Interchanging Simulations with Other Tools

No capability is provided to translate between DSSL and other simulation tools in either direction.

Sharing Simulations with Others

You may share simulations with others in source and executable form under the terms of the license information on the CD-ROM.

Support for Embedded Code Generation

No code generation capability is provided with DSSL. The code used to implement algorithms in a DSSL simulation is standard C++, so the same code can be implemented in an embedded application using the same algorithms. The algorithms used in DSSL are reasonably efficient, so they are suitable for implementation within an embedded product as well.

Support for Monte Carlo Simulation

No direct support is provided for Monte Carlo simulation. Implementation of this capability is up to the simulation developer.

Support for Data Analysis and Visualization

No support is provided. The example program in Listing 9.1 shows one way to store data during execution and use a separate tool (Excel, in this case) for post-run data analysis and plotting.

User Interface

The user interface for C++/DSSL is the C++ development and compilation environment selected by the user.

9.2.2 MATLAB/Simulink

MATLAB is a software tool from the MathWorks that provides a command-line environment and graphical tools to perform numerical analysis with emphasis on vector/matrix manipulations. MATLAB includes an extensive set of graphing tools for creating 2-D and 3-D plots. To use any of the other products available from the MathWorks, MATLAB is required as a basis.

Simulink is an add-on to MATLAB that provides the ability to develop and execute dynamic system simulations in a block diagram environment. Real Time Workshop is an add-on to Simulink that takes a simulation block diagram and generates equivalent C or Ada code suitable for use in an HIL simulation or in an embedded processor.

Figure 9.3 is the top-level Simulink block diagram of the example turntable system. The block in this figure labeled "Digital Controller" is a subsystem block. Subsystem blocks allow the Simulink user to develop hierarchical sets of diagrams to control complexity during simulation development. Subsystems can be nested to any level in much the same manner that function calls can be nested within other functions in a text-based programming language.

The contents of the "Digital Controller" subsystem block are shown in Figure 9.4. The blocks labeled "Zero-Order Hold1," "Zero-Order Hold2," and "Unit Delay" make this a discrete-time subsystem. Each of these blocks has a parameter associated with it that has been set to indicate 5-millisecond updates.

As Figures 9.3 and 9.4 indicate, Simulink provides blocks for the direct entry of transfer functions in the s and z domains. In addition, blocks are provided that model effects such as quantization, saturation, and transport delay. Many other types of blocks are included in the Simulink library. Additional special-purpose libraries of blocks are available as options from MathWorks at extra cost.

Figure 9.3   Simulink model of turntable system.

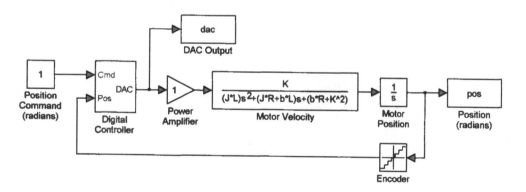

Figure 9.4   Simulink model of turntable controller.

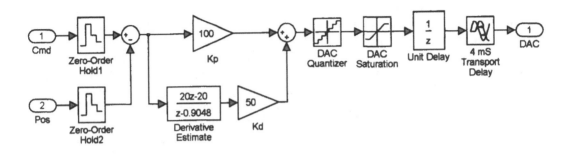

Figure 9.5   Simulink plot of DAC output signal.

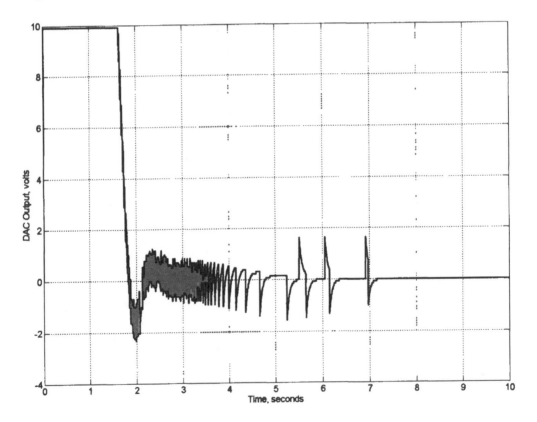

Figures 9.5 and 9.6 are plots of the output variables from a run of the Simulink turntable model. These results are close to those shown in Figures 9.1 and 9.2, but they do not agree exactly. The differences are minor and are probably related to different implementation techniques of the simulation algorithms. If this were an actual product development project, we

would want to determine the reason for the discrepancy between the simulations. This exercise is left to the reader.

Figure 9.6 Simulink plot of motor position.

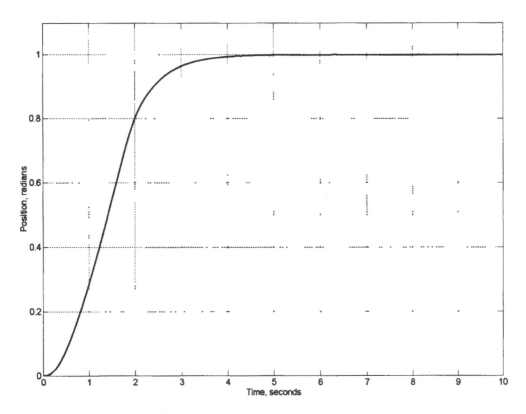

Product Name and Version

The products used in the example were MATLAB v6.0, Simulink v4.0, Stateflow v4.0, Real Time Workshop v4.0, Real Time Windows Target v2.0, and xPC Target v1.1.

Pricing

A variety of options are available for purchasing groups of MathWorks products in suites, which reduces the cost compared to purchasing individual products. The single-item costs for the products as of March 2001 are MATLAB: $1,900; Simulink: $2,800; Stateflow: $2,800; Real Time Workshop: $7,500; Real Time Windows Target: $2,000; and xPC Target: $4,000.

Supported Platforms

MATLAB and Simulink run on the following operating systems: AIX, Digital UNIX, HP-UX, HP-UX 10, HP-UX 11, IRIX, IRIX/IRIX64, Linux, Macintosh 68000, Open VMS, Power Macintosh, Solaris, SunOS 4, and Microsoft Windows.

Capabilities of Core Product

MATLAB is a command-line environment for manipulating, analyzing, and plotting data, with an emphasis on vector/matrix manipulation. Simulink is an add-on to MATLAB that provides a block diagram environment for developing and executing simulations. Simulink provides the ability to place "scopes" in a simulation that plot simulation results during execution. Simulink can also transfer simulation output data in the form of time histories to the MATLAB environment for further analysis and plotting.

Simulink comes with a library of blocks suitable for modeling dynamic systems. A variety of linear, nonlinear, continuous-time, and discrete-time blocks is included.

Add-On Products

A variety of toolboxes is available as add-ons to MATLAB, some of which provide additional library blocks for Simulink. For example, the Stateflow tool provides a Simulink block that encapsulates a state transition diagram. Some add-ons that are specific to Simulink are available which are called "blocksets" because they consist entirely of Simulink blocks. Some Simulink blocksets are listed below.

DSP (Digital Signal Processing) Blockset   The blocks in this blockset contain a variety of DSP-oriented algorithms for tasks such as digital filtering and signal estimation, and transforms, including the fast Fourier transform and the discrete cosine transform.

Fixed-Point Blockset   This blockset enables the implementation and execution of algorithms using fixed-point mathematics. This permits the Simulink simulation to accurately represent the behavior of the algorithm executing on a processor that uses fixed-point mathematical operations.

System Identification Blockset   The blocks in this blockset implement a variety of algorithms for developing linear models of dynamic systems from measured data.

Dials & Gauges Blockset   This blockset provides a variety of graphical input and output devices that can be placed directly in a Simulink diagram. The input and output devices are active when the simulation is executing.

Real Time Workshop is an add-on to Simulink that provides the ability to generate efficient C or Ada source code from Simulink models. The generated code can be compiled and executed on the Simulink host system or cross-compiled and downloaded to an embedded target system. Real Time Workshop provides a number of additional capabilities that are not part of typical system simulations, such as interrupt handling. The generated source code requires an operating system or real-time kernel to schedule its execution. Support for the VxWorks real-time operating system is provided with Real Time Workshop. Other supported execution environments include the Real Time Windows Target and xPC Target add-ons.

Real Time Windows Target is an add-on that enables Real Time Workshop-generated code to execute in real time in a Windows (95, 98, or NT 4.0) environment. The Real Time Windows Target software preempts the Windows operating system when necessary so that normal use of the computer can continue even while running a real-time simulation. Real

Time Windows Target supports a variety of I/O devices such as analog-to-digital converters, digital-to-analog converters, and digital I/O ports. A potential application of Real Time Windows Target is as the real-time simulation computer for an HIL simulation. The ability to execute the real-time simulation on the same system used for the simulation development and post-run data analysis greatly simplifies the entire process.

xPC Target is another add-on that provides a real-time execution environment for Real Time Workshop-generated code on standard PC hardware. This environment requires that a host computer running MATLAB and Simulink be connected to a target PC through a serial cable or network interface. xPC Target provides an execution environment that includes a real-time kernel and support for a variety of I/O devices. No additional real-time operating system is required. With another add-on called xPC Target Embedded Option, it is possible to deploy complete, embedded software systems that do not require a connection to a host system running Simulink.

Product Availability

See http://www.mathworks.com for complete product literature, documentation, pricing, and ordering information.

Installation and Licensing

Almost all MathWorks products are included on a single distribution CD. An unlocking code is provided to the customer that enables installation of only the products that have been purchased.

Development of an HIL Simulation

Development of an HIL simulation begins with the development of a non-real-time simulation of the elements of the dynamic system as well as the interactions between the system and its external environment. Usually, the non-real-time simulation includes models of the components that will be implemented in the HIL simulation using actual system hardware. This provides a variety of benefits, such as the ability to perform simulation runs without using the system hardware and the ability to perform HIL simulations in ridealong mode (see Section 4.9).

Using the non-real-time simulation as a basis, an HIL simulation is then developed. This step requires the addition of I/O device interfaces to pass signals to and from the system hardware. To maintain the ability to run simulations without the system hardware, switches must be placed in the block diagram to enable selection of either the software-only simulation mode or the HIL simulation mode.

Using Real Time Workshop, the simulation is translated to source code and compiled for a real-time environment such as Real Time Windows Target. The resulting simulation can then be executed in real time in conjunction with the system hardware.

Development of a Distributed Simulation

Simulink does not provide support for distributed simulation. This would require developing a software distrbuted simulation capability (for example, to the RTSP protocol discussed in Section 5.7) using the S-function interface. The S-Function interface is provided by Simulink to interface user-provided source code to Simulink block diagrams.

Technical Support

Complete online help is provided for all installed MathWorks products. Additional help is available on the MathWorks web site at http://www.mathworks.com. If this information does not resolve the problem, MathWorks application support engineers provide assistance via email and telephone calls, as long as the product is under maintenance. One year of maintenance is provided with the purchase of each product and additional maintenance is available for purchase on a yearly basis.

Available Integration Methods

A variety of fixed-step and variable-step integration methods is provided with Simulink. The selection of an appropriate algorithm for a particular problem depends on
- the stiffness of the simulated system,
- the accuracy required in the simulation results,
- the execution speed required for the simulation, and
- whether or not the simulation is a real-time application.

Real-time simulations generally require fixed-step integration algorithms. Non-real-time simulations usually execute most efficiently with variable-step algorithms, although sometimes the step size selection algorithm fails to function effectively and a fixed-step algorithm provides better results. The variable step algorithms are:

ode45 (Dormand-Prince)   This algorithm provides medium accuracy and works well on nonstiff problems.

ode23 (Bogacki-Shampine)   This algorithm provides lower accuracy than ode45 and works well on moderately stiff problems.

ode113s (Adams)   This algorithm can provide a high level of accuracy with reasonable efficiency on nonstiff problems if the error tolerance is sufficiently stringent.

ode15s (stiff/NDF)   This algorithm works well on stiff systems where ode45 executes slowly because of the stiffness.

ode23s (stiff/Mod. Rosenbrock)   This algorithm provides lower accuracy in solving stiff systems.

ode23t (mod. stiff/trapezoidal)   This algorithm is for moderately stiff systems and avoids numerical damping.

ode23tb (stiff/TR-BDF2)   This algorithm is good for low-accuracy solutions of stiff systems.

The fixed-step algorithms are as follows.

ode5 (Dormand-Prince)   This is a fixed-step version of ode45. It is a good general-purpose integration algorithm.

ode4 (Runge-Kutta)   This is the fourth-order Runge-Kutta integration algorithm. It provides good performance in the presence of discontinuities in the derivative function.

ode3 (Bogacki-Shampine)   This is a fixed-step version of ode23.

ode2 (Heun)   This is Heun's method, also known as the improved Euler method. It provides second-order accuracy.

ode1 (Euler)   This is the forward Euler integration algorithm. Because of its low accuracy, its use normally should be avoided, except when performing experimental comparisons of different algorithms.

Supported I/O Devices

Real Time Workshop and the add-ons Real Time Windows Target and xPC Target support dozens of I/O devices from a variety of vendors. See the MathWorks web site for a complete listing.

Interchanging Simulations with Other Tools

Simulink comes with a tool called SB2SL that translates MATRIX$_X$ SystemBuild (see Section 9.2.4) superblocks into Simulink diagrams. This tool translates most, but not all, of the block types available in SystemBuild into the equivalent Simulink blocks. SB2SL allows the user to select a SystemBuild superblock at any point in the simulation hierarchy for translation. The selected block and its contents are then translated into a Simulink model.

Simulink does not provide any tools for translating its model files into formats readable by other programs. However, the Simulink files are in ASCII format and the contents of these files are fully documented, so it may be possible to write a translator to another format.

Sharing Simulations with Others

There is no capability provided for distributing Simulink simulations to others who do not have their own copies of MATLAB and Simulink.

Support for Embedded Code Generation

Real Time Workshop provides the ability to generate C or Ada source code from Simulink diagrams. The code produced by Real Time Workshop is efficient and is intended to be used directly in embedded applications. The code generation activity performed by Real Time Workshop is highly configurable to match a variety of development and execution environments.

Support for Monte Carlo Simulation

There is no capability to perform sets of Monte Carlo simulation runs entirely within Simulink. However, it is possible to perform Monte Carlo simulation by controlling the simulation runs from the MATLAB environment.

The key to performing Monte Carlo runs with Simulink is to use MATLAB variables as parameters within the model — for example, where the "Motor Velocity" block (Figure 9.3) contains the MATLAB variables K, J, L, R, and b. It is then possible to set these variables to any desired value within MATLAB prior to starting a simulation run. Listing 9.2 shows the MATLAB commands required to perform a single simulation run with a specific set of parameter values.

Listing 9.2 MATLAB commands to set up and execute a simulation run.

```
J = 0.012
b = 0.2
K = 0.013
R = 1.1
L = 0.6


sim('Turntable')
```

To perform a set of Monte Carlo runs, it is necessary to place statements similar to Listing 9.2 inside a loop and set the value of each parameter by drawing a number from a probability distribution. The MATLAB script to perform the Monte Carlo run must also save the output data from each simulation run after it completes.

Support for Data Analysis and Visualization

Simulink provides a "Scope" block that can be placed in a diagram and connected to display one or more signals. As the simulation runs, each Scope displays a time plot of its input signal(s) in a separate window. Several other types of run-time displays are provided, such as a numerical display, an *x-y* plot, and a spectrum analyzer plot.

Simulink provides the ability to store time history data to a file or to the MATLAB workspace during simulation execution. Any number of files and MATLAB variables can be created in this manner. However, there is no provision for saving different runs in a Monte Carlo set to different filenames, so it is necessary to rename the files or otherwise store the data from each run before starting a new run.

MATLAB provides an extensive set of capabilities for manipulating and plotting data saved to files or to the MATLAB workspace during Simulink runs. Using MATLAB commands, it is possible to perform actions such as subtracting one signal from another (assuming both are sampled at the same time points), integrating a signal, and computing the discrete Fourier transform of a signal. Additional MATLAB commands are available for producing time plots, *x-y* plots, 3-D surface plots, and several other plot formats.

User Interface

The Simulink user interface conforms closely to the PC Windows conventions. The user places blocks in a diagram by dragging them from a palette and dropping them at the desired location. Blocks can be moved at any time by clicking and dragging. Clicking on the output port of one block and dragging to the input port of another block creates a connection, which displays as a solid line with an arrow indicating the direction of the signal flow. Clicking on a connecting line selects it and permits it to be moved or deleted.

A subsystem is a block that is placed in a diagram like any other. Double clicking the subsystem block opens a new Simulink diagram window that is identical to the original window, except that it is initially empty. Input and output port icons can be placed in the subsystem window to pass signals between the subsystem and the upper level diagram.

9.2.3 VisSim

VisSim is a block diagram-oriented tool for building dynamic system simulations, which is produced by Visual Solutions, Inc. In addition to the usual dynamic system simulation capabilities, VisSim provides several useful features such as the ability to solve implicit equations, perform global optimizations, and design digital filters. Add-ons are available for VisSim that perform frequency domain analysis, constrained optimization, C code generation, and HIL simulation.

VisSim provides the ability to integrate its operation with MATLAB and Mathcad. The MATLAB integration enables the transfer of variable values and linear system models between MATLAB and VisSim. In addition, a block can be placed into a VisSim simulation that contains an arbitrary MATLAB expression. This expression is passed to MATLAB for evaluation during the VisSim simulation execution.

Mathcad is a software tool from MathSoft (http://www.mathsoft.com) that performs symbolic and numerical mathematics in a worksheet environment. Mathcad displays mathematical expressions in a typeset, textbook-like format. The integration between VisSim and Mathcad allows the user to place blocks into a VisSim simulation that contain Mathcad expressions and to pass data between Mathcad and VisSim. It is also possible to control the execution of a VisSim simulation from Mathcad, which is useful for performing sets of Monte Carlo simulation runs.

VisSim includes a tool that translates Simulink models into equivalent VisSim Models. VisSim also includes a "viewer" program that enables the distribution of executable VisSim simulations to individuals who do not own copies of VisSim. The viewer program does not permit modifications to the simulation other than changing the values of block and simulation parameters.

Figures 9.7 and 9.8 show a VisSim simulation of the example turntable and controller simulation. As Figure 9.7 indicates, VisSim plots are placed directly into the simulation block diagram. During a simulation run, the plot y-axis autoscales to contain the full range of signal data on the plot.

Note that the plot of the DAC Output signal in Figure 9.7 displays an ongoing oscillation that is different from the results of the equivalent DSSL and Simulink simulations. The reason for this difference in behavior is not completely clear. As mentioned previously, the same integration methods and integration step sizes were used in all of these simulations.

The one known difference between the VisSim simulation and the other simulations of the turntable system in this chapter is the behavior of the VisSim quantization block. In the other simulations, the quantization function rounds the input value to select the nearest quantization step. VisSim, however, performs a truncation operation that selects the nearest quantization step that is less than the input signal. There is no option for rounding to the nearest step when using the VisSim quantization block.

Figure 9.7   VisSim model of turntable including plots of output signals.

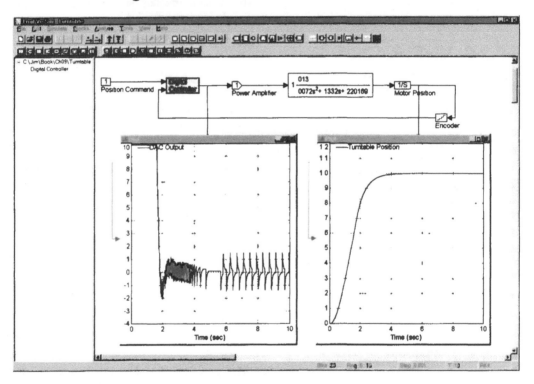

The compound block is used in VisSim to create a diagram hierarchy. In Figure 9.7, the "Digital Controller" block is a compound block. Figure 9.8 shows the contents of the compound block, which is displayed by clicking on the block name in the list of diagrams in the leftmost pane. Inputs to the compound block appear as incoming arrows at the diagram left edge and outputs are outgoing arrows at the right edge. This subsystem is specified to have discrete-time behavior through the use of the sample-and-hold block (labeled "S/H") and the discrete-time transfer function block, both of which are set to operate with a 5-millisecond update interval.

Figure 9.8 VisSim model of digital controller.

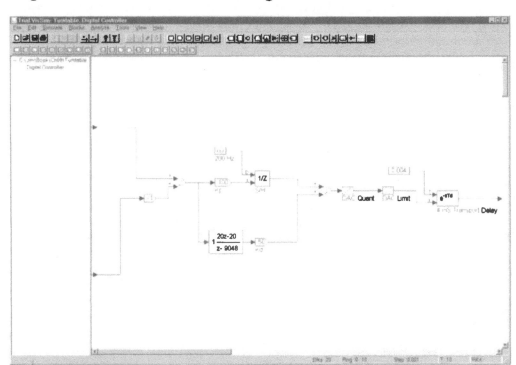

Product Name and Version

The product tested was Trial VisSim v4.0e. The trial version can be downloaded from the VisSim web site. It is identical to the purchased version, except that the license will expire after an evaluation period.

Pricing

The prices as of March 2001 for VisSim products are: Professional VisSim: $2,495; VisSim/Analyze: $995; VisSim/OptimizePRO: $995; and VisSim/Real-TimePRO: $1,995. An entry-level product called VisSim Personal Edition costs $495. VisSim Personal Edition is the same as Professional VisSim except that the number of blocks in a simulation is limited to 100, and custom block creation is not available.

Supported Platforms

VisSim runs on Microsoft Windows 95, 98, and NT 4.0.

Capabilities of Core Product

VisSim is a block diagram-oriented tool for modeling and simulation of continuous, discrete, multirate, and combined discrete–continuous systems. It allows complex models to be represented as a hierarchy of diagrams and comes with a library of over 100 blocks.

VisSim provides capabilities for solving implicit equations, performing constrained optimization, and designing digital filters. It includes facilities for transferring data between VisSim and other applications using ActiveX and dynamic data exchange (DDE). These communication techniques are supported by a variety of applications in the Microsoft Windows operating environments. VisSim also provides a mechanism to directly access MATLAB (if it is installed on the same computer) to perform matrix calculations and transfer data between the two applications.

Add-on Products

VisSim/Analyze performs linearization of a nonlinear system model about a given operating point. This linear model can be used to perform frequency domain analysis. Several forms of analysis are available: pole-zero analysis, root locus analysis, Bode analysis, and Nyquist stability analysis.

VisSim/OptimizePRO determines optimal values of design parameters subject to user-specified constraints. An example application for this tool is the selection of controller gains that optimize some function, such as minimum rise time or minimum steady-state error.

VisSim/C-Code generates standard ANSI C source code from a VisSim diagram. The generated code is suitable for use in an HIL simulation or as source code for an embedded controller.

VisSim/Real-TimePRO provides the ability to run a VisSim simulation in real time on a PC and to communicate with system hardware through I/O boards installed in the PC. A variety of I/O boards from different manufacturers is supported. The I/O board capabilities include analog and digital input and output, counter-timers, quadrature encoders, and many others.

Product Availability

See `http://www.vissim.com` for complete product literature, documentation, pricing, and ordering information.

Installation and Licensing

The demonstration version of VisSim can be downloaded from the VisSim web site. Installation is a straightforward procedure. It is necessary to get a license code from VisSim to enable the software for the evaluation period.

Development of an HIL Simulation

An HIL simulation usually starts out as a non-real-time VisSim simulation of the system hardware. To convert the simulation to a real-time HIL simulation, the VisSim/Real-TimePRO product is required, along with a set of supported I/O boards that meets the needs of the application. To produce the real-time simulation,

1. select the I/O cards to be used from the list of supported cards and
2. in the VisSim diagram, connect the I/O cards to the appropriate simulation signals using the real-time `dataIn` and `dataOut` blocks.

As discussed previously, it is a good idea when implementing an HIL simulation based on a non-real-time simulation to maintain the ability to run the simulation without system hardware. This allows the simulation to run in a software-only mode and permits use of the ridealong mode to support hardware integration and debugging.

Development of a Distributed Simulation

VisSim does not provide a capability for distributed simulation, other than perhaps through the use of ActiveX communication. This approach does not appear to be useful for real-time simulation of systems with frame times measured in milliseconds.

VisSim allows the user to develop and add new blocks to the list of available blocks when building simulations. It would be possible to add a distributed simulation capability using this mechanism.

Technical Support

Technical support is available from online help files, the VisSim web site, and the VisSim technical support staff via email or telephone.

Available Integration Methods

VisSim provides the following variable-step integration methods.

Adaptive Runge-Kutta 5th order   This method obtains fifth-order accuracy and provides good performance in the presence of discontinuities in the derivative function.

Adaptive Bulirsh-Stoer   This algorithm uses rational polynomials to extrapolate a final estimate using a series of substeps. It is very accurate when the derivative function is smooth.

VisSim provides the following fixed-step integration methods.

Euler   This is the forward Euler integration algorithm. Because of its low accuracy, its use is to be avoided except when performing experimental comparisons of different algorithms.

Trapezoidal   This is an implicit second-order algorithm.

Runge-Kutta 2nd order   This algorithm estimates the derivative at the step midpoint and uses that estimate to integrate over the entire step. It provides good performance in the presence of discontinuities in the derivative function and has second-order accuracy.

Runge-Kutta 4th order   This is the fourth-order Runge-Kutta integration algorithm. It provides good performance in the presence of discontinuities in the derivative function and has fourth-order accuracy.

Backward Euler   This algorithm is good for simulating stiff systems but has low accuracy because it is a first-order method.

Supported I/O Devices

VisSim/Real-TimePRO supports a variety of I/O boards from Advantech, Analog Devices, ComputerBoards, DataTranslation, MetraByte, National Instruments, Precision Micro Dynamics, and Technology 80. A complete list of supported boards is a available on the VisSim web site.

Interchanging Simulations with Other Tools

The VisSim/Simulink Translator converts Simulink block diagrams into VisSim block diagrams. It does not support all of the available Simulink blocks. If the Simulink diagram includes MATLAB statements, the VisSim block diagram will attempt to use MATLAB to execute those statements.

No capability is provided to translate VisSim diagrams into other formats. VisSim diagram files are composed of ASCII characters, but the file format does not appear to be documented publicly.

Sharing Simulations with Others

VisSim includes VisSim Viewer, which is a run-time simulation engine for VisSim block diagrams. VisSim Viewer does not allow the modification of block diagrams other than to change the values of block and simulation parameters. With this tool, it is possible to hide the contents of compound blocks from users to maintain the security of proprietary models.

VisSim users can distribute up to 100 copies of VisSim Viewer without paying royalties. VisSim Viewer runs on the same platforms as VisSim.

Support for Embedded Code Generation

VisSim/C-Code generates ANSI C source code from VisSim diagrams. The source code can be compiled for any target processor for which an ANSI C compiler is available. The VisSim/C-Code product can produce executable applications on MS-DOS, Windows 98, Windows NT, and Windows 2000. The compiled simulation can be executed from the VisSim environment just like a normal simulation. The major difference in this configuration is that the compiled simulation runs up to 10 times faster.

To build executable applications for platforms other than the MS-DOS and Windows operating systems requires the purchase of the Support Library Source Code from Visual Solutions. This library provides ANSI C source code to implement the capabilities of the VisSim blocks and the simulation engine.

Support for Monte Carlo Simulation

VisSim does not provide a useful Monte Carlo simulation capability. Integrating a VisSim simulation with Mathcad provides a way to set up and execute Monte Carlo run sets. However, this approach requires that the simulation developer and user purchase and learn to use both products. It also requires that upgrades to each product be coordinated to maintain compatibility with each other and with the features used in the system simulation.

Support for Data Analysis and Visualization

Data generated during a simulation run can be displayed directly in VisSim in the form of time plots, strip charts, histograms, bar graphs, meters, and simple animation. The animation capability allows bitmap pictures (using the .BMP file format) to move around the screen and change size and allows the selection of a picture from a group of pictures based on simulation signal values during execution. It is also possible to draw straight lines in an animated manner so that the lines move as the simulation executes.

User Interface

The VisSim user interface conforms closely to the PC Windows conventions. The user places a block in a diagram by selecting one on a menu and then clicking in the diagram at the desired location. Blocks can be moved at any time by clicking and dragging. Clicking on the output port of one block and dragging to the input port of another block creates a connection, which displays as a solid line with an arrow indicating the direction of signal flow.

It is not possible to change the position of the interconnecting lines between blocks other than by moving the blocks or connecting a wirePositioner between the two blocks. A wirePositioner is a "handle" that allows the wire to be moved around. This is a somewhat more tedious approach to arranging diagrams than that provided by Simulink.

A compound block is created by selecting a group of blocks in a diagram and then selecting Create Compound Block on the Edit menu. A dialog prompt appears, requesting the name of the block. This creates a compound block that has the same number of input and output signals as the group of blocks that were selected. The name of the compound block will appear in the tree list showing the diagram hierarchy at the left side of the VisSim window.

Right-clicking on a compound block in the diagram or left-clicking on a compound block name in the hierarchy window causes that subsystem to occupy the main editing window. When editing a compound block, input signals appear at the left side of the editing window and output signals appear at the right side of the window.

9.2.4 MATRIX$_X$ SystemBuild

MATRIX$_X$, from Wind River Systems, Inc., is a family of products that supports dynamic system simulation and embedded software development. MATRIX$_X$ includes the following products.

Xmath is a command-line numerical computation environment that provides data analysis, visualization, and scripting capabilities.

SystemBuild is a graphical block diagram tool for developing and executing dynamic system simulations. SystemBuild is the core element of the MATRIX$_X$ product family.

AutoCode translates SystemBuild block diagrams into C or Ada source code for implementation as an HIL simulation or as embedded system software.

RealSim provides an integrated hardware and software environment for executing SystemBuild HIL simulations.

Documentlt   extracts information from SystemBuild block diagrams and generates format-ted documentation files. The primary use for this tool is to create software specification and design documents in formats that comply with industry or company standards.

Xmath and SystemBuild are the minimum MATRIX$_X$ products required for simulation development and execution. DocumentIt, AutoCode, and RealSim are optional, but RealSim requires AutoCode.

The relationship between Xmath and SystemBuild is similar to that of MATLAB and Simulink. Xmath and SystemBuild run concurrently, which allows simultaneous editing of SystemBuild models, analysis of results in Xmath, and display of data in 2-D and 3-D plots. Xmath has a built-in programming language with an extensive set of capabilities, including support for complex numbers, linear algebra, and statistics. Xmath has programming access to the SystemBuild environment for changing parameter values and performing simulation runs, which supports Monte Carlo simulation.

Figure 9.9 is a SystemBuild diagram of the turntable system. SystemBuild uses the name "superblock" to identify a block that contains a group of blocks. The top-level diagram in a SystemBuild model is a superblock. Each superblock in a diagram is defined to be continuous time or discrete time. In the turntable simulation, the top-level superblock is continuous time and the Digital Controller superblock (Figure 9.10) is discrete time.

In Figure 9.9, the output of the Digital Controller block and the output of the Motor Position block are specified as outputs of the superblock, indicated by the flags with "1" and "2" near each block output. At the end of a simulation run, SystemBuild can plot the output signals from the top-level superblock, as shown in Figure 9.11 (page 266).

Figure 9.9   SystemBuild diagram of turntable system.

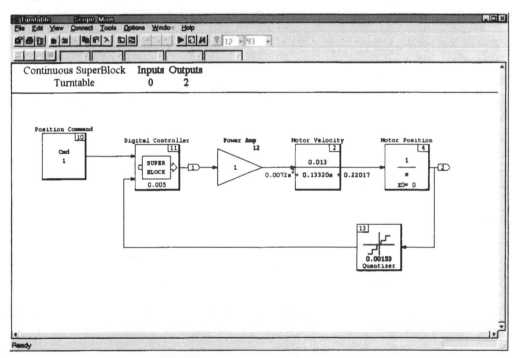

Figure 9.10 SystemBuild diagram of digital controller.

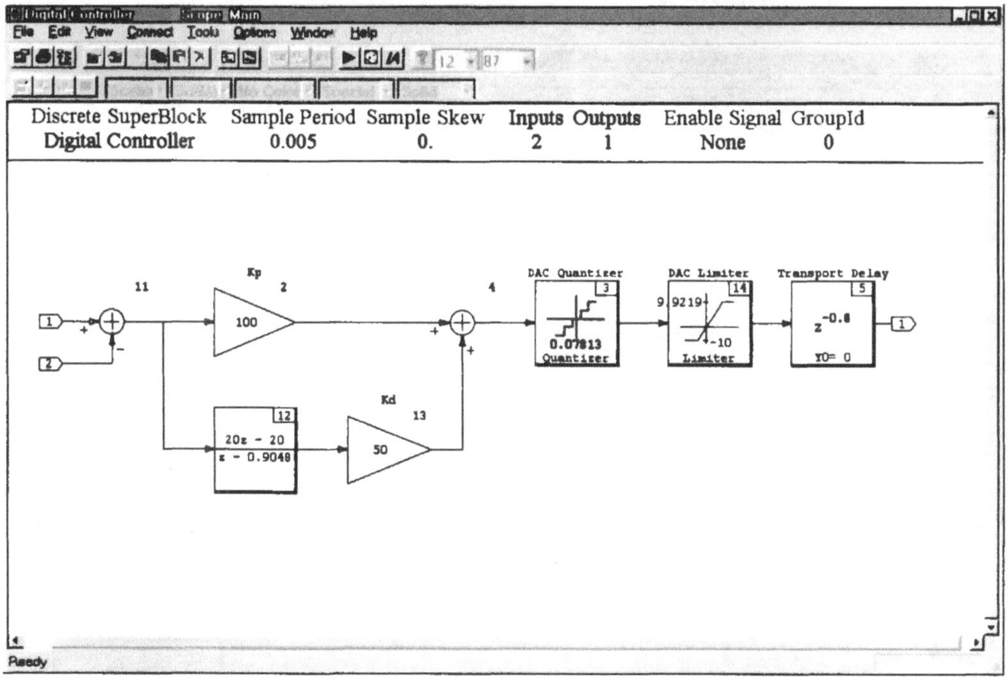

Product Name and Version

The products examined were the MATRIX$_X$ Product Family v62.2 build 62mx1118 (Win32) for Windows NT v4.0.

Pricing

At the time of this writing, the distribution rights for the MATRIX$_X$ Product Family had recently been acquired by MathWorks. According to information provided on the Math-Works web site (at http://www.mathworks.com/company/pressroom/windriver_faq.shtml), "Wind River and The MathWorks do not anticipate doing any further development work on MATRIX$_X$." In addition, the RealSim hardware products are being discontinued. I was unable to obtain price information for the MATRIX$_X$ Product Family from either Wind River or MathWorks.

Supported Platforms

MATRIX$_X$ is supported on DEC True 64UNIX 4.0D; SunOS 4.1.4; Sun Solaris 2.6 and 2.7; Microsoft Windows 95, 98, and NT 4.0; HP-UX 10.2; and SGI IRIX 6.5.4.

Figure 9.11 Xmath plots of DAC output signal and motor position.

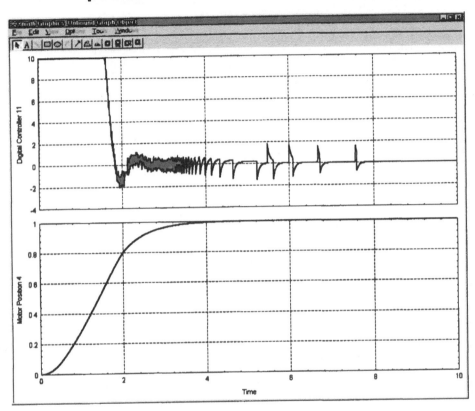

Capabilities of Core Product

Xmath is a command-line environment that is required for any of the other products in the MATRIX$_X$ family. Xmath provides capabilities for mathematical data analysis, visualization, and scripting that complement the abilities of SystemBuild. This environment is used for analysis and plotting of SystemBuild simulation results. Xmath and SystemBuild run concurrently, so both environments are available when developing simulations and analyzing results. Xmath uses the MathScript programming language, which is similar in syntax and capabilities to the MATLAB programming language.

SystemBuild is an add-on to the Xmath product that provides the ability to develop and execute simulations of dynamic systems in a block diagram environment. SystemBuild provides the usual capabilities for developing models of complex systems using a hierarchy of block diagrams and has several other useful features. One of these is the ability to perform linearization and frequency response analysis of a system represented in a block diagram. Another is support for fixed-point arithmetic, which allows accurate simulation of an algorithm as it will execute on a fixed-point target processor.

The SystemBuild block palette includes blocks that provide for conditional execution, repetitive execution, and ordered execution of other blocks and superblocks. The conditional execution capability maps to the `if-then-else` statements, and the repetitive execution capability maps to the `while` statements of a text-based programming language.

Add-On Products

AutoCode is a highly customizable tool for generating source code in C or Ada from System-Build models. The generated code is suitable for use as a fast-executing version of the simulation, as the basis for a RealSim HIL simulation, or as embedded code on a target processor.

DocumentIt uses a SystemBuild model as its input and creates design documentation automatically. It uses templates to format and select the contents of documents. The tool can create output files in FrameMaker, InterLeaf, Microsoft Word, or ASCII format, and it can generate documentation that adheres to the MIL-STD 2167A standard, among others. The document templates can be modified to meet a variety of formatting requirements.

RealSim is a hardware/software environment for executing SystemBuild models in a real-time HIL environment. The hardware component is called a RealSim controller, which is a real-time computer system based on the 80486, Pentium, Pentium Pro, or Pentium II. The RealSim/104 hardware series is designed for desktop and laboratory use. It is based on the PC/104 architecture and supports standard PC/104 I/O boards and Industry Pack modules. RealSim also supports standard PC computer hardware. In addition, there is a high-end hardware configuration based on the VME backplane and Motorola PowerPC 604 processors called the AC-1000 series. The AC-1000 series is intended for simulation computation and I/O applications requiring maximum performance.

Several additional products are available as add-ons to Xmath and to SystemBuild. The Xmath add-ons include modules for control system design, optimization, and system identification. SystemBuild add-ons include products such as fuzzy logic and neural network blocks.

Product Availability

The product home page is at `http://www.windriver.com/products/html/matrixx.html`.

Installation and Licensing

MATRIX$_X$ is installed from a set of two CDs. One CD contains all the application software and online help. The online help system requires that Netscape be installed, which may be a bit disconcerting for Internet Explorer users. The second CD contains Adobe PDF versions of the full documentation set. A one-month free evaluation period is available on request. The license system is based on the FLEXlm product.

Development of an HIL Simulation

As with the other tools discussed here, HIL simulation development begins with a software-only simulation of the system and its interactions with its environment. This requires the Xmath and SystemBuild products for simulation development and execution. To implement an HIL simulation requires the additional tools AutoCode and RealSim, as well as suitable real-time computing and I/O hardware. The real-time computing hardware can be a standard PC, an AC-104 series system, or an AC-1000 series system.

The host computer must be connected to the real-time computer through Ethernet. The MATRIX$_X$ software uses this connection for downloading the software to the real-time computer, controlling its operation, and logging data and error information during execution. If the real-time computer system has multiple processors, the SystemBuild model can be distributed across those processors by assigning subsystems to specific processors for execution.

Simulation development, code generation, compilation, downloading, and execution of the real-time software all occur in the Xmath/SystemBuild environment. Beginning with the software-only version of the simulation, it is necessary to modify the SystemBuild diagrams to include inputs and outputs for hardware signals. It is also necessary to add selection logic that allows switching between a software-only simulation mode and an HIL simulation mode that uses external hardware inputs. A Hardware Connection Editor is used to connect the input and output signals to specific I/O device channels.

After these steps are finished, it is necessary to generate source code, compile the simulation, and download it to the real-time computer. Control of the real-time computer during execution is managed from the Xmath environment, as is data collection, storage, and analysis.

Development of a Distributed Simulation

$MATRIX_X$ provides no direct support for distributed simulation. Complete documentation is included for interfacing user-provided code to SystemBuild models, so it would be possible to implement a distributed simulation using the RTSP protocol, for example.

Technical Support

Support is available through the $MATRIX_X$ web site, by email, or by calling a toll-free telephone number.

Available Integration Methods

SystemBuild provides the following variable-step integration methods.

Variable-Step Kutta-Merson   This algorithm uses the fixed-step Kutta-Merson (see below) method as its basis and estimates the local truncation error to adjust the integration step size. This is the default method used by SystemBuild.

Differential Algebraic Stiff System Solver (DASSL)   This algorithm works well with stiff systems and with systems described by differential algebraic equations. A differential algebraic equation contains a derivative that is defined by an implicit equation, rather than in the explicit manner assumed in this book. In the case of implicit systems, the DASSL algorithm uses a Newton-Raphson search to determine the value of the derivative at each step.

Variable-Step Adams-Bashforth-Moulton   This is a variable-step, variable-order predictor–corrector method that works well with smooth derivative functions. It is usually more computationally efficient than any of the other SystemBuild algorithms.

Over-Determined Differential Algebraic Stiff System Solver (ODASSL)   This algorithm is useful for solving systems of differential or differential algebraic equations involving constraints. These are problems where there are more equations than state variables. Problems involving multibody motion such as vehicles, satellites, and robots often lead to systems of equations in this form.

Gear's Method   This method is designed to handle a mixture of ordinary differential equations, nonlinear equations, and linear equations. Gear's method is a variable-step, variable-order, predictor–corrector algorithm. It is a good algorithm for implicit systems and is appropriate in cases where ODASSL fails to provide reasonable results. Gear's method is several times slower than ODASSL, however.

SystemBuild provides the following fixed-step integration methods.

Euler   This is the forward Euler method. Because of its low accuracy, its use normally should be avoided except when performing experimental comparisons of different algorithms.

Runge-Kutta 2nd order   This algorithm estimates the derivative at the step midpoint and uses that estimate to integrate over the entire step. It provides good performance in the presence of discontinuities in the derivative function and has second-order accuracy.

Runge-Kutta 4th order   This is the fourth-order Runge-Kutta integration algorithm. It provides good performance in the presence of discontinuities in the derivative function and has fourth-order accuracy.

Fixed-Step Kutta-Merson   This algorithm improves on the Runge-Kutta fourth-order algorithm by adding a fifth step that improves accuracy at a small cost in execution speed.

QuickSim   This is an explicit algorithm intended for solving stiff systems. It has good efficiency and good accuracy for linear and nearly linear systems.

Supported I/O Devices

The available I/O devices depend on the particular configuration of real-time computing hardware in use. A variety of analog, digital, and specialized I/O interfaces is available for each of the supported RealSim hardware configurations.

Interchanging Simulations with Other Tools

No support is provided for translating from other model formats to SystemBuild or from SystemBuild to other formats.

Sharing Simulations with Others

There is no supported method of sharing a SystemBuild simulation with a user that does not have a licensed copy of SystemBuild.

Support for Embedded Code Generation

The AutoCode product provides the ability to generate C or Ada source code from SystemBuild block diagrams for embedded processors. The code generation process is highly customizable and can be tailored for a variety of specialized purposes.

The generated source code includes the following components, which provide a complete real-time kernel and application implementation.

- A manager/scheduler component that performs I/O operations for the application program and generates the dispatch list of subsystems that are ready for execution. This component can be tailored by modifying or rewriting the provided real-time scheduler.

- A dispatcher component that enables the execution of subsystems at appropriate times according to a prioritized list. This component can be tailored to customize the dispatching logic.

- Subsystem components implement the SystemBuild block diagram models.

- I/O routines provide input data to the real-time application and collect output data from the application.

- A timer interrupt handler invokes the real-time scheduler at appropriate intervals. This routine must be tailored to function properly in the target execution environment.

- A background function that performs non-time-critical idle-time tasks such as self-testing or display updates. This function can be tailored to implement any desired activity, as long as it is interruptible.

The AutoCode code generation procedure can be performed from the Xmath command line, from SystemBuild, or from the operating system command line. It is usually easiest to generate code from within SystemBuild.

AutoCode supports the Euler, Runge-Kutta second-order, Runge-Kutta fourth-order, and fixed-step Kutta-Merson integration algorithms. It does not support operations that lead to indeterminate execution times, such as algebraic loops (which require the iterative solution of an implicit equation) and zero-crossing location. AutoCode also does not support complex numbers.

The default target for AutoCode is a simulation that runs on the host computer and saves its output in a data file that can be loaded into Xmath for analysis. AutoCode can also generate code to run within a real-time operating system such as pSOS+ or VxWorks.

AutoCode provides the source code for a complete execution environment. This enables code generated from SystemBuild models to be executed on an arbitrary target processor as long as a C or Ada compiler is available for that target.

Support for Monte Carlo Simulation

From the Xmath command line, the user can modify parameters in SystemBuild models and execute simulation runs. These functions can also be performed from Xmath script files. These capabilities enable the execution of sets of Monte Carlo runs in a manner similar to the MATLAB/Simulink technique described in Section 9.2.2.

Support for Data Analysis and Visualization

Time history output data from SystemBuild simulations is accessible for analysis and display in the Xmath environment. Xmath can perform data manipulation and computations much like MATLAB and has capabilities for creating 2-D and 3-D plots similar to those available in MATLAB.

User Interface

SystemBuild is the dynamic system simulation component of MATRIX$_X$ and is the tool in which the simulation developer spends the most time. SystemBuild maintains all the information related to a simulation in a file called a catalog. A catalog contains four folders: superblocks, state diagrams, data stores, and components. A superblock is a collection of primitive blocks, state transition diagrams, data stores, and references to other superblocks. A state diagram is a graphical representation of a finite state machine. A data store is a mechanism that provides global data storage. Components are encapsulated superblock hierarchies, each of which contains its own catalog.

Simulation block diagrams are created from the elements in the catalog and from the primitive blocks contained in the block palette. The developer drags each block from its source location and drops it in the SystemBuild editor window at the desired position. Once positioned in a diagram, blocks can be moved by dragging them.

Connecting blocks together in SystemBuild is a more complex process than with Simulink or VisSim. To connect an output from one block to an input of another block, the user first Ctrl-right clicks on the source block to highlight it then Ctrl-right clicks on the destination block. If there is more than one output on the source block or more than one input on the destination block, a dialog box will appear that allows the user to specify the desired connection.

Interconnecting lines between blocks are positioned automatically by SystemBuild, however, it is possible to manually route them when desired with more Ctrl-right clicks. These Ctrl-right clicks are necessary because the SystemBuild software originally was designed for use on a UNIX workstation with a three-button mouse. On a PC with a two-button mouse, Ctrl-right clicks serve the same function as the middle mouse button on the three-button mouse.

9.2.5 20-sim

20-sim is a graphical dynamic system modeling and simulation tool that runs in a Microsoft Windows environment. This product is developed, sold, and supported by Controllab Products BV, which is affiliated with the University of Twente in the Netherlands. It is a successor to the TUTSIM dynamic system modeling and simulation package, which was also developed at the University of Twente. 20-sim is fully compatible with TUTSIM and includes all the standard TUTSIM library submodels, plus many more. Model development in 20-sim is very similar to the approach used in TUTSIM. The first commercial version of 20-sim was released in 1995.

20-sim supports modeling with iconic diagrams, block diagrams, bond graphs, and equations. Iconic diagrams are icons and the connections between them, which transfer energy between components. Block diagrams use the same modeling technique as the graphical modeling tools discussed previously. Bond graphs are drawings that show the physical structure, as well as the nature of subsystems, in an idealized manner that relates to Kirchoff's laws for electrical circuits. Equation models are created using the programming language SIDOPS+, which permits the specification of model parameters, variables, and mathematical equations in a straightforward manner.

All of these model representations can be mixed together as needed so that each element of a simulated system is developed using the most appropriate approach. 20-sim supports modeling of a variety of dynamic system types, including linear, nonlinear, continuous-time, discrete-time, and combined systems. This product supports hierarchical model representation by allowing an unlimited number of diagram levels. It also supports vector and matrix operations.

Figure 9.12 shows the turntable system model in block diagram form. The contents of the block labeled "Digital Controller" are shown in Figure 9.13.

Figure 9.12 20-sim diagram of turntable system.

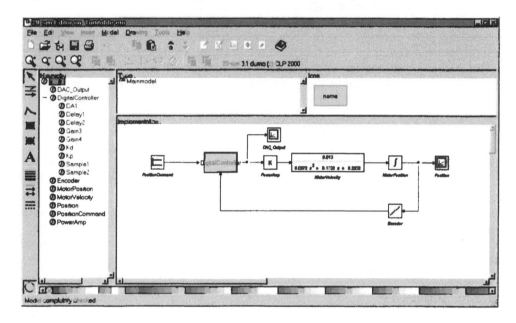

Product Name and Version

The product examined was the demonstration version of 20-sim v3.1 Pro.

Pricing

A corporate single-user license for a new purchase of 20-sim v3.1 Pro cost $4,000 in March 2001. This price was for an Internet download of the software and manuals. The 20-sim v3.1 product (without the "Pro") has fewer features and costs $2,000.

Supported Platforms

20-sim v3.1 Pro is supported on Windows 95/98/NT 4/ME/2000.

Capabilities of Core Product

20-sim v3.1 Pro provides the typical block diagram modeling capabilities of the other products discussed in this chapter, as well as several interesting additional features. Besides the block diagram modeling technique, it is also possible to create model elements using iconic diagrams, bond graphs, and equations.

Figure 9.13 20-sim diagram of digital controller.

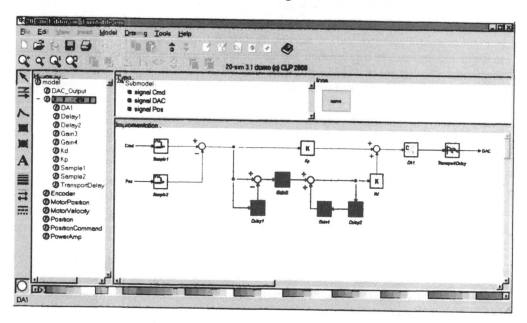

Iconic diagrams are similar to block diagrams, except that each element in the diagram is represented by a graphical icon. This allows, for example, the construction of electrical circuit simulations using standard symbols to represent components such as op-amps and capacitors. Bond graphs are useful for developing ideal physical models of components in domains such as electrical, mechanical, and hydraulic.

In 20-sim, all models are internally represented in equation form. The user can define models in terms of equations, or equations can be encapsulated within graphical components used in the other supported modeling techniques. When preparing a simulation for execution, 20-sim processes the model elements into a set of equations and compiles these equations into fast-executing code for the host processor.

20-sim can be used to develop linear and nonlinear models of continuous-time, discrete-time, and combined continuous–discrete-time systems. It has a built-in capability for developing a linear model from a nonlinear system about a selected operating point. The linear model can be saved as a 20-sim submodel or exported to a file for import into MATLAB. 20-sim can also export data from a single simulation run or from a run set to a file in a MATLAB-compatible format.

20-sim includes a debugging capability that allows single-stepping, the use of breakpoints, and variable browsing. One nice feature is that after stopping at a breakpoint, the user can place the mouse pointer on a signal line (in graphical models) or on a variable name (in equation models) and the numerical value of the signal or variable will be displayed.

20-sim provides capabilities for performing run sets that include parameter sweeps, optimization, and Monte Carlo parameter variations. A parameter sweep involves performing a set of simulation runs while varying the values of one or more model parameters by steps over a specified range. The optimization capability performs minimization or maximization of a user-specified cost function through automated variation of a set of model parameters and initial conditions. Eight different search algorithms are provided for performing optimization searches. A Monte Carlo simulation run set performs a specified number of runs with parameter values selected from a normal (Gaussian) or uniform distribution. Results from multiple run sets can be displayed in histogram form, examined numerically, or exported in a format suitable for use in MATLAB.

20-sim includes some useful visualization capabilities. It can animate a graphical model during execution so that the thickness and color of signal lines vary as the signal values change. Red lines indicates negative values, and green lines indicate positive values. The thickness of the lines indicates the magnitude of the signal value. 20-sim can also create 3-D animations during simulation execution. Any variable in the simulation can be used to control the behavior of an object in the 3-D animation.

3-D animations can be constructed from a variety of primitive objects including lines, cubes, spheres, cylinders, cones, squares, circles, and DirectX data files. A variety of lighting and camera options is also provided. The animation engine is based on Microsoft Direct3D technology, which automatically makes full use of any 3-D acceleration capabilities available in the computer's video card.

20-sim includes the ability to generate ANSI-standard C source code from any 20-sim model. The generated code can be targeted to become a standalone application, a C function for use in another application, or an S-Function, which can be compiled and used as a block in a Simulink diagram.

20-sim also has a controller design editor, which supports the design of feedback control systems using Bode plots, Nyquist diagrams, and pole-zero maps of linear systems. Changes to the model or controller parameters cause the graphical diagrams to update immediately. Models developed in the controller design editor can be stored as 20-sim submodels or saved in MATLAB format files.

Add-On Products

There are no add-ons available for the 20-sim Pro product. The 20-sim (without the "Pro") product is a lower cost version that does not include the built-in simulation compiler, optimization capability, Monte Carlo analysis, linearization, C source code generation, graph animation, 3-D animation, or the controller design editor.

Product Availability

20-sim is available for purchase and download from the 20-sim website at http://www.20sim.com. A free limited-time demonstration version is also available for download, along with a full set of documentation in PDF format.

Installation and Licensing

Installation is straightforward and uses standard Windows install/uninstall procedures. The demonstration version of 20-sim 3.1 Pro includes a license that is valid for several months.

Development of an HIL Simulation

20-sim is not targeted to real-time applications. It is possible to generate C source code for any 20-sim model and compile it for execution in a real-time environment that has an ANSI

C compiler. However, 20-sim does not support any real-time I/O devices, so the developer is responsible for integrating any needed I/O devices into the simulation. Unfortunately, there does not appear to be a way to integrate user-supplied source code (in C, for instance) with a 20-sim model. This means that every time the developer generates C code from a 20-sim diagram it is necessary to modify the generated code to include support for items such as real-time I/O and execution scheduling.

This may be a feasible approach to implement HIL simulations for some applications, but in most cases, other tools discussed in this chapter would be more appropriate.

Development of a Distributed Simulation

20-sim does not include a capability for distributed simulation. Because there is no straight-forward way to integrate user-supplied source code in a language such as C, it does not appear to be possible for a developer to easily add this capability.

Technical Support

Support is available through the 20-sim online help, through the 20-sim web site, and through telephone, fax, and email communication with Controllab Products.

Available Integration Methods

20-sim provides the following variable-step integration algorithms.

Runge-Kutta-Dormand-Prince 8th order   This method provides good performance for solving stiff and nonstiff systems.

Runge-Kutta-Fehlberg   This is a fourth/fifth-order integration algorithm intended for solving nonstiff and mildly stiff systems. It has relatively low overhead, which leads to efficient execution of simulations with modest accuracy requirements.

Vode-Adams   This is an explicit algorithm that is well suited for stiff systems.

Backward Differentiation Formula   This is an implicit variable-order algorithm that implements Gear's backward differentiation formula. It uses code from the DASSL library (see previous SystemBuild description) and is suitable for models that contain algebraic loops. An algebraic loop occurs when an algebraically-computed variable that is a block output is also an input (either directly or indirectly) to that block.

20-sim provides the following fixed-step integration algorithms.

Euler   This is the forward Euler method. Because of its low accuracy, its use normally should be avoided, except when performing experimental comparisons of different algorithms.

Adams-Bashforth 2nd order   This is an explicit algorithm with second-order accuracy. It is a good choice for real-time simulations of systems with relatively smooth derivative functions.

Runge-Kutta 4th order This is the fourth-order Runge-Kutta integration algorithm. It provides good performance in the presence of discontinuities in the derivative function and has fourth-order accuracy.

Only the Euler and Runge-Kutta fourth-order integration algorithms are supported in C code generated from 20-sim models.

Supported I/O Devices

20-sim does not provide support for real-time I/O devices. It does support standard PC I/O operations to disk and to a monitor screen, including 3-D animation.

Interchanging Simulations with Other Tools

No support is provided for importing simulations from other simulation tool formats or for exporting them to formats readable by other simulation tools. 20-sim does have the ability to read and write linear model descriptions in a format suitable for use with MATLAB.

Sharing Simulations with Others

There is no supported method of sharing a 20-sim simulation with a user that does not have a copy of 20-sim.

Support for Embedded Code Generation

A capability for generating ANSI C source code is provided with 20-sim, but there is very little capability for tailoring the code generation process. The generated code is intended for use as a fast-executing version of the simulation and is not really geared to the common restrictions of embedded computing environments.

Support for Monte Carlo Simulation

20-sim provides the ability to perform Monte Carlo parameter variations during sets of simulation runs. The typical application of this approach is to investigate the sensitivity of a result variable to statistical variations in a set of model parameters.

Two statistical distributions are provided for the parameter variations: the normal (Gaussian) distribution and the uniform distribution. Results collected during Monte Carlo run sets can be displayed in histogram format, examined numerically, or exported to a file in a format suitable for input to MATLAB.

Support for Data Analysis and Visualization

20-sim provides capabilities for creating 2-D plots and 3-D animations. When performing a single run, multiple plotted variables will appear on a single set of axes, as shown in Figure 9.14. When performing multiple-run sets, 20-sim can create 2-D overplots of a set of simulation variables showing the results from all the runs. Simulation data can also be stored to a file and redisplayed later.

It is easy to zoom in on an area of interest in a 2-D plot and to display the numerical values of data points using the mouse. The data analysis environment includes a capability for performing a fast Fourier transform on time history data and displaying the resulting power spectral density.

When performing multiple-run sets, 20-sim saves the final value of the selected simulation variables and parameters for each run. This data can be examined numerically in 20-sim and can be exported to MATLAB for 2-D and 3-D plotting.

The 3-D animation capability is unique among the simulation tools discussed in this chapter. Using Direct3D technology, high-fidelity animation of complex scenes can be performed in 20-sim. Direct3D uses the full capabilities of modern video cards, many of which provide hardware support for high-performance 3-D animation. 3-D rendering capabilities that are not supported by hardware are performed in software, which means that Direct3D animations are portable across computers regardless of the 3-D capabilities of the system video card.

In 20-sim, the simulation developer can create 3-D animations that contain collections of primitive objects and complex 3-D objects described in the DirectX file format. The available primitive objects are: circle, cone, cube, cylinder, line, sphere, and square. The DirectX file format enables the specification of arbitrarily complex 3-D objects in a text or binary file format. DirectX files can be created with a text editor or by exporting object descriptions from a 3-D modeling program that has a DirectX output option.

The values of variables in a 20-sim simulation can control the position, orientation, scaling, and color of the objects in the 3-D scene. By placing a set of primitive elements and DirectX file elements into a scene and controlling their behavior with simulation variables, it is possible to build impressive animations of complex systems.

Figure 9.14 20-sim plots of DAC output signal and motor position.

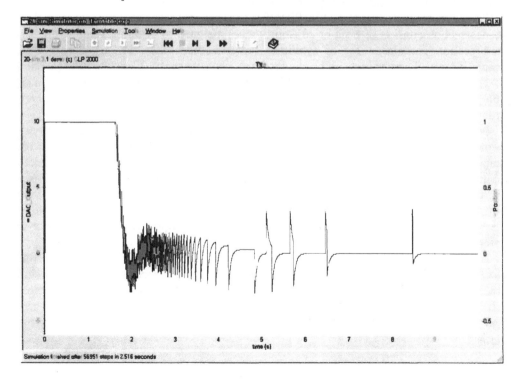

20-sim can display an animation as the simulation executes and can replay the animation after execution has completed. During execution, animations play at the speed of simulation execution, so the animated behavior may be much faster or slower than real time. If the replay animation runs faster than real time, 20-sim can play it at real-time speed.

Although 3-D animation provides a qualitative view of system performance rather than the quantitative view required for detailed performance analysis, this type of animation does provide some significant benefits for simulation. One application for animation is verifying that the simulation is operating properly after setting up and starting a run. Many times, an incorrect parameter setting will be apparent by observing the animation for a short time. The user can stop the run, change the parameter value, and restart the run. This is more efficient than waiting for the run to complete before analyzing the results and detecting the problem.

User Interface

20-sim differs from the other simulation tools discussed in this chapter in that it supports four methods for modeling dynamic systems: iconic diagrams, block diagrams, bond graphs, and equations. All four of these methods can be combined to model a particular system or subsystem. All of the graphical representations are converted to equations prior to execution. The language used for entering models in equation format and for the inner representation of graphical model elements is called SIDOPS+.

Equation models in SIDOPS+ are based on four keywords, each of which describes a section of code: `constants`, `parameters`, `variables`, and `equations`. A complete model may contain all four of these sections, although the first two are optional. The sections must appear in the order listed. The first three keywords are each followed by a set of declarations. The `equations` keyword is followed by the model equations.

Four data types are supported by SIDOP+: `boolean`, `integer`, `real`, and `string`. The constants section consists of a set of constant values assigned to symbolic names. The `parameters` section contains a set of symbolic representations that do not change during a simulation run. These values can be changed between runs in the 20-sim simulator. The `variables` section is a list of symbolic names for numerical quantities that change during a simulation run. The `equations` section is a list of one or more equations that describe the model behavior.

In 20-sim, equations are true mathematical equations rather than the assignment statements of other programming languages. During compilation, 20-sim will attempt to rearrange all the equations into a causal form, where all output variables become a function of input variables. Equations containing derivatives or integrals can also be entered. 20-sim will attempt to rewrite equations containing derivatives into a form containing only integrals, because this allows any of the integration algorithms to be used. If this is not possible, only the backward differentiation method is available. 20-sim supports the use of vector-matrix notation in SIDOPS+ equations.

Listing 9.3 shows the equations contained within the MotorVelocity transfer function block of Figure 9.12. This model does not contain a `constants` section, but it does include the other three sections. Note that each SIDOPS+ statement is terminated with a semicolon. The first two lines in the model are comments that use C++ syntax. Vectors and matrices are specified using syntax similar to MATLAB. The input to the model is defined to be u and the output is y.

In the first equation, ddt() indicates that the derivative of the two-element vector x (with initial condition x0) is the value to the right of the equal sign. Note that it is not necessary to manually enter these equations. 20-sim includes a linear system editing tool that allows entry of transfer functions just by specifying the numerator and denominator polynomial coefficients. That tool automatically created the equations of Listing 9.3.

Listing 9.3 20-sim equations for MotorVelocity block in G in Figure 9.12.

```
// 20-sim Linear System Editor
// tf
parameters
real hidden A [2, 2] = [0.0, -3.0579027777778; 10.0, -18.5];
real hidden B [2, 1] = [-0.013; 0.0];
real hidden C [1, 2] = [0.0, -13.888888888889];
real hidden x0 [2] = [0.0; 0.0];
variables
real x [2];
equations
ddt (x, x0) = A * x + B * u;
y = C * x;
```

20-sim does not provide a capability for entering transfer function models of discrete-time systems, so it was necessary to implement the digital controller derivative transfer function using delay elements, as shown in Figure 9.13. It is also possible to create a discrete-time transfer function using an equation model.

After creating the structure of the model shown in Figures 9.12 and 9.13, a separate window called the Simulator is used for setting up and executing runs and for creating 2-D plots. This window is shown in Figure 9.14. In addition to the basic single run capability, the Simulator can perform multiple run sets for parameter sweep and optimization applications. The Tools menu in the Simulator contains options for performing FFT analysis of simulation results, linearizing models, generating C source code, and setting breakpoints for simulation debugging.

I encountered a few problems using 20-sim. Occasionally a small dialog box would appear with the message "An error occurred! Please restart 20-sim as soon as possible." This message appeared when performing seemingly harmless tasks such as adding a splitter to a signal line (so the signal could be passed to multiple blocks) and when trying to generate C code from a 20-sim model. The message "Matrices are not yet supported!" appeared another time when I tried to generate C code from a 20-sim model. The source of this problem was the matrix implementation of the MotorVelocity block, as shown in Listing 9.3. When I contacted 20-sim technical support about this problem, I was informed that a version of the C code generator that supports vector-matrix operations is planned for a future release.

9.3   Other Software Tools

This section contains a list of additional tools for dynamic system simulation. These products were not included in the previous section because many of them have limited applicability compared to the tools already discussed, or they are based on dated software technology and may be more difficult to use. The products included here are by no means a complete list of available simulation software tools. These products are only a small sample of the available tools for dynamic system modeling and simulation.

9.3.1   DESIRE

DESIRE (which stands for Direct Executing SImulation in REal time) is a dynamic system modeling and simulation tool that has been in use since 1986. The current version (DESIRE/2000) runs on Microsoft Windows 95/98/NT and on the Sun Solaris operating system. Programming in DESIRE is based on an equation-oriented text language for creating models. The language supports differential equations and vector/matrix operations. It also includes a capability for modeling neural networks and fuzzy logic systems.

The user interface for this product is somewhat primitive. It provides text windows for source code editing and command input. Even when the program has just been started and no simulation is running, DESIRE consumes 100% of the available CPU time under Windows NT.

For more information, see `http://hometown.aol.com/gatmkorn/index.htm`.

9.3.2   Dymola

Dymola is a modeling and simulation tool that is geared primarily to the simulation of electromechanical systems such as robots and power systems. Dymola uses the modeling language Modelica, which is intended to facilitate the exchange of dynamic system models among tools and the reuse of models. Dymola supports graphical modeling using icons and provides a 3-D animation capability similar to that of 20-sim.

Dymola supports modeling systems as ordinary differential equations and as differential algebraic equations. It performs symbolic manipulation of equations to put them in the best form for simulation. Several integration algorithms are provided that are suitable for stiff systems and for handling discontinuous events.

Dymola is an appropriate simulation tool for systems of the electrical, mechanical, hydraulic, thermodynamic, and chemical types. It appears to be less well-suited to applications in other areas, such as aircraft flight simulation. For information on Dymola, see `http://www.dynasim.se`.

9.3.3   EASY5

EASY5 is a simulation tool developed by Boeing that supports the modeling and simulation of complex aerospace, electrical, multiphase fluid, powertrain, hydraulic, and pneumatic systems. EASY5 provides a graphical environment similar to that of SystemBuild, along with a variety of optional toolkits that cover areas such as matrix algebra and real-time simulation. EASY5 includes a code generator that automatically translates models into FORTRAN or C for compilation prior to execution. This results in high-speed simulation execution.

EASY5 is clearly oriented toward FORTRAN. It includes a FORTRAN block, into which the user can type FORTRAN source code. If the user prefers to use another language (such as C), it must be called from FORTRAN code. This is the result of the development history of EASY5, which dates back to the mid-1970s. EASY5 runs on a variety of UNIX workstations and on Microsoft Windows 95/98/NT.

For system simulations that involve the application areas supported by EASY5, it may be the best available tool. For other applications, the tools discussed earlier in this chapter probably will be more appropriate and will avoid the quirks associated with the FORTRAN language. For more information, see `http://www.boeing.com/assocproducts/easy5`.

9.3.4 SD/FAST

SD/FAST accepts a textual description of a set of rigid bodies connected by joints and derives the complete nonlinear equations of motion for that system. The resulting equations are then output as source code in C or FORTRAN. This code can be compiled into a larger system simulation or it can be used to perform a variety of engineering analyses.

Some examples of the systems that SD/FAST can model are: mechanisms and machine components; vehicles, such as automobiles and bicycles; articulated spacecraft; robotic manipulators; and electromechanical systems, such as cameras and photocopiers. SD/FAST supports the connection of rigid bodies using a variety of joint types that include: pin joints, ball joints, gimbal joints, and universal joints. Constraints can be applied to the motion of any joint or body in the system. The code generated by SD/FAST is very efficient and is suitable for use with a variety of integration algorithms.

SD/FAST performs one step of the simulation process: the generation of equations of motion for a mechanical system. For systems of even moderate complexity, these equations are typically very difficult to derive by hand. The value of SD/FAST lies in its ability to generate these equations given a description of the mechanical system. SD/FAST is available from Symbolic Dynamics, Inc., at `http://www.symdyn.com`.

9.3.5 EngineSim

EngineSim is a Simulink model of an automotive engine intended for use by control system engineers. It simulates a sequential port-fuel-injected, spark ignition engine. It includes air, fuel, and EGR dynamics modeling, as well as process delays inherent in the four-stroke cycle engine. Inputs to the model include atmospheric effects, external load torque, throttle input, and all the engine actuator inputs, such as fuel injectors and EGR valve.

EngineSim is intended for use in real-time simulation, in non-real-time simulation, as a subsystem model for sensor and actuator testing, and as a subsystem in a complete powertrain model. Extensive testing of an actual engine on a dynamometer was performed to validate the EngineSim model.

This is an example of a model that a simulation developer can purchase rather than develop in-house. Depending on the budget and time constraints of a development project, the approach of buying models like this rather than developing them may be preferable much of the time.

EngineSim is produced and marketed by simcar.com. For more information, see `http://www.simcar.com/products.htm`.

9.4 Real-Time Simulation Computing Systems

A number of companies market computer systems intended for use in HIL simulation applications. Some of these products include a complete software environment for model and simulation development, while others are intended for use with models created using software tools from other vendors.

9.4.1 ADI Simsystem

Simsystem is the hardware and software system produced by Applied Dynamics International for high-performance HIL simulation. The hardware consists of a VME-based system using Motorola PowerPC processors as high-performance simulation engines. A separate PowerPC running a UNIX operating system provides the interface between a host computer (PC or UNIX) and the real-time simulation. A variety of I/O devices is supported, including analog and digital I/O, CAN bus, MIL STD 1553 bus, and many others.

Simulations can be created using the C, Fortran, and ACSL programming languages; Simulink; SystemBuild; or EASY5. Models developed in various environments can be combined into a single simulation using a software tool called the ADvantage IDE. The ADvantage IDE adapts models for real-time use and provides a communication infrastructure between models running on separate processors within the VME chassis.

The high performance provided by the PowerPC processors and the VME backplane make the ADI Simsystem appropriate for the real-time simulation of complex systems at very high frame rates. For more information see http://www.adi.com.

9.4.2 dSpace

dSpace provides hardware and software tools for real-time HIL simulation. Real-time simulation processor options include the Texas Instruments TMS320C31 DSP and the Motorola PowerPC 750. A variety of hardware configurations is available, including a single board computer that plugs into a PC slot and a miniaturized system intended for onboard use in vehicle road testing. A modular system configuration is provided for laboratory use, which has the ability to support several processors and a variety of I/O boards in a high-performance real-time computing system.

The dSpace processors run simulations developed in the MATLAB/Simulink environment. The Real Time Workshop product from MathWorks processes the simulation model into source code form, which is then compiled and linked for the dSpace execution environment. The dSpace software environment supports the development of graphical control and instrument panels for real-time use and for the automation of experiment sequences. Graphical techniques are used to configure I/O interfaces and to set up scheduling for multitasking applications and for multiprocessor systems.

For more information, see http://www.dspace.de.

Exercises

1. Select one of the graphical simulation software tools in Section 9.2 that is appropriate for your needs and acquire a demonstration version from the vendor. You can usually download a free version from the web site listed in the description, or you may need to contact

the company and request a demo disk. Install the product and try out some of the included examples.

2. Implement the turntable model that was used as an example in Section 9.2. Run the model and plot the DAC output signal and the turntable position. Compare your plots with those shown in Section 9.2. Time how long it takes your simulation to run using fourth-order Runge-Kutta integration and a 1-millisecond time step for a simulated time period of 10 seconds. Make your measurement as accurate as possible.

3. Generate C source code for your simulation using the facilities of the simulation software tool. Examine the generated code and see if you understand the function of each source file and routine. Compile and link the source code so that the simulation can run as a standalone application on your computer. Set up the simulation to save the output variables (DAC output signal and turntable position) to a data file at intervals of 1 millisecond.

4. Execute the simulation and measure how long it takes to execute using fourth-order Runge-Kutta integration and a 1-millisecond time step for a simulated time period of 10 seconds. Make your measurement as accurate as possible. Compare the execution time of this simulation to the execution time of the simulation that you measured in Exercise 2.

5. Compare the results of the simulation in Exercise 4 to the results of the simulation in Exercise 2. Produce overplots and difference plots for the two variables (DAC output signal and turntable position) from the two simulation runs. If there are differences between the two runs, determine whether those differences are significant and identify the cause(s).

Glossary

6DOF An abbreviation that stands for "six degrees of freedom." A 6DOF simulation models the motion of bodies using three degrees of freedom for translational motion and three degrees of freedom for rotational motion. 6DOF motion accurately represents the motion of rigid bodies in the real world.

Algebraic Variable Any simulation variable that does not represent a continuous or discrete state. See *State Variable*.

Aliasing A form of distortion that occurs when a continuous signal is sampled at too low of a frequency. It occurs when the continuous signal contains components with frequencies greater than one-half the sampling frequency. Aliasing can be reduced or eliminated by sampling at a higher frequency or by filtering the continuous signal to attenuate signal components at frequencies above half the sampling frequency.

Bode Plot Bode plots display the amplitude and phase of the response of a system to a sine wave input signal across a range of frequencies. In a Bode magnitude plot, the frequency appears on the horizontal and the response magnitude appears on the vertical axes using logarithmic scaling. In a Bode phase plot, the frequency appears on the horizontal axis with logarithmic scaling and the response phase appears on the vertical axis using linear scaling. Bode plots are widely used in stability analysis and control system design.

Combined System A dynamic system described by a combination of differential equations and difference equations. Combined systems contain both continuous-time elements and discrete-time elements.

Continuous-Time System A dynamic system that has behavior described by differential equations. The state of the system can change over any nonzero time interval.

Decibel The decibel measure is the ratio of two power values. Given two power values, the formula for computing this ratio is

$$10 \log\left(\frac{\text{power}_1}{\text{power}_2}\right).$$

If the signal amplitude is used instead of the power, the expression for computing the decibel ratio is

$$20 \log\left(\frac{\text{amplitude}_1}{\text{amplitude}_2}\right).$$

The multiplying factors are different because power is proportional to the square of the signal amplitude.

Difference Equation Difference equations model the behavior of discrete-time systems. It is a recursive algebraic equation that computes the next value of a discrete state variable as a function of its current and previous values and the equation input variables. Difference equations are used in numerical integration algorithms to approximate on digital computers the integration of continuous signals in a discrete-time manner.

Differential Equation A differential equation contains one or more derivatives of an unknown function. When it contains only ordinary derivatives, it is an ordinary differential equation. When it contains partial derivatives, it is a *partial differential equation.* In a simulation of a dynamic system, numerical integration algorithms can estimate the unknown function in an ordinary differential equation.

Direction Cosine Matrix When simulating the motion of a body in N-dimensional space, a direction cosine matrix is an $N \times N$ matrix that transforms a vector in one coordinate system into another coordinate system. A common application of direction cosine matrices is to transform vectors between earth-fixed coordinates and body-fixed coordinates.

Discrete-Time System A dynamic system that has behavior described by difference equations. The state of the system can change only at the update times of the difference equations.

Distributed Simulation A simulation made up of components that execute on separate computers connected together by a communication network. A distributed simulation may include components that are not simulations, such as real aircraft or other systems.

Dynamic Embedded System A system that contains embedded computing resources that control dynamic aspects of its behavior. Some examples of dynamic embedded systems are an aircraft with an altitude-hold autopilot and an automobile with cruise control.

Dynamic Equations Equations that describe the dynamic behavior of a system. These may include differential equations, difference equations, and algebraic equations.

Dynamic System   A system with behavior that evolves over time. This behavior can be described by differential equations, difference equations, or a combination of both.

Empirical Modeling   A technique for determining the dynamic equations that describe the behavior of a system from experimentally measured data. This approach is useful for developing models of dynamic systems, as well as for systems that do not exhibit dynamic behavior. The approach of building models of dynamic systems from noisy, measured data is called system identification (see *System Identification*).

Euler Angles   A set of Euler angles defines an ordered sequence of rotations about coordinate system axes that transform a vector from one coordinate system to another. For example, the yaw, pitch, and roll angles of an aircraft define the angular relationship between the earth coordinates and the aircraft body coordinates.

Fixed-Step Integration Algorithms   These numerical integration algorithms perform updates at fixed intervals of simulation time. See *Variable-Step Integration Algorithms*.

Frame Overrun   A frame overrun occurs in a real-time simulation when the time to execute computations and perform I/O for a particular frame exceeds the available time.

Frame Ratio   In a multiframe simulation (see *Multiframing*), the frame ratio is the ratio of the faster frame rate to the slower frame rate. This ratio is usually an integer.

Interpolation   Interpolation techniques are used to estimate the value of a function between known values at breakpoints. The function may be of one or more dimensions. The number of dimensions corresponds to the number of function inputs. Various techniques are used for performing the interpolation, including linear interpolation and cubic spline interpolation.

Linear Time-Invariant Model   A linear model of a dynamic system has an output signal amplitude that is proportional to the amplitude of the input signal, regardless of how small or large it is. A model is time-invariant if its dynamic equations do not change as a function of time. A linear time-invariant model combines both of these properties and is valuable because it lends itself to a variety of mathematical analysis techniques. These models can also be used in simulations, but they often leave out significant nonlinearities that are present in real-world systems.

Linearization   The process of converting a nonlinear model of a dynamic system into a linear model that approximates the response of the nonlinear model over some region of the system behavior.

Mathematical Model   An algorithm or set of equations and a set of data values that together represent the significant behavior of a system, process, or phenomenon.

Multiframing   Multiframe simulations break a simulation into multiple pieces that execute at different frame rates. The reason for doing this is to increase efficiency by not executing models at a higher rate than necessary.

Monte Carlo Simulation A Monte Carlo simulation performs a large number of simulation under identical conditions, except that a different pseudorandom sequence is used for each random parameter or process in each run. The different sequences of pseudorandom numbers generate performance variations that involve combinations of random behaviors.

Neural Network Modeling Neural networks provide a method for developing models from data using a method that is conceptually similar to the system identification technique. A neural network is based on simple mathematical models of biological neurons, which are the fundamental cognitive units of the brain. This technique can be used to model highly non-linear systems and phenomena that do not have any associated models based in physics.

Non-Real-Time Simulation A simulation that executes as fast as it can. This may result in the passage of simulation time at a rate higher or lower than that of real time. The actual rate of execution does not affect the results of a non-real-time simulation because it does not use inputs from the real world.

Nyquist Sampling Theorem This theorem states that the sampling frequency of an ADC must be at least twice the highest frequency component of its input signal in order to permit accurate reconstruction. Reconstruction in this sense means the ability to accurately convert the input signal back to an analog signal using a DAC.

Operational Testing Testing a dynamic system by placing it into its intended operational environment and exercising it to determine its capabilities. This is the most realistic type of testing available, but for many types of systems it can be very costly to perform.

Ordinary Differential Equations A differential equation that contains ordinary derivatives and does not contain partial derivatives.

Partial Differential Equation A differential equation that contains partial derivatives.

Probability Density Function If x is a continuous random variable, the probability density function (or PDF) $f(x)$ defines the probability that x is in the range $x_1 < x \leq x_2$ using the formula

$$P(x_1 < x \leq x_2) = \int_{x_1}^{x_2} f(x)dx.$$

A continuous PDF satisfies the condition

$$\int_{-\infty}^{\infty} f(x)dx = 1.$$

If x is a discrete random variable, the PDF $f(x)$ defines the probability p_i that x takes on each possible discrete value x_1. A discrete PDF satisfies the condition

$$\sum_i p_i = 1.$$

Profiler A powerful software tool that helps developers isolate and resolve performance problems in applications. A profiler tells the developer where the application spends its time during execution. These tools use techniques, such as sampling the instruction counter at regular intervals and inserting instrumentation code into the application, to collect the necessary data. Executing an application under a profiler may cause it to run much more slowly than normal. This may cause problems when working with real-time applications.

Quality In a complex embedded product, quality has many dimensions. A straightforward definition is that a product has high quality if it performs its intended functions adequately without significant negative attributes or behaviors from the user's point of view. Additional quality factors include the maintainability and testability of the product and its software. The quest for quality must be balanced against the need to deliver the product on schedule and within budget constraints.

Rate Monotonic Scheduling Rate monotonic scheduling (RMS) is a technique for scheduling multiple software tasks for execution in a prioritized, preemptive multitasking environment. To use RMS, the execution frequency of each task must first be identified. In an HIL simulation application, this frequency will be the inverse of the task integration step size, h. The scheduling priority of the tasks is then assigned so that the task with the highest frequency has the highest priority and the task with the lowest frequency has the lowest priority. This assignment of priorities, as a monotonic function of task execution rate, is what gives RMS its name.

Random Process A sequence of random variables that occurs over time. An example of a random process is the sequence of additive noise values that appear in the result of an analog-to-digital converter that performs conversions at regular time intervals.

Random Variable A number assigned to every outcome of an experiment that contains some element of randomness. For example, if heads = 0 and tails = 1, the outcome of a coin flip is a random variable taking on the value 0 or 1. The output of a software pseudorandom number generator approximates the behavior of a random variable, even though it is not truly random.

Real-Time Simulation A real-time simulation is constrained to execute so that simulation time passes at the same rate as real time. If the execution of any frame of the simulation takes longer than the allowed time step size, a frame overrun occurs (See *Frame Overrun*).

Regression Testing Regression tests attempt to verify that existing system capabilities are not lost or degraded when enhancements or repairs are made. Regression testing consists of repeating tests that have been performed successfully in the past. Because this type of testing involves repeating identical test sequences, it is desirable to automate it as much as possible.

Ridealong Mode Ridealong mode applies to HIL simulations that contain a software model of the system hardware that is used in the simulation. It addresses the problem of getting the simulation to work with the hardware when the software-only system simulation works well. Ridealong mode runs the software-only simulation in real time and uses the outputs of this simulation to drive the hardware. This makes it easier to examine the hardware outputs and compare them to the outputs of the software model of the hardware. Ridealong mode is useful during system integration of an HIL simulation and when troubleshooting problems with an HIL simulation.

Roundoff Error The result of a computation that uses finite-precision rational numbers (such as the floating-point numbers used by computers) to approximate infinite-precision real numbers. The amount of roundoff error in a particular computation depends on the number of arithmetic operations performed and the precision of the floating-point representation used.

RTOS An abbreviation for real-time operating system, which is the type of system software used in embedded systems when they must respond to inputs within a deterministic length of time. This contrasts with a general-purpose operating system, such as in a desktop computer, which takes varying amounts of time to perform actions depending on factors such as system loading.

Simulation A mathematical model of a system or a group of systems that executes over time. The mathematical model describes the behavior of the systems and their interactions with the external environment. The rate of time passage in the simulation may be arbitrary (see *Non-Real-Time Simulation*) or it may be constrained to match the passage of real time (see *Real-Time Simulation*), depending on the simulation application.

State Variable A continuous state variable is the result of integrating a differential equation. A discrete variable is the result of computing the next value of a difference equation.

System Identification A set of techniques used to develop mathematical models of dynamic systems from noisy measured data. The model resulting from system identification is usually linear and time-invariant (see *Linear Time-Invariant Model*).

Table Interpolation Table interpolation uses a data table and an interpolation algorithm to estimate the value of a function of one or more variables. This approach is often used when the function output must be determined experimentally. It is also applicable as a speed optimization technique when used as an alternative to a lengthy computation (perhaps an iterative procedure) for evaluating the function.

Taylor Series Expansion The Taylor series expansion of an arbitrary function about the point a is

$$f(x) = \sum_{n=0}^{\infty} \frac{f^{(n)}(a)}{n!}(x-a),$$

where $f^{(n)}(a)$ is the nth derivative of the function evaluated at a. Linearization of a nonlinear function is frequently performed by using only the terms for $n = 0$ and $n = 1$ and discarding the remaining terms of the expansion.

Timestamp   A reading of the current time taken in response to an event. Timestamps are used to record when the event occurred for later use. One application of timestamps is the extrapolation of continuous values to the current time following a latency period.

Transfer Function   A mathematical description of the relation between the input and output of a dynamic system or component.

Truncation Error   The error that would result from a single step of a numerical integration algorithm if the roundoff error were zero. In other words, it is the error if the algorithm step had been executed on a computer with infinite numerical precision.

Variable-Step Integration Algorithms   Variable-step integration algorithms change the size of the integration time step in response to the behavior of the simulated system. When the system state changes rapidly, the algorithm will use smaller time steps to reduce truncation error. When the system state changes slowly, the algorithm will use larger time steps to reduce the simulation execution time.

Zero-Order Hold   A zero-order hold samples its input signal at (usually) a constant rate and holds that value as its output until the next sample is taken.

Answers to Selected Exercises

Chapter 2

(from page 69)

1. (a) Yes.
   (b) Possibly, if the circuit includes feedback (either directly or indirectly) from a gate's output to its input, such as in a flip-flop circuit. When this is true, the circuit output following an input signal transition depends on the input signals as well as the previous state of the circuit.
   (c) Yes.
   (d) Yes.

2. $x'_3 = ax_3 + bx_2 + cx_1 + d$

   $x'_2 = x_3$

   $x'_1 = x_2$

   where $x = x_1$.

3. $\theta'' = -\frac{g}{l}\sin\theta - Cl^2\theta'|\theta'|$

7. 0.7091, 0.5121, and 0.3310

Chapter 3
(from page 98)

2. $y'' = 1000 - 1001y' - 1000y$
$y(0) = y'(0) = 0$

10. The furnace switches on 3 times during the hour of operation.

Chapter 6
(from page 201)

2. The expected value of the TIC for sequences of uncorrelated random numbers with zero mean and unit variance is

$$\frac{\sqrt{2}}{2}.$$

Index

T - #0256 - 101024 - C0 - 229/179/17 [19] - CB - 9781138436411 - Gloss Lamination